Dimensions of Shared Agency

A Study on Joint, Collective and Group Intentional Action

Giulia Lasagni

Europa-Universität Flensburg, Germany

Critical Perspectives on Social Science

VERNON PRESS

www.vernonpress.com

In the Americas:
Vernon Press
1000 N West Street, Suite 1200
Wilmington, Delaware, 19801
United States

In the rest of the world:
Vernon Press
C/Sancti Espiritu 17,
Malaga, 29006
Spain

Critical Perspectives on Social Science

Library of Congress Control Number: 2021942359

ISBN: 978-1-64889-370-4

Also available: 978-1-64889-127-4 [Hardback]; 978-1-64889-318-6 [PDF, E-Book]

Cover design by Vernon Press using elements designed by Freepik.

Table of contents

List of tables and figures

Acknowledgments

A few days after the defense of my doctoral dissertation, my supervisor, Italo Testa, told me not to follow his example but to publish my thesis in a short time. As a matter of fact, I ended up following his example rather than his advice, and now, three years after that day, I can finally thank him for all the encouragement and support he has always been able to provide me with.

I would also like to extend my deepest gratitude to Beatrice Centi and to the entire philosophy department of the University of Parma, which gave me the opportunity to start and pursue the research presented in this book. I am extremely grateful to the members of the doctoral committee—Matteo Bianchin, Arto Laitinen, and Michael Schmitz—for the intense discussion, constructive criticism, and practical suggestions, which helped me improve my research and develop it into this book. I am also grateful to Alessandro Salice and David Schweikard for helpful comments on the first version of my dissertation. I am even more grateful for what followed.

I would like to extend my sincere thanks to Carol Rovane for giving me the opportunity to enjoy the privileges of a visiting student in the philosophy department at the Columbia University in the City of New York and for the inspiring conversations we had when this project was just beginning. I also wish to thank Mihnea Dobre, Iulia Nitescu, and Matthew Dentith, who made possible and pleasant my stay as a visiting student at the Research Institute of the University of Bucharest.

Thanks also to Chiara Lasagni, Jessica Mambreani, and all the friends and colleagues from Vita Activa, who have provided me with unrelenting encouragement and patience throughout the duration of this project.

I cannot even begin to express my thanks to Timothy Tambassi, my partner in life and first reader of the book manuscript in all its many versions. I dedicate this book to you.

Introduction

1. The topic

The notion of shared agency is at the core of many philosophical debates, such as social philosophy, philosophy of mind, action theory, and social ontology. In particular, social ontology, a crosscutting area of research, is interested in shared agency due to its double relation with the social environment. On the one hand, shared agency is important for how we make the social world: our doing things together powers the establishment of rules and patterns of behavior, shaping the social context. In this sense, the creation of social institutions is one of the most fundamental issues investigated. On the other hand, shared agency helps to understand to what extent the social world might affect how we, as human beings, act together. The question is about the influence that both institutional and habitual regulations have on agency, be it individual or shared with others. Assuming agency is described as an intentional behavior, rationally oriented towards action, 'shared agency' refers to all phenomena where two or more individuals act together intentionally. Developing thorough explanations accounting for how we act together intentionally is complex, and the contemporary debate has proposed a variety of frameworks that are sometimes complementary and other times at odds with one another.

This book endeavors to explore some of the most influential theories of shared agency, concentrating primarily on the proposals of 'the Big Five of Social Ontology'—Michael E. Bratman, Margaret Gilbert, John R. Searle, Raimo Tuomela, and Philip Pettit (considered mainly for his works with Christian List).[1] This investigation pursues three main purposes: first, it intends to offer a critical survey of some of the most influential theories of shared action and provide an original conceptual framework suited to capture points of consensus and conflict emerging between different accounts. Second, the book attempts to establish whether the theories in question also aim to approach shared agency in terms of group agency and ascertain

---

[1] The group of theorists including Bratman, Gilbert, Tuomela, Searle, and Pettit can be found in Chant, Hindriks & Preyer (2014) as 'the Big Five of social ontology'. Although the present investigation refers primarily to the pieces Pettit has written together with List, the expression 'Big Five' is not changed into 'Big Six', because it is beyond the scope of this book to account for what Pettit and List have been writing individually. The fifth in my list will thus be the plural subject formed by List and Pettit taken together.

whether this shift (if any) is adequately supported. I will establish that not all of the Big Five aim to approach shared agency as group agency. Authors who take this path propose theories that, in some regards, do not match the theoretical desideratum. Therefore, the third objective is to sketch a non-reductive account based on a functional and performative notion of agency that applies to both individual-sized and group-sized forms of agency.

Each chapter pursues each goal, respectively, from first to third. Part One provides a critical survey of different accounts of shared agency, aiming to clarify how two or more individuals can act together intentionally and how extensive previous explanations of shared agency have been. Part One focuses intensively on the theory of Bratman, Gilbert, Searle, and Tuomela, known as 'the Big Four of Collective Intentionality' (Chant, Hindriks & Preyer 2014).[2] They have illuminated the question of shared agency by providing indispensable explanations and theoretical tools to account for how two or more individuals act together intentionally. Part Two considers shared agency in terms of group agency and asks whether the subject of group agency is the individuals who contribute to the performance or the group that they form. As the scope broadens, the Big Four's analysis is enriched by List and Pettit's proposal (2011). Part Two then moves to discuss the contributions of the Big Five. The question then becomes: has someone from the Big Five of social ontology offered a group-level account of shared agency? By 'group-level account', I mean an account that defends the idea that sometimes groups, not individuals, are the subject of intentions and actions. Part Three explores the received accounts by showing how adhering to a particular form of individualism has undermined most attempts to treat groups as agents. The thesis developed here is to drop such an individualistic premise and offer a functionalist and performative notion of agent: an agent is what is capable of agency. In the wake of Carol Rovane's action theory (Rovane 1998, 2004, 2014), I will maintain that in so far as social groups can act intentionally—by committing to a rational plan—they can be regarded as agents. It is only in these cases that shared agency can be regarded as group agency.

To begin, we need to establish what shared agency is. There are various occurrences that intuitively cause us to suppose that two or more individuals do something together. Here are just some of many possible examples: looking out the window, one can see people walking and chatting with one

---

[2] 'Big Four' thus denotes the group of philosophers who focused specifically on collective action. 'Big Five' denotes the Big Four in addition to Pettit (here, List and Pettit) as a group interested more generally in social ontology and agency in collective and group contexts.

another, friends grabbing a coffee together, children crossing the street in line by pairs, and neighbors greeting each other. One can also think about more complex contexts of agency happening in private life and at work. In those circumstances, it is common to experience situations where obtaining a goal is a complex challenge that can be easily overcome through a concert of individual contributions rather than by a single individual effort. Meeting strict deadlines, moving heavy obstacles, and preparing amazing shows are just some targets better reached with the help of others. Sometimes, it may also happen that people act together moved by altruistic motives, feelings of solidarity, or empathy. Contrariwise, one might do something with others instrumentally, aiming for a particular goal. Other times people share an action just by obeying pre-existing rules or customs, unaware that the act implies collective efforts. For instance, standing in line at the supermarket is not a matter of deliberation; we stand together and wait for our turn because we are habituated and expected to do it. It is a custom, and respecting that custom can be seen as a way of acting together—although no joint action was voluntarily started. Shared agency may also arise from intimate relationships binding individuals together, as in the case of individuals getting married, becoming friends, or business partners. Another interesting phenomenon concerns worshippers, people who do something together by praying to the same God in which everyone believes. Setting differences aside, all these examples have at least one thing in common: each describes a performance in which several individual contributions are conducive to the same goal. Nevertheless, the scenario may be different and concern "cases of joint action with an inbuilt element of conflict" (Tuomela 2000, p. 7). For example, in the case of a tennis match, the activity requires two or more players, rules, the referee, a suitable court, and the right equipment; moreover, the expected end of playing together is based on each individual's aim to defeat the opponent(s) and win the match. This example demonstrates that shared agency sometimes involves competition.

The list is long and could even be longer. By allowing our imagination to run wild and find examples of shared agency without restraints, we might end up with a bountiful variety of situations where two or more people do something together. Still, the diversification offered by empirical descriptions is not the only source of complexity. To the variety of ways people act with others, we should further consider the various dimensions that emerge from the observer's perspective and situatedness. In fact, if we were to focus our research on a single definition of 'acting together', such as 'collective actions pursuing some common goal', the entire reflection may dismiss some classes of examples not involving a shared aim, like in the tennis case. Thus, the expression 'shared agency' will be used to identify only events of a specific sort while excluding others. Although it is not possible, or even productive, to eliminate the specificity imposed by the theory, it is essential to consider that different approaches use the same concept in ways that do not always overlap and sometimes have distinct meanings. This is the reason why different theories apply the same expression to domains that may differ from one another.

A cornerstone of this work is to investigate philosophical concepts without overlooking their theoretical standpoint and explanatory power. Thus, the next section delineates the philosophical perspective from which the concept of shared agency is defined, analyzed, and criticized in this book. Broadly, the philosophical approach is grounded in the contemporary debate in social ontology and situated within the analytical branch. Although this general perspective encompasses many variables, some common points make it feasible to merge several theories into a single approach. The most important point of consensus is the *intentionalistic model of action*, adopted by most analytical accounts.

2. The debate

Social ontology is a regional ontology that attempts "to put to use the rigorous tools of philosophical ontology in the development of category systems which can be of use in the formalization and systematization of knowledge of a given domain" (Zaibert & Smith 2007, p. 1). In particular, the domain of social ontology can be identified through the social world, a realm formed by the totality of individuals, relationships, groups of people, institutions and all other patterns of behavior that are a part of society. To better specify the scope, we need some preliminary clarifications about the specific concerns associated with the discipline. There are many different branches, varyingly characterized by specific methodological choices, tasks, and background references.[3]

First, there is social ontology of phenomenology, rooted in the Münich and Göttingen Circles, particularly in the doctrine of Edmund G. A. Husserl (1973, 1975, 1984), Max Scheler (1954), and Adolf P. B. Reinach (1989). These philosophers studied the experience of the subject and the nature of the object, referring to the notions of consciousness and intentionality—two constitutive moments of social objects, subjects, and the relationship between the two poles.[4] Second, and strictly intertwined with the phenomenological approach, there are discussions in social ontology close to the philosophy of law. This branch is related to theorists such as Reinach

---

[3] For a thorough introduction to the discipline, see Epstein 2018.
[4] About phenomenological social ontology, see Andina 2016, Salice 2013, Salice & Smith 2016.

(1989), Wilhelm A. J. Schapp (1930, 1959), and Czeslaw Znamierowski (1912), who devoted their research to the study of social entities—including laws, codes, norms, and institutions—characterized by normative features. Third, agency and social entities/structures have been studied in connection with one another by the proponents of critical realism (Archer 1995, 1998a, 1998b, 2010, Bhaskar 1998, Bhaskar & Lawson 1998, Elder-Vass 2007, 2010, 2014), a line of thought in contemporary sociology intertwined with social philosophy and action theory.

In addition, social ontology can be associated with critical theory. For example, György Lukács' ontology of social reality (1984) proposed an ontology concerning the reality established through human labor and the modifications it enacts on the natural and causally determined world.[5] Critical theory has also helped advance another way of reasoning related to the development of analytical social ontology, which spread notably among the exponents of the second Frankfurt School generation. The approach is the one drawn on John L. Austin's speech acts theory (1962) and embraced in Jürgen Habermas' theory of communicative action (1981a, 1981b). Apart from being true or false, the guideline is that some statements can represent a proper way of acting due to three main features: locutory, illocutory, and performative power. The first aspect concerns the production of a meaningful linguistic expression; the second element involves the action performed by the speaker in uttering that phrase; while the third is related to the power of the speech act to affect the audience and change the way things are. These features are typical of utterances expressed by performative verbs such as promising, asserting, claiming, forgiving, etc., which do not have any true or false value. Take, for example, the statement: 'I assert that the race is on'. This assertion communicates a meaning (locutory act), i.e., the beginning of the race; it expresses the intention to start the game (illocutory act); and it makes the race begin (performative act). Speaking out the statement consists of doing something and impacting the social world.

Speech act theory is important to introduce the analytical perspective into social ontology, which has found its starting point precisely in the study of language and the human capacity to make things with words. In particular, John R. Searle's contribution (1995) deeply impacted the debate on the construction, composition, and nature of social reality, influencing philosophers of mind, epistemologists, and researchers interested in

---

[5] On the relation between analytical social ontology and critical theory, see Testa 2015, 2016.

decision and game theory.[6] Briefly, Searle's philosophy of language holds that "speaking in a language is a matter of performing illocutionary acts with certain intentions, according to constitutive rules. These constitutive rules typically have the form 'X counts as Y', or 'X counts as Y in C'" (Searle 2002, p. 4). To speak in a language means saying things that one intends to do, while being formed by constitutive rules, and having the performative power to generate a new state of affairs, which is then represented in the mental attitude as Y.[7] While the X of constitutive rules represents a physical object (e.g., a piece of paper), Y indicates a new mind-dependent function covered by X (e.g., money) in context C (e.g., this piece of paper now counts as money in the context). The power of language is to add a new function to a slice of the world that did not have that meaning before the intention to implement it (Searle 2014).[8] Therefore, social ontology's main object is the mind-dependent world, considered as the portion of reality populated by functions, norms, and institutions, constructed by human language and interaction.[9] The core of Searle's theory asserts that the act of making something with language is an intrinsically collective performance, which gains its power through shared understandings by many individuals in context C.[10] In this sense, shared agency is involved in the creation,

---

[6] For a comprehensive introduction to Searle's philosophy, see Smith 2003.

[7] For the sake of simplicity, I use the expression 'constitutive rule' as mentioned in the quote (Searle 1995, 2002). It is worth noting that Searle subsequently modified and replaced the notion with the broader concept of declaration, which embraces a richer variety of ways of accepting status functions (cf., Searle 2010, pp. 19–24).

[8] In addition to standard cases in which a status function (Y) is attributed to a physical object, Searle has considered free-standing Y terms existing as long as "a status function is created without there being an existing person or object who is counted as the bearer of the status" (Searle 2010, p. 20). Examples of free-standing Y terms are corporations, electronic money, and blindfold chess. In response to Smith's critique (2003), taking freestanding Y terms to be exceptions to Searle's former account of constitutive rules, in Searle (2010, pp. 97–100) those cases are treated as characteristic products of complex societies, where collective intentionality is somehow integrated with the exercise of individual imagination. Thus, the declarations involved in the creation of any status function can generate social facts that are not based on prior brute facts.

[9] An introduction to social objects is offered by Gallotti & Michael 2014, especially, Gallotti 2014 and Guala 2014.

[10] Sharing an intention has a weak meaning on Searle's view as it regards the belief that other individuals in C may participate in the effort planned by the intention. The collective nature of the action is fixed by the form of the attitude, 'we-intention', which is a trait of individual psychology. Cooperating with others is not necessary for the exercise of collective intentionality (Searle 1990, 1995, 2007, 2010). Searle's perspective will be explored in Section 2.2.

maintenance, and modification of objects generated by declarations and classified as mind-dependent entities (Searle 2003).[11]

Shared agency is not only a structuring element of the social world, but it is also structured by such reality and regulated by established practices, customs, and institutions. Accordingly, shared agency refers to performances carried out by two or more individuals together and through the mediation of social facts. The presence of a normative regulation may determine some sort of organization in the context, which allows complex ways of doing things together. When doing things together in these contexts, everyone plays a role and participates in the action, bearing a function that is fixed by the system of rules and realizable by anyone who is suitable.[12]

3. The theory

Current accounts in analytical social ontology investigate shared agency by adopting the doctrine of intentionality. This theory is a philosophical model approaching the study of human behavior that has acquired its full dignity in the contemporary debate, especially after the theory's diffusion through the innovative works proposed by Elizabeth Anscombe (1957) and Donald Davidson (1963, 1970).[13] According to Anscombe, an intention is the reason for someone to do something—the reason for the action—which makes an intentional action an action "to which a certain sense of the question 'why?' has application" (Anscombe 1957, p. 11). This means that intentional actions are those events of human behavior for which the agent can account. Insofar as a particular action has been done for a reason, we can ask the agent why she has acted in that way, and since the action was an intentional one, the agent should be able to give us an answer—making it possible to hold the agent responsible for her actions. Similarly, Davidson maintains that an action is intentional if and only if the event (i.e., the action or the activity of doing it) can be considered and described as something done for a reason. For Davidson, "a reason rationalizes the action only if it leads us to see something the agent saw, or thought he saw, in the action—some feature, consequence or aspect of the action the agent wanted, desired, prized [...]" (Davidson 1963, p. 685). Importantly, in order to take an agent's action as an accountable

---

[11] On collective intentionality and the creation of the social world, see Seddone 2014. For an analysis and critique regarding the strict focus on collective intentionality, see Ylikoski & Mäkelä 2002.

[12] On complex forms of social behavior see, among others, Descombes 2011, Hodgson 2007b, List & Pettit 2011, Thomasson 2002, Tuomela 2007, 2013a.

[13] A concise introduction to intentional agency can be found in De Caro 2008, pp. 111–134.

event, a description must be provided based on which the agent is moved to action by a goal that she wanted to realize.[14]

A major part of the debate in social ontology has followed a similar intentionalistic framework by combining it with some principles of speech acts theory, particularly the importance of language in the making of the social world.[15] As Searle first suggested, the unique way in which humans communicate and give a structure to their life represents a primary feature in establishing what is social and what is physical. Socially created aspects are set through performative language use, which is the act people realize by attributing a specific function (e.g., money) to a neutral object, such as a piece of paper chosen to become a form of currency. In this sense, when people recognize the existence of a new object in the context, they are acting together. Their action consists of the performance they realize by sharing and uttering their common intention as it happens, for example, with the intention to make some piece of paper function as a form of currency. Thus, the intention is a mental attitude expressed by the speech act and connected with the willingness to do what the speech act effectively says and does. In other words, the intention can be described as a mental state representing (in a proposition) the task the agent wants to realize through the action, be it a verbal or physical performance.

Following this line of thought, Searle assumes that "an intentional action is simply the condition of satisfaction of an intention" (Searle 1983, p. 80). Apart from offering a different formulation of the issue, this statement focuses on at least three aspects characterizing the intentionalistic model of agency: the action, the mental state, and its conditions of satisfaction.[16] Let us start with the mental state, i.e., the intention. According to Searle, an intention for the

---

[14] The emphasis on accountability explains why intentional actions have been considered so important to become almost the exclusive focus of action theory. The fact that we can describe an action by attributing some willingness or rational guidance to the agent is the aspect that makes the action a relevant topic of research, especially in relation to moral and ethical issues (De Caro 2008).

[15] The book focuses specifically on the 'rationalistic' side of the debate, but it is worth mentioning that part of social ontology that has also considered aspects pertaining to the emotional and phenomenological experience of the subjects. The contributions of Hans-Bernard Schmid are particularly interesting in this regard (see Schmid 2009, 2014, 2017a, 2017b).

[16] It is important to observe that Searle rejects Davidson's idea that an action is intentional insofar as it is describable in terms of intentionality. Searle thinks that what is relevant is not the way of describing something but the nature of that something, i.e., the mental attitude (Searle 1980, pp. 47–70).

action is a kind of attitude which, together with desires, beliefs, and other mental states, shows a propositional form: 'I intend to do x' or 'I intend x'. Meaning that an intention for an action requires a subject having the attitude in mind, an external object to which the mental state refers, and a content that is the mental representation of the object. Moreover, the intentional attitude has a form that indicates the specific way in which the subject is relating herself to the object (the x term) when she is intentionally approaching it (Crane 2014). In this sense, an intention for the action has the form of a mental state planning for the action. This kind of reference makes the intentional case a specific one; if we consider other attitudes, for instance, beliefs and desires, the way of approaching the x term would present a different situation. Take the case of a belief. Here the subject has the mental state 'I believe that x' or 'I believe x', where x represents the object of the word with which the subject has a relation of believing it. For a belief to be satisfied, the content of the mental state must correspond with the object it wants to represent. Thus, if the mental state is 'I believe that it is raining', such a mental state will be satisfied—it will be true—only if the state of affairs in the world confirms the attitude's content. That said, it is easy to observe that intentions for the action work otherwise.

> Unlike beliefs and desires (broadly construed), the conditions of satisfaction of intentions are not mere states of affairs that coincide with the representational contents of the intentional state. These states of affairs must in addition be appropriately caused by the intentional state of intending, and agents who intend them must also wish that their intentional state of intending causes the appropriate state of affairs in the appropriate ways. The condition of satisfaction of an intention refers back to the representational contents of the intention. (Zeibert 2003, p. 212)

To rephrase, an intention for the action is satisfied insofar as the intention itself makes the agent do what the content represents as the intended action (performative power). If the action is realized by someone else or by the subject herself only by chance, the mental state will not be satisfied. In order for the intention to be fulfilled, it is necessary for it to play a causal role in the performance of the action. In this sense, "a given human behavior counts as an action, if and only if an agent having the intention to perform the action in question has caused it" (Schulte-Ostermann 2008, p. 191). As stated by Anscombe, the intention is the reason why a certain activity has been performed, and according to Searle, such an activity is what makes the intention realized.[17]

The notion of intentionality can be related to agency in several ways to generate, as Searle suggests, various kinds of intentional attitudes. First, there is the prior-intention, "that is the intention that one forms prior to the performance of an intentional action" (Searle 2010, p. 33), otherwise called the plan for the action and considered the outcome of the process of deliberation that leads the agent to the formation of the attitude in question. Additionally, there is the occurrence that Searle has named intention-in-action, which indicates a primitive and actual component of the action: "it is the psychological event that accompanies the bodily movement when I successfully perform an intentional action involving a bodily movement" (Searle 2010, p. 33). While prior-intentions come before the action, intentions-in-action happen with the performance itself.[18] Moreover, for an intentional action to be realized, a condition where (one or more) intentions-in-action are present is always necessary, whereas prior-intentions can be missing (as in the case of extemporary behaviors). The point is that one can do something without having planned it before, as the intentional character of the action will be guaranteed by the presence of intentions-in-action that occur even in the absence of full awareness. Further, by comparing and contrasting the two intentional phenomena, it becomes clear that they require different conditions of satisfaction. For example, if I plan to eat an apple, my prior intention will be satisfied by me eating the piece of fruit. Differently, intentions-in-action require me moving my hand to grasp the apple and then moving it again to lift it to my lips: these conditions of satisfaction will be encountered if and only if I effectively make the gestures the conditions prescribe.[19]

---

[17] According to Bratman there should be something more than the conditions of satisfaction that make intentions special mental states. Bratman proposes a distinction between intentions and other volitional attitudes (such as beliefs and desires) and connects intentions with the function of planning the action. The plan is a background framework on which the agent can weigh her beliefs and desires for and against the action. While beliefs and desires provide reasons concerning the action, intentions have the power to move the agent, to control her conduct, and to have an influence on it. Intentions create expectations that other attitudes do not generate (Bratman 1987, 1990).

[18] On the notion of intention-in-action, see McDowell 2011.

[19] In general, it is not necessary for the agent to be aware of the mental phenomenon involved in the action. Even though it is always possible to focus on the content of a mental state, such an acknowledgment is not necessitated by the event. Unaware intentions are more frequent in the case of intentions-in-action, while intentional plans—as the results of a deliberation process—are generally clear to the agent (Searle 2010, Crane 2014).

4. The approach

To better delineate the model of shared agency studied in this book, it is important to identify four dimensions of intentional agency that can be found in the case of both individual and shared agency. The investigation aims to clarify the extent to which the intentional faculty is involved in the definition of agency as an intentional behavior, and how strict the connection between the intention and the action may be. While the debate has introduced each relation, not all dimensions are a part of every account.[20]

    a.   **Constitutive relation.** Intentions and actions are constitutive parts of agency (Stahl 2013): "Actions and intentions, in other words, are interlocking components of a system of practical activity" (Epstein 2015, p. 218), within which the mental attitude is an essential constituent of agency and not just a descriptive feature, as Davidson would say. The intention—especially in the case of intention-in-action—is associated with bodily movement. Together, both intention and bodily movement realize the entire performance of action. In this sense, intentional attitudes are defined as psychological counterparts of physical acts and as constitutive elements of the whole activity (Searle 2007, 2010, Tuomela 2007).[21]

    b.   **Structural relation.** Intentions do not only occur with and within the action, especially as prior intentions; they also provide structure to the event by representing the plan that the action (gesture + intentions-in-action) is going to realize. Intentions for the action are plan states: "they are embedded in forms of planning central to our intentionally organized temporally extended agency and to our associated abilities to achieve complex goals across time" (Bratman 2014a, p. 15). According to this, intending and acting are connected by a

---

[20] It is a task of Part One to show the heterogeneity dominating analytical social ontology and the way of theorizing intentional agency. More precisely, in that part, the focus is on the dimensions of shared agency characterizing the theories proposed by Bratman, Gilbert, Searle, and Tuomela, namely the 'Big Four' of collective intentionality.
[21] In other words, intentions are constitutive of agency because they are essential components of any phenomenon of agency. Thus, a behavior is an intentional action if and only if it is moved by intentions or if there are intentions related to that act. Furthermore, a system can be said to be an agent if and only if it can bear and satisfy intentions for the action.

structural relation in which the mental state indicates the direction towards which the activity is oriented;[22]

c. **Normative relation.** Apart from representing the scope of the performance, the content of intention can also be considered as the aim to which the agent commits herself when she formulates, in her mind, the willingness to act on that basis. Any intention for the action creates some sort of normative bond between the action and the content of the attitude—by having the goal in mind, the agent commits herself to the action of realizing the goal (performative trait). The intention represents in its content a task that, to be obtained, requires the effective performance of the activity;[23]

d. **Causal relation.** An intention is the cause of the action as it has the power to trigger and start the performance planned by the mental state. To be more precise, a distinction needs to be made: prior intentions exert a causal power on the formation of intentions-in-action, whereas the latter—at least in Searle's perspective (2010)—have a direct causal influence on the bodily movements with which they occur. Therefore, prior intentions do not trigger the act straightforwardly.

Thus, according to intentionalistic action theory, the connection between intentions and actions can be regarded as an inner, multifold relation, which shows at least four different connotations: constitutive, structural, normative, and causal effectiveness. The challenge is to understand how it could be possible to combine the idea of intentional actions with that of shared agency. In particular, the difficult question is to identify how an individual's internal mental state might relevantly (constitutive, structural, causal, and normative) influence the performance of an entire group of people (Velleman 1997).

---

[22] It is important to underline that the kind of guidance provided by the intentional faculty is a form of rational control that does not exclude other structuring forces from the picture. Instincts, emotions, habits, and dispositions might be seen as further elements that orient the human capacity to act (Clarke 2015, Mele 2003, Pacherie 2002, Small 2017, Testa 2017, Thompson 2008). Still, the focus of the present book is specifically on intentional actions.

[23] A rejection of the normative agency relation might be difficult to defend especially when the agent expresses her willingness verbally or makes it public somehow. Such a declaration will create expectations in the observers that are difficult to deny (Schmid 2009).

How could we possibly relate the mental attitude of each participant with the activity of a group? And how should we interpret the assumption that a group of individuals can act by following a shared intention for the action and be moved by a shared intention-in-action? On this point, the debate is still divided. On one side, some scholars argue that intentional shared activities involve the same faculty that underlies individual intentional behavior (Ludwig 2014, 2016, Miller 2007, Pacherie 2007, Salice 2015); on the other side, there are the advocates of so-called collective intentionality, the human faculty to have collective intentions for the action.[24] Bratman, the reference point of the former position, proposes a way to classify the diatribe by distinguishing between the continuity thesis and the discontinuity thesis of intentionality. The continuity thesis indicates the perspective that "the theory of individual planning agency puts us in a position to provide a model of modest sociality (in our terms, a model of shared agency) without the introduction of fundamentally new practical elements" (Bratman 2014a, p. 9) that go beyond the theoretical apparatus required to explain individual behavior. Regarding the 'discontinuity thesis', Bratman notes that proponents, especially Searle and Gilbert, "see the step from individual to shared agency as involving a new basic practical resource" (Bratman 2014a, p. 9).

Differences aside, one of the purposes of this book is to delineate how various debates approach the notion of shared agency. More precisely, Part One considers the theories proposed by the Big Four as member-level accounts (MLA) of shared agency, which analyze events by focusing on what each participant thinks and does when she contributes to the fulfillment of a joint effort. Then, Part Two widens the scope of the investigation and questions whether the theories offered by the Big Five manage to provide a group-level account (GLA) that is suitable to treat shared agency as a phenomenon related to the group of individuals treated as a whole. Finally, Part Three argues that the acknowledged theories of shared agency propose different and well-working MLAs but do not present stable GLAs. So, an alternative approach is suggested.

5. The desideratum

Throughout this book, I argue that member-level accounts are merely one side of the coin. Even shared agency can be seen from another perspective—the group-level account (GLA)—which treats groups as the subject of intentional actions. As opposed to the MLA, the GLA assumes shared agency

---

[24] An overview of the main approaches to collective intentionality can be found in Jankovic & Ludwig 2018, Schweikard & Schmid 2012.

as a complex event that cannot be understood through concepts and descriptions suitable for explaining individual-level forms of agency. In other words, the GLA attempts to approach (at least, some) phenomena of shared agency through concepts and descriptions that refer specifically to high-level notions, such as 'group attitude', 'group action', and 'group agent'.

Thus, we will first examine shared agency and its member-level explanation(s). In this respect, the main concern is to understand how the discipline has described the event of individuals sharing mental states located in the mind of each and familiar to everyone in the context. The purpose is to grasp features typical of shared agency and show how the philosophical debate has accounted for these features. The approach is, at the same time, critical and meta-theoretical. Its critical side aims at outlining prominent positions, revisiting interpretations, and suggesting points of agreement. Its meta-theoretical side calls into question the theoretical premises and explicative objectives of social ontology rather than its content. The investigation regards second-order assumptions, methodological choices, epistemological perspectives, and explicative targets characteristic of MLAs.[25]

Following the study of MLA, the book addresses the issue of shared agency as group agency. Close attention is given to the most influential accounts proposed in social ontology, with special focus on the theory rooted in the Big Four of collective intentionality alongside the account proposed by List and Pettit (2011). Hence, I will refer to the group as 'the Big Five'. As the issue of high-level social explanations is not a new topic in philosophy, the present research does not claim to illustrate all positions exhaustively.[26] The focus here remains the Big Five's attempts to propose high-level accounts of shared agency. The core argument being: the debate has aimed at but not managed to find a consistent GLA for shared agency. Setting differences aside—each approach has conceived the group-level account as being somehow reducible to what happens at the members level. This reduction reveals ties to an individualistic mindset, which fixes some priority of individual agents over groups. 'Individualistic mindset' denotes the conjunction of several forms of individualism:

---

[25] I use 'second-order assumptions' with reference to the meta-theoretical level of reflection, considering the theory as an object of study. Consistently, the expression 'first-order assumptions' refers to considerations that are part of the theory and concern the contents investigated by it.

[26] An overview of the debate is offered by Zahle & Collin 2014.

    i.   ontological individualism: "the thesis that facts about individuals exhaustively determine social facts" (Epstein 2009, p. 187),

    ii.   normative (moral) individualism:[27] "the principle according to which the design of our socio-political institutions should ultimately be sensitive only to the concerns of human beings" (Hindriks 2014, p. 1566), since "something is good only if it is good for individual human or, more generally, sentient beings" (List & Pettit 2011, p. 182),

    iii.   intentional individualism: the conception that "[A]ny interpretation of an individual's behavior has to be given in terms of individual intentional states" (Schmid 2009, p. 23),

    iv.   metaphysical individualism: the claim that rational human beings are *natural persons* or agents (List & Pettit 2011, pp. 170-74),

    v.   second-level normative individualism (NI_2): the meta-theoretical characterization of intentional action theory for which agency is first and foremost human agency.

As I will argue, if shared agency has been conceptualized primarily as a phenomenon about individual agents and their intentional behavior, it is because the study of shared agency as group agency has been set up on misleading premises. More specifically, what has most compromised the attempt to treat groups as agents is the idea that if groups are capable of agency, they are so only in a derivative sense, whereas individuals are agents by nature, originally. Therefore, the natural agentive skills of individuals would be the starting point for building the agency of groups. Instead, I will contend that there is no natural agency; the ability to act always comes as the result of a process of deliberation and rational commitment. This applies to both individuals and groups.

In brief, the desideratum of the book is to clarify to what extent the GLAs proposed by the Big Five have been derived from MLAs and treated as reducible. Further, the desideratum suggests that—on different premises—the

---

[27] I use the expression 'normative individualism' as defined by Hindriks (2014) and Rovane (2014). Both have employed the adjective 'normative' to refer to the moral salience of the position, which gives priority to individual agents over group agents. Thus, I will consider normative individualism to be the view that attributes special moral status to individual agents.

two accounts could coexist as alternative readings of (at least, some cases of) shared agency—theories concerned with distinct levels of reality and reflection (Fodor 1998, List 2018).

6. The structure

The book is organized into three parts, respectively devoted to presenting, criticizing, and revising the debate.

Part One introduces the most influential member-level accounts of shared agency. This reconstruction considers the relation between mental states and actions by treating collective intentional activities as a multi-layered connection with constitutive, structural, normative, and causal features. Then, the investigation takes into consideration the account of Bratman, Searle, Tuomela and Gilbert, showing how the doctrine of intentionality has been adopted to describe actions done by two or more individuals together. The argument builds on a double alternative: the continuity and discontinuity thesis of intentionality. The former interprets shared agency with concepts and laws taken from the explanation of individual intentional action (Chapter One). The latter introduces specific notions and principles suitable for grasping facts with an intrinsic collective nature (Chapter Two). Differences aside, the debate is committed to notions—such as 'group' and 'collectivity'— that make the description of shared agency a different issue when compared to individual agency (Chapter Three). The point is maintained based on the analysis of the four agency relations between intending and acting (i.e., constitutive, structural, normative, and causal relation).

Part Two questions whether the debate has managed to provide an interpretation of shared agency that goes beyond the member-level account (MLA) to propose a non-redundant group-level account (GLA). I argue that, although most authors (including Gilbert, List, Pettit, Tuomela and, in some sense, Bratman) claim to grasp shared agency by means of high-level concepts and descriptions, the explanation they provide is still bound to specific forms of individualism. Assuming all intentionality happens in each individual mind, the debate takes individual agents as the ultimate motors of any intentional action. Moreover, no ontological commitment has been endorsed to the existence of group agents. Consequently, notions such as 'group agent', 'group action', and 'group attitude' have acquired meaning only for descriptive purposes (Chapter Four). This framework takes the name of holistic individualism as it combines methodological holism with ontological individualism (Chapter Five). By outlining the GLA of holistic individualism, I will discuss whether high-level descriptions of reducible entities have proved stable enough to reach the proposed goal: to explain shared agency in terms of group agency (Chapter Six).

Part Three begins with a survey of the four dimensions characterizing the relation between intentions and actions showing the flaws hidden in the GLA of holistic individualism (Chapter Seven). Apparently, the main problem is that given ontological individualism, analyzing shared agency through concepts directly referred to groups cannot avoid contradictions as the claim of describing shared agency with a holistic lexicon is not strong enough to avoid returning the discussion to the individual members (Chapter Eight). Such a reductive force finds its source in deep metaphysical individualism, attributing special rational and normative status to individual agents. This premise generates ontological individualism and exerts its side effects on constitutive, structural, normative, and causal dimensions of shared agency. Consequently, holistic individualism hardly supports stable high-level descriptions.

Solving contradictions is, however, possible. The task requires questioning the metaphysical priority of individual agents and considering rational systems of agency as fully-fledged subjects of agency (Chapter Nine). Once the metaphysical priority of individual agents is abandoned, both individual and group agents can be considered rational systems, equally established over time and through the interaction with the social environment (Chapter Ten). In defense of this account, I maintain that the capacity to act intentionally results from an identity-giving process, constituting the rational stability and continuity of any system working as an agent. Thus, the notion of group agent and the GLA concerned with it are not reducible to the MLA because each account refers to specific dimensions of the social world and assumes a particular perspective on it.[28] In group contexts, the MLA focuses on acting as a group member; the GLA studies the group as a unique subject.

---

[28] This book is based on my doctoral thesis, entitled *Dimensions of Shared Agency: In Search of a Group-Level Account in Social Ontology* (University of Parma, 2018).

Part One.
Shared agency

Chapter 1

The continuity-thesis account

1.1 Survey of Part One

Conceptually, the dimensions of shared agency are dramatically open to different interpretations, each of which views shared agency based on particular definitions, perspectives, and purposes. The intertwining of such varied accounts, all claiming to speak of the same event, makes studying the debate challenging—perhaps nearly as difficult as investigating shared agency itself. For this reason, the following section will identify points of agreement, overlapping theoretical frameworks, and similar objectives. By drawing clear guidelines throughout various approaches to shared agency, it becomes possible to understand its limitations more easily. In other words, clarifying the premises is a good starting point for identifying eventual problems of misframing and possible foundations for alternative interpretations. Later on, we will discuss critiques and revisions of current accounts, but we need to consider shared agency through the lens of social ontology for that to take shape. Using social ontology, I suggest considering three dimensions of shared agency. First, shared agency, in the case of collective intentional behavior, concerns a class of intentional actions composed by the intentional subject, the mental state, and the action. In this sense, shared agency has many descriptive parts that constitute the event. Second, the case that dimensions of shared agency are the conceptual definitions applied to the study of those descriptive components. As with all philosophical investigations, how one might approach a particular object of study involves specific definitions, notions, and principles that are characteristic of the position. These theoretical tools can be so different from account to account that overlooking the theoretical dimensions would lead to serious misunderstandings about how shared agency is regarded. Thus, dimensions of shared agency can be located both in the event and in the theoretical account. Third, the case that different dimensions refer to different perspectives of analysis, according to which shared agency can concern either collective actions or actions of collectives (Ware 1988). In this case, each dimension identifies the portion of reality considered on a case-by-case basis and the perspective from which each slice is viewed.[1] We will see that accounting for a social phenomenon of agency can be done by focusing on the actions of the group's members or by looking at the entire group-scale event as one.[2]

With these cases in mind, this book argues that dimensions of shared agency appear in three kinds, each of which raises specific issues:

1. descriptive dimensions: what are the distinctive components of shared agency? What is collective in shared intentional activities? Is it the subject, the mode, or the content of the attitude? What are the agency relations between a shared plan and a joint action?

2. Conceptual dimensions: what are the main accounts of shared agency? In what way do they differ from one another? Do they speak of the same object? Is there any point of agreement?

3. Micro-macro dimensions: how could it possibly be that shared agency allows different levels of description? Is shared agency at the participant level a different event from shared agency at the group level? Could we speak of group agency? If so, would group-level accounts be irreducible to member-level accounts?

Answers will be provided based on the following categorizations:

1. descriptive dimensions:
    (1a) intentional behavior: intention (subject-mode-content) + action,
    (1b) agency relations: constitutive, structural, normative, and causal relation.

---

[1] The set of distinctions here proposed is not aimed at being exhaustive as there may be other meanings for which shared agency has dimensions, such as the dimensions of experience and emotion captured by phenomenology. Although the issue is of utmost importance and has become the center of thriving philosophical researches and discussions (Pacherie 2017, Salice & Schmid 2016, Salmela 2012, Schmid 2014), this book is mainly focused on aspects regarding the rational planning of collective actions as conceived by the Big Five.

[2] Section 3.3 adds some further considerations on interpreting 'dimension'.

2. Conceptual dimensions:
   (2a) continuity-thesis account,
   (2b) discontinuity-thesis account.
3. Micro-macro dimensions:
   (3a) member-level account (MLA),
   (3b) group-level account (GLA).

According to this framework, Part One proceeds as follows: Chapter One outlines how shared intentional behaviors (1a) have been interpreted by the continuity-thesis account (2a) proposed, in particular, by Bratman as one of the most influencing philosophers interested in member-level accounts of shared agency (3a). Then, Chapter Two concerns shared agency (1a) and the MLA (3a) of the discontinuity-thesis account (2b), with special attention drawn to the interpretations given by Searle, Tuomela, and Gilbert. Finally, Chapter Three describes the four agency relations (1b) as presented in all the MLAs outlined in Chapter One and Chapter Two (3a).

As suggested in the introduction, member-level accounts explain shared agency in terms of individual psychology, behavior, and relation with the social environment by considering the individual-level portion of reality as the focus of analysis. Hence, I focus on the descriptive components of shared agency by questioning whether the event shows a common trait that sets the phenomena of this kind completely apart from events of one single agent personally realizing her own plan for the action. Answering this question has generated a variety of accounts, many of which have found it reasonable to locate the distinctive aspect of shared agency in the mental state planning it— the intention for the action. Thus, although current member-level accounts in analytical social ontology differ widely from one another, it seems to be generally accepted that intentions in the case of shared actions differ from intentions planning individual agency either in kind or content (Tollefsen 2002a). When the discrepancy between attitudes occurs in the content of the mental state, I will discuss the continuity-thesis account of shared agency (2a). According to this view, best exemplified by Bratman's theory, each individual who takes part in the action is considered to have an intention that expresses its shared nature by representing the group dimension in the content: 'I intend that we do x together'. By contrast, intentionality in joint action can differ from intentionality in individual action due to a change in kind. Thus, shared agency involves intentions that are typical of collective contexts of agency since they are the product of a special rational capacity that is collective intentionality as opposed to individual intentionality. The phrase for we-intentions is 'we intend to do x together', which is formally different from 'I intend to do x' as well as from 'I intend that we do x together'.

The introduction of we-intentionality allows the clustering of some approaches, including Searle's, Gilbert's, and Tuomela's theory, all endorsing a form of discontinuity-thesis account (2b). Accordingly, the next sections explore the member-level account proposed in Bratman's works as a case of the continuity-thesis account of intentionality.

1.2 Agency according to Bratman

Some authors have approached intentional shared actions by leaning into the theoretical sources provided by research on individual intentionality. The reason being, no relevant discrepancy between individual and collective agency, neither metaphysical nor descriptive, has been found. On the one hand, the same structure that regulates individual conduct is assumed to regulate activities done by many agents together; and on the other hand, the same theoretical tools one employs to describe one's own or others' personal behavior should suffice for explaining shared agency.

Bratman (Bratman 1987, 1999, 2007, 2009d, 2014a, 2014b, 2015, 2018) has scrupulously developed this line of thought and further theorized a reductive, yet multifaceted, model of shared agency. The perspective he has promoted is reductive in the sense of considering shared agency as a phenomenon constructed and explained by aspects of individual intentional agency. Additionally, Bratman's perspective reduces the subject of shared agency to the network of individual agents, which rejects any attempts to introduce collective subjects of action. Still, Bratman's approach conceives a multifaceted idea of shared agency because it assumes that individual intentions for the action can coordinate themselves in various ways and generate different kinds of social activities. Consequently, the rejection of new concepts for explaining group phenomena does not imply a homogeneous interpretation of agency. Relevantly, from an ontological and methodological viewpoint, Bratman elaborates a form of individualism that he calls *augmented individualism*, which distinguishes itself from a reductive approach—it includes the possibility to enrich the explanation of what happens to singular individuals with a network of interlocking attitudes. Even if it is true that the attitudes of which Bratman speaks are individual states of mind, the complex interconnection and influence that such an entanglement may have on individual intentions generate a different scenario from the one in which a single person acts based on her own intentions for the action. Despite this, shared agency is still comparable to individual intentional action, especially when the latter is considered in relation to its unfolding over time. In fact, in Bratman's proposal, the study of different states of mind held by the same agent over time is analogous to different states of mind belonging to various agents at the same time. Therefore, the kind of augmented individualism he proposes holds a thesis of continuity and applies the same methods to investigate both the issues, namely the interconnection of intentions over time and the interconnection of intentions among persons:

> The *shared-ness* or *joint-ness* of shared intention consists of relevant contents of the plan states of each and relevant interconnections and interdependencies between the planning psychologies of each, all in relevant contexts. This augmented individualism depends then on a rich model of individual agent as a planning agent whose agency is temporally extended. (Bratman 2014a, p. 12)

Insofar as the target is to understand what shared agency is and how to approach it, we need to define first a theory of individual intentional agency. Bratman's aim is to find a way to relate individual intentionality at a specific time (synchronic level) to individual intentionality over time (diachronic dimension).[3] The main undercurrent of Bratman's research is that the theory of individual agency as a temporally structured phenomenon should provide all the conceptual tools we need to reflect upon shared agency. The author has suggestively called such tools the *building blocks of shared agency* (Bratman 2014a).

To better comprehend what the building blocks are, as constitutive parts of the notion of shared agency, giving a brief introduction of Bratman's understanding of individual intentional agency is an unavoidable step. It is important to mention two general considerations on intentionality: the first is that an intention for the action is a state of mind, a rational aspect that the agent formulates in planning her action. In this sense, and in opposition to Davidson's proposal (Davidson 1963), intentions are not just descriptive features; on the contrary, they have a metaphysical cogency, meaning that they exist in the individuals' minds. Due to this fact, speaking of intentionality, for Bratman, is always a matter of both metaphysics and description—concerning what happens in the mind and what is told about it, respectively. The second assumption is that intentions are plan states, i.e., attitudes planning for the action with a structuring function over the action. In this sense, we might say that intentions are meant to be the kind of mental phenomena that Searle called 'prior intentions' (Searle 2010). In addition to this notion of plan states, Bratman assumes that actions are complex phenomena composed of many different aspects and, in some sense, composed of many 'lower' intentions held

---

[3] On the comparison between synchronic and diachronic reason (self-governance), see Bratman 2004, 2009a, 2009b, 2009c, 2010, 2012.

by the agent over time or in connection with various facets of the same action.[4] In this respect, intentions are characterized as partial plans that need to be filled in as time goes by. For example, today I intend to go swimming tomorrow. That intention will be completed through additional deliberations and intentions about how to go there, when, and with whom. Thus, the plan of swimming tomorrow is just a single part of the story. Nevertheless, such partiality is accompanied by another typical character—confirming the complexity ingrained within individual agency—the hierarchical structure of intentions. An intention for the action generally involves other components that are definable as sub-plans. Regarding my plan to go swimming tomorrow, possible sub-plans could be: having fun, driving the car, or putting on a swimsuit. I can keep certain aspects of the activity, while deciding to discard other components, without losing the original plan of swimming tomorrow.

By defining intentions as plans for the action, Bratman affirms that "plans […] are mental states involving an appropriate sort of commitment to action: I have a plan to A only if it is true of me that I plan to A" (Bratman 1990, p.19). Thus, besides the characters of partiality and hierarchy, intentions as plan states also have a normative salience. Intentions for the action have the power to guide what the agent does by generating some sort of commitment—a bundle of expectations about the action.[5] In this sense, Bratman identifies plans as norms: a plan for the action endows the agent with a rational standpoint from which one can exert a rational control on the action and guide further deliberations about its realization. This normative feature connects the capacity of having plans with self-governance. Having a plan confers a rational self-control on one's performances, which is guaranteed by two fundamental principles related to intentionality: *consistency* and *means-end coherence*. According to the former, intentions need to be consistent in a double sense: first, a plan has to be composed of sub-plans that do not prevent the fulfillment of the other parts concerned and of the plan as a whole—this is *internal consistency*. Second, intentions must be *consistent with beliefs*. Implying that for a plan state to be effective, it is crucial that the plan is compatible with the network of beliefs held by the agent. Bratman writes:

---

[4] Bratman conceives the structure of intentions in accordance to Harman's insight: "In a typical intentional action, you have an end E which you intend to achieve by means M, possibly foreseeing side effects S of M and consequences C of E: ACT -> M -> E -> C -> S. Normally we would suppose that although M and E are intended, S and C need not be intended but might be merely foreseen", (Harman 1983, p. 123). Bratman (1984) discusses and diverges from Harman (1976, 1983).

[5] Normativity is what distinguishes intentions from beliefs and desires (Bratman 1990, 2009d, 2013, 2014a).

a good coordinating plan is a plan for the world I find myself in. So, assuming my beliefs are consistent, such a plan should be consistent with my beliefs, other things equal. Roughly, it should be possible for my entire plan to be successfully executed given that my beliefs are true. This is a demand that my plans be *strongly consistent, relative to my beliefs*. (Bratman 1987, p. 31)

This principle represents the first way to connect intentions with reflection and self-governance. Moreover, the idea of self-control is based on the *means-end coherence principle* of intentionality, which implies a balance between the goal of the plan and the means one chooses to pursue it. If one has the plan to go to the library and needs to use the car to go there, the intention to drive the car should be compatible with that of going to the library. Such a case could be further enriched by considering intentions that are fulfilled over time. On those occasions, the construction of an entire plan for the action may require various sub-plans related to activities that are the means to realize the end, and the agent needs to make multiple coherent deliberations over time (Bratman 1984, 1987).

This brief survey on Bratman's theory of individual intentional agency has shown the following main assumptions:

- intentions are plan states,

- plan states are partial,

- plans have a hierarchical structure,

- there are two normative principles. The former is about consistency, the latter regards means-end coherence.

Moreover, being consistent with beliefs and coherent with means is related to the capacity of exerting self-governance; for intentions to be successfully fulfilled, the agent must reflect on her plans and give them a stable structure. Reflection is an important aspect to open the path towards shared agency. In particular, it introduces the possibility of the diachronic dimension of individual agency, providing a framework for a cross temporally organized activity that, in Bratman's theory, is analogous of shared agency. Behind an individual temporal organization of agency (based upon the coherence and consistency of plans over time), there is a planning capacity common to the action's social organization: the common core consists of the control people have upon their own action through exercising the planning faculty.

1.3 The building blocks of shared agency

As the capacity for planning represents the core of Bratman's proposal about intentional agency, it is time to enrich such a view by individuating the building blocks of shared agency. As already mentioned, these structural elements are first taken from the theoretical apparatus involved in the explanation of individual agency. Then, the building blocks are used to formulate the explanation of shared intentional actions. The result is an understanding of shared agency grounded in normative and metaphysical continuity to individual intentional agency and its unfolding over time.

The first brick laid by Bratman assumes that shared intentions have the form 'intending that we J'—meaning that the intention is conceived as a mental attitude in which 'we' appears in the content. In particular, 'intending that we' is different from 'we-intentionality'. 'We-intentionality' is used to identify a mental capacity, typical of phenomena of shared agency—the *discontinuity thesis* of intentionality (Chapter Two)—or a capacity shown by a plural subject coinciding with the 'we' (Schmid 2009) (Chapter Four). Contrariwise, following the expression 'intending that we' is the idea that everyone involved in the context holds, in their mind, a shared intention. Such a mental state encompasses, in its content, the representation of a performance realized by all the individuals bearing the plan state. This discrepancy between the subject of the mental state (a single agent) and the actor (the 'we') makes it necessary to use the form 'intending that we J' rather than 'intending to J'. In fact, in the case of the latter expression, we would not know who performs the action, as the subject is omitted. Even though an ambiguous subject does not represent a problem for individual agency—where the intention is held by the same individual who performs the act—the case of a shared intention would become problematic for group agency because the intention is held by each individual but realized by many individuals together.[6]

---

[6] Bratman's concern is about the so-called own-action condition discussed by Stoutland (2002). The problem, for Bratman, is that if we assume—as Stoutland does—that an intention for the action is fulfilled insofar as the subject of the mental state is also its executor, how could we guarantee the own-action condition in shared agency? And how could we explain cases in which an agent *a* has the intention *x* that another agent *b* will fulfill *a*'s intention that *b* realizes *x*? Both cases are difficult showing a situation in which the fulfillment of the intention is not completely up to the subject having the intention. Bratman's suggestion is to use the form 'intending that we J' instead of 'intending to J'. The expression specifies the one who is expected to realize the intention and then the own-action condition decays accordingly (Bratman 2014a, p. 60–64).

Insofar as shared action is a plan realized by many individuals together, the second building block underlines the importance of each contribution and each plan state for composing the entire plan. In this sense, the meaning of 'I intend that we J' is not to be interpreted as if I had an all-embracing intention that supplants others' plans; instead, Bratman's idea is that when I have a shared intention, I include the reference to the shared intention of the other participants in its content. To exemplify, our shared intention to go to NYC implies we each intend the following: that we go to NYC *by way of* the intentions of each individual that we go to NYC (Bratman 1992). Thus, each one's mental state represents in its content the intention held by the other agents. This aspect leads us to the third construction element: the agents' mutual responsiveness concerning the intentions and actions of the others. In this element, everyone observes what the others do, or plan to do, in order to better deliberate about what to intend and how to behave in view of the final goal. Thus, 'intending that we J' by way of 'others' intentions that we J' is possible only if it is out in the open that everybody in the context has the shared intention in question, and each individual is aware of the others' attitudes towards the action. This is what Bratman calls the building block of publicity, which can also be formulated in terms of common knowledge. As he says:

> To fix ideas, however, we can here think of common knowledge as consisting in a hierarchy of cognitive aspects of the relevant individuals: it is common knowledge among A and B that p just when (a) A knows that p, (b) B knows that p, (c) A knows that B knows that p, (d) B knows that A knows that p, (e} A is in an epistemic position to know that (d), (f) B is in an epistemic position to know that (c), and so on. And what we want is that a constituent of our shared intention to j is a form of such common knowledge of that very intention. (Bratman 2014a, p. 57)

What emerges from this passage is that the condition of common knowledge refers to the presence in shared intentional agency of many components and mutually interlocked contributions. One's intention to be a part of the content of the intention of a partner is a way to be included in her plan and be considered a co-participant in the action (connection condition) (cf., Bratman 2014a, pp. 48–52). Moreover, similarly to individual plan states, shared intentions must show consistency and coherence. According to the first requirement, for a co-participant to be considered as such, she is expected to think—and this should be out in the open—that the intention she has in mind is conducive to the shared intention pursued by every individual in the context. The means-end coherence principle regulates the context so that each individual plan is a step towards realizing the entire plan: each individual plan represents a sub-plan functional to the realization of the shared goal.[7] Within this arrangement, each individual plan is a sub-plan of the shared intention, and it meshes with the others by enhancing the effort towards the shared end. Despite the sharedness of the final goal, for Bratman, meshing sub-plans are not necessarily matching intentions; even though the contribution of each has the structure of a shared intention and is conducive to the shared end, this does not require that everyone has the same intentional content. One can participate in a shared activity while moved by a reason compatible with the shared intention but divergent from that of the other agents in the context. If we consider cases of a shared activity, such as painting a house together, having different sub-plans is possible and often necessary. When making various plans, it makes sense to speak of meshing sub-plans for the action.

Considering the above outline, to construct the theory of shared intentional action proposed by Bratman, the following building blocks—in addition to the fulfillment of consistency and means-end coherence principles—are required:

- each intends that we do J,

- each intends that we do J by way of the intention of each that we do J,

- mutual responsiveness and satisfaction of the connection condition,

- publicity/common knowledge,

- intention on the part of each in favor of the shared intention for the action by way of meshing sub-plans of the intention of each.

Finally, it is important to integrate another feature: the interdependence among each participant's intentions. Interdependency supplements the

---

[7] The two principles work in the same way as in individual temporally extended action, where each sub-plan is coherent and consistent with the more general plan realized over time and with all the other sub-plans of the subject. In the case of a social performance, the interconnection is not among different attitudes at different times, but it is among the attitudes of different subjects. The common feature consists in the capacity for planning, establishing—in accordance with the two normative principles— a consistent and means-end coherent organization of the entire intentional plan.

previous blocks with the idea of persistent, stable relation among the parts. Persistence-interdependence is described by Bratman as a mutual rational support that we can formulate as

- the intention of each that we J persists, until the intention of the other's that we J persists, and *vice versa*.[8]

1.4 Bratman and the participatory-intention account

The model of shared agency proposed by Bratman and consistent with the continuity thesis of intentionality might allow for comparison with the participatory-intention account (PIA). This theory seeks to reduce shared agency to individual intentions taken singularly.[9] Participatory intentions are basically individual intentions. Those attitudes are considered participatory because they are plans for individual action in contexts where the activity of each actor aims at a goal that cannot be accomplished alone. Thus, participatory intentions involve emergent coordination, i.e., a form of intentional behavior in which the collective dimension emerges from automatic mechanisms of entrainment, alignment, and simulation.[10] Such mechanisms can be eventually rationalized into intentional attitudes and can also be made explicit among the participants. Such a behavioral pattern can still happen even in the absence of shared norms regulating the entire activity. This aspect is part of the reason that makes emergent coordination of PIA different from the joint intentional behavior discussed in Bratman's account.[11]

---

[8] Bratman identifies three kinds of interdependence: desirable, feasible, and obligated interdependence. In case of desirability-based interdependence, the persistence of intentions is based on each agent holding the intention as long as each participant keeps doing the same. This form of interdependence is stable since each participant judges such an intending a desirable activity. For what concerns feasibility-based interdependence, Bratman explains it as a kind of opportunistic attitude. The attitude occurs when each agent finds the goal of joint activity a feasible purpose to pursue, depending on the fact that each participant may hold the intention that we J as a feasible goal to pursue jointly. Finally, obligation-based interdependence is about the joint intentions that rely on the mutual obligations supporting the attitude. The introduction of these three kinds of persistence interdependence explains why in Bratman's list we can find eight building blocks instead of five (see Bratman 2014a, pp. 70–78).

[9] For an introduction to reductive interpretations of shared agency, see Alonso 2018.

[10] On entrainment, alignment, and simulation: Butterfill 2017; Castelfranchi 2015; Gallotti, Fairhurst & Frith 2017; Garrod & Pickering 2009; Knoblich & Sebanz 2008; Vesper, Wel, Knoblich & Sebanz 2012.

[11] On the distinction between planned and emergent coordination, see Butterfill 2017.

In particular, what distinguishes the former case from the latter is the intervention of rationality in terms of normative regulation. Although both forms of coordination require the use of rationality as a form of intentionality to govern individual behavior, for PIA this faculty is expected to regulate the actions of each actor, without necessarily securing any norm of coherence and consistency regarding the contributions (eventually) given by the others. In fact, in the case of emergent coordination, the interaction among subjects could happen even without rational capacities geared toward governing the collective effort. On the contrary, the kind of planned coordination proposed by Bratman necessarily involves intertwining individual plan states, making it feasible for the members to act jointly based on intentions for the action — the shared goal being the intentional content. In this case, the action is the fulfillment of an individual plan-state involving norms and structural organization of the parts. Therefore, we could observe that since PIA is based on a weak, even fortuitous, form of coordination of individual intentional actions, the account is not committed with planned and normatively regulated coordination. In fact, it does not involve any 'shared' rational control and normative constraint among the parties.[12]

So, according to PIA, "what makes my behavior participatory is nothing more (and nothing less) than my conception of what I do as related to the group act" (Kutz 2000, p. 11). In this sense, the participatory-intention account (PIA) seems to explain shared intentions by reducing the issue of joint action to individual contributory intentions where the only irreducible aspect might be identified in the cognitive horizon within which the agent locates (the representation of) her conduct. The group dimension appears from a set of beliefs held by each individual and gathered from the environment in which she lives. However, such a cognitive understanding does not affect the intentional nature of the act that, after all, is still an individual event.

It has been observed that:

> A participatory intention has two representational components, or sets of conditions of satisfaction: individual role and collective end. By "individual role" I mean the act an individual performs in order to foster a collective end; and "by collective end" I mean the object of a description that is constituted by or is a causal product of different individual's act. This is to say that individual participatory actions aim at two goals: accomplishment of a primary individual task that

---

[12] In other words, we could say that Bratman thinks of a more demanding form of coordination, which can be identified in terms of cooperation.

contributes to a secondary collective achievement, be it an activity or an outcome. (Kutz 2000, p. 10)

Although PIA and Bratman's theory depicts the group dimension as a feature accountable through individual attitudes, the role of the 'we' plays a slightly different function. On the one hand, for the PIA the mental representation of the group is a functional/cognitive element that makes it possible for the agent to conceive of her own contribution as part of a wider effort. Nevertheless, the group is neither introduced as part of the intentional content of the individual sub-plan nor as a normative milieu to which it belongs. On the other hand, Bratman maintains that the 'we' enters the attitude as a part of the representational content referred to in the sub-plan intended by each party. Moreover, the collective horizon has a normative influence on distinguishing what is appropriate from what is inconsistent with the activity pursued jointly with others. In this sense, Bratman takes the group as the outcome of cooperation, the executor who realizes the whole activity in practice (Bratman 2017). By concentrating on the network of individual participants—instead of focusing just on each individual participant—Bratman thinks it is plausible to ascribe the action to the 'we'. Far from being the subject of any intentional state of mind, the 'we' could instead be considered a functional notion—connected to the idea of networking, according to which a complex system can realize the plan devised by all participants through meshing sub-plans. Bratman concedes that "being the agent of the shared action can come apart from being the subject of the shared intention, even given that shared action is organized by the shared intention" (Bratman 2014a, p. 127). The main idea behind this assumption is that the general plan guiding the group activity is not an individual participatory intention but the outcome of a network of individual sub-plans, beliefs, expectations, commitments, and mutual responsiveness not reducible to the attitude held in the mind of each actor taken singularly. Consequently, to deny—as Bratman does—that shared agency requires more than interlocking individual attitudes towards the action does not coincide with the rejection of a wider perspective, which relates the action to the group as a whole (Bratman 2017). The group can be seen as the by-product of individual agency, becoming the system to which the action is functionally referred—a claim that the participatory approach is not inclined to accept. Bratman writes:

if a group has a shared intention to bring about an untoward effect and succeeds in doing that, we may want in some sense to hold that group accountable. But then what we need is an interpretation of such accountability that does not require a group subject (though it may require a group agent in the weak sense we have been discussing). (Bratman 2017, p. 128)

From this quotation, it seems clear that although the introduction of a plural subject of agency is profiled, the move is restricted only to the interpretation of the action and not extended to the subject of shared intentionality. In fact, the intentional viewpoint is bounded to every single individual. Taking the group as the actor is plausible because Bratman's position, i.e., augmented individualism (Bratman 2014a), assumes that, similarly to the case of individual action over time, agency in shared contexts is regulated by a network of intentions brought together in a consistent and coherent way by two normative principles (i.e., consistency and means-end coherence). Those principles transform emergent coordination into planned coordination and guarantee the entire plan's realization under the participants' shared rational control. Each sub-plan relates to that of the others and acquires its function only under conditions of publicity and common knowledge among the parties. Even though none of these elements exceeds individual psychology, reaching the final goal would require the fulfillment of the entire planning activity in addition to the satisfaction of every single contributory intention. The salience of that 'entire planning activity' represents the reason why speaking of a group as the actor realizing shared intentions might have, at least, an explanatory meaning, which could not be defended by the PIA.[13]

In conclusion, Bratman's continuity-thesis account of intentionality offers a different picture than the one proposed by the PIA, mainly because the former assigns the 'we' to a group dimension that is not just a matter of individual psychology.[14] Instead, the representation of the 'we' alludes to a system of

---

[13] Shared agency might be considered also by the discontinuity-thesis account in its divergence from purely individual agency. In this case, differences would concern the specific kind of attitudes introduced for the explanation of shared intentional behaviors, namely we-attitudes. Searle (2010), Tuomela (2007) and Gilbert (1989) have provided different versions of this position introducing collective/we-mode intentions for the action without violating the distributive principle, locating all intentionality in the individuals' mind. Therefore, it would be quite easy to argue against the association of the PIA to the discontinuity-thesis account, because we-attitudes are originally collective and cannot be explained in terms of individual intentionality (Chapter Two). We could define this kind of divergence as a categorical gap.

[14] A difference can be found also at the cognitive level: while the PIA does not consider the group dimension as a constitutive part of individual contributory intentions, but as an additional representation connected with the individual goal, the continuity thesis of intentionality regards the 'we' as a part of the content of the attitude. Thus, the 'we' is no more an additional representation associated with the individual goal, but an intrinsic component of intentionality. To say it otherwise, while the PIA takes contributory intentions to be made up of two different representational contents, Bratman's MLA assumes just one content of the attitude. The aspect multiplied in Bratman's MLA is

meshing plans, expectations, and norms locating the individual mental state in a broader context. This system of goals can be satisfied only through a complex and shared effort—an effort that can be ascribed to the entire collective. We will see that such an acknowledgment has both cognitive significance and methodological and normative implications.

As an alternative to PIA and Bratman's proposal, Chapter Two will consider explanations of shared agency that find relevant discontinuities between individual and shared intentional actions. In such accounts, what most marks the specificity of shared agency, is the so-called collective intentionality, a faculty in each person's mind meant to plan shared actions.

---

rather the number of intentions (i.e., sub-plans) relevant for the realization of a complex goal obtained over time and through social interaction. The point relates to Bratman's criticism of the simple view, which is meant to relate each intentional behavior to a single attitude planning it (Bratman 1984).

Chapter 2

The discontinuity-thesis account

2.1 The discontinuity thesis of intentionality

Current accounts in social ontology have treated the issue of shared agency by questioning the distinctive features of the event. Chapter One introduced Bratman's theory (Bratman 2007, 2010, 2014a), which considers shared intentional actions as the outcome of interrelated individual efforts that are bound together by the mediation of two normative principles. Consistency and coherency, respectively, secure each individual's contribution to the activity of the network. Bratman describes shared agency in terms of individual psychology, behavior, and mutual relationship; meaning, the entire event emerges from individual-level facts. The interrelation among the subjects is so important that it makes Bratman's account different from the narrower, individualistic approach, i.e., the participatory-intention account (PIA), which considers shared agency as the result of individual intentions and actions, taken singularly (Kutz 2000). In the framework of PIA, it is possible to account for the event of two or more individuals acting together by applying only concepts and principles concerning individual mind and behavior, casting networking to the periphery. Setting differences aside, I argued that—compared to the concepts used to understand individual agency—both Bratman's MLA and PIA defend a kind of formal continuity in the study of shared agency as they avoid introducing any formal discontinuity in the way in which individuals think and act together. In this sense, the continuity-thesis of intentionality is maintained, assuming that shared intentional behaviors can be spelled out in terms of individual (I-mode) intentionality.[1]

Alternatively to continuous accounts of intentionality, views that consider events of shared agency different from cases of individual agency (due to the

---

[1] Assuming that the mode of intentionality is an I-mode does not imply establishing the content of the intentional attitude as a proposition referring to the individual agent taken singularly as it is, for example, with 'I intend that I do x'. In fact, one might participate in a shared activity with the I-mode intention that 'we' realize the plan in practice. Considering the peripheral role attributed to the network, we argued that the minimalist account of PIA does not embrace such a collectivity-oriented content (Kutz 2000), which is instead a feature plainly accepted by Bratman (Section 1.4).

kind of attitudes required on each occasion) have received much attention. While individual agency is based on I-mode intentionality, psychologically speaking, shared agency is the outcome of we-mode intentionality. We-mode intentionality is a specific way of thinking in which each individual agent has plans in a plural grammatical form. Examples of we-mode intentions are 'we intend to do *x* together', 'we collectively intend to *x*', 'we have the collective intention to do *x*'. 'Intending together', 'intending collectively', and 'having the collective intention' are all ways of saying that each individual in the context has the we-mode intention to do something with the other participants. The possibility of creating such a connection among the agents is based on mutual beliefs that each one in the context is willing to participate in the activity with personal contributions. Even though mutual beliefs are important for gaining a full understanding of shared agency, the specificity of accounts focused on we-mode attitudes can already be found in studying the intentional state of mind. Indeed, the formal discontinuity introduced by this side of the debate surrounds the mode of intention: the way in which individuals think of what they are going to do together with others. We-mode thinking generates collective mental states, showing the collective dimension in the form of intentionality. Such a specific form of intentionality is collective intentionality, and the accounts that endorse that faculty are mentioned in this book as proponents of discontinuity-thesis accounts of intentionality.[2]

Thus, we-mode thinking is different from I-mode thinking in the way that the form of the attitude changes. On one side, this modification in kind has been interpreted as a phenomenological feature—a filter of individual experience that occurs every time the subject feels her own thoughts and actions as thoughts and actions of the group to which she belongs.[3] From this perspective, we-mode intentionality has to do with the specificity of "experiences had and shared by individuals as members of some group" (Pacherie 2018, p. 166) that are also associated with bodily mechanisms of alignment, simulation, resonance, and relevant social emotions such as empathy and solidarity (Rizzolatti & Sinigaglia 2008, Salmela 2012). Then, on the other side, contemporary analytical investigations have focused on we-mode as a specific aspect of intentional states of mind: a mode of thinking that makes collective intentions genuinely different from individual plan

---

[2] For an introduction to non-reductive views of shared intention, see Tuomela 2018.
[3] On collective intentionality in the history of philosophy and phenomenology, see Salice 2013.

states.[4] Insofar as intentional attitudes require (a) a subject who has intentions in mind, (b) a content represented or just meant by the mental state, and (c) a mode through which the subject refers to it, modifying the mode involves a variation of just one of these constitutive features. While Chapter One has dealt with accounts focused on the content of individual intentionality (b), this chapter treats some of the most influential theories of collective intentionality. The approach considers the collective nature of shared agency to be about the mode of the attitude (c). Searle, Tuomela, and Gilbert will be the protagonists of the following sections, which are going to show how differently those authors have interpreted the discontinuity-thesis of intentionality as a mode-account.

We will see that, besides the acceptance of collective intentionality, it is possible to find a point of disagreement among mode-account proponents. This disagreement is analogous to the discrepancy detected in content-accounts between Bratman's theory and the PIA. In fact, as observed about PIA already, Searle considers shared agency to be explained by studying the psychology of individuals, taken singularly, as if they were brains in a vat. Contrariwise, Tuomela and Gilbert argue that the foundations of shared agency are situated within the inter-relation among those who participate in the action. In line with Bratman's account, Tuomela and Gilbert take the difference between individual and shared agency to be the outcome of mutual beliefs, joint attention, and commitment: these aspects bring the individual agents together in a network and make them think in the we-mode as group members.[5]

---

[4] The mode of intentions has been introduced in social ontology by Tuomela, who proposes a notion of mode that is fundamentally different from the mode of intentions meant by Brentano (Brentano 1874). While the phenomenological notion captures the way in which the subject refers to the object of intention through the mediation of specific attitudes such as desire, belief, concern, and so forth, according to Tuomela, the mode has an adverbial function as it grasps the mode of experience. On the adverbial function of mode, see Tuomela 2013a, pp. 36-37.

[5] Searle elaborates on the network (Searle 2010) in a way that might seem at odds with considering Searle's position being a theory of original collective intentionality. In fact, Searle's account of collective intentionality especially refers to individuals taken singularly, by leaving aside the important function played by mutual relationships and by the interaction with the social environment. Still, Searle finds the network is a key aspect for the construction and maintenance of the social world, as it represents a cognitive structure of beliefs, intentions, desires, and knowledge. The network helps to create a common ground for all the individuals who belong to the same social environment. However, being the outcome of intertwining intentional states, the network is not a necessary condition for the exercise of collective intentionality, which

Importantly, in addition to the content- and the mode-account, one could see shared agency as a collective event due to a modification in the subject of intentionality (a). In this case, shared agency is different from individual agency because it refers to a collective subject.[6] Among the Big Four, this position has been generally attributed to Gilbert's view as a plural subject-account of collective intentionality (Chant, Hindriks & Preyer 2014). I will suggest that the theory proposed by Gilbert should instead be counted among the mode-accounts, since it offers a concept of the plural subject that is not strong enough to entitle the group to the status of an autonomous agent (Section 2.4). The concept of autonomous agent refers to groups "not in a non-reductive, but rather in a reductive fashion, for it takes the group as intending to perform some action X only in virtue of the group members' jointly committing themselves to the performance of X" (Schweikard 2008, p. 10). Here, the thesis defended is that the most essential aspects of Gilbert's view are the inter-subjective relationships and the mutual acts of commitment that make the individuals think and act together in the we-mode. Individuals think and act as if they were a single body, but they are not one; rather, they are a collectivity that incorporates the members' strong social unity. Member-level features characterize the account as a mode-account, in which individual agents are the ultimate subjects of shared agency.

2.2 Searle's collective intentionality

Searle (1990) asserts that shared agency relies on the fundamental principle that collective actions are primitive phenomena in the sense that "there really is such a thing as collective intentional behavior that is not the same as the summation of individual intentional behavior" (Searle 1990, p. 402). In particular, shared agency acquires its specificity from the kind of intentionality exerted by the individuals, who orient their plans towards a group performance. This approach brings together two seemingly divergent assumptions that Searle wants to reconcile: (1) all intentionality is in the individuals' head; (2) shared agency involves collective intentionality and collective intentionality is a primitive phenomenon. To defend this

---

is viewed as an original mental faculty that can be performed by the individual independently of whether she has relevant social relations. In this sense, understanding the cognitive possibility of shared agency does not necessary require considering the agential context, which could still serve to gain understanding of the action. In other words, one might say that, for Searle, the network is important for social ontology in general, although it is not a precondition of collective intentionality.

[6] See Section 4.2.

connection, Searle claims, "there is no reason why you could not have intentionality in individual heads that took the form of the first person plural" (Searle 2007, p. 12). Even though all intentionality is ascribable to individuals, an intention can have both a singular and a plural form, which gives rise to I-intentions and we-intentions for the action, respectively.[7]

From these few considerations, it should be clear that a collective intention for action is an attitude belonging to individual psychology and refers to the 'we' as the subject to which the shared effort is attributed. The 'we' gives the form to the state of mind thought by each participant. Whereas Bratman associated shared intentionality with events represented by 'I intend that we', Searle's proposal introduces the concept of we-attitudes built upon expressions such as 'we intend that...', 'we have the collective intention to...' and so forth. While Bratman's interpreted the shared phenomenon as a continuity of the form with the individual-oriented usage of the intentional faculty, Searle's proposal marks a formal discontinuity. It introduces we-attitudes for the action besides individual intentions.

Despite the discontinuity thesis on the form of the intention, the model of collective intentionality Searle proposes to explain cases of shared agency can be considered a linear development of his notion of individual intentional agency. In this sense, both individual and collective intentionality have the same structure, which involves two phases:[8] prior intentions and intentions-in-action. Prior intentions are general plans that may be held by the agent as an overall guideline for the action. Instead, intentions-in-action are a necessary aspect of any intentional behavior and the psychological counterpart of the bodily movement intended by the plan state.

---

[7] Searle holds that the double form can be associated with many kinds of attitudes and, especially, with mental states with propositional structure. Examples are beliefs (I-belief/we-belief), desires (I-desire/we-desire), claims (I-claim/we-claim) and so forth, (Searle 2007). The changing aspect in the nature of the attitude is the grammatical form in which the agent has it in mind. In the event of a collective intention, 'we have the intention that...', the state of mind is held by each individual and each singular attitude is independent of the fact that it is getting things right. One could have a collective intention for the action even though such a plan does not match what really happens outside of the mind, for the nature of the intention is only based on individual thinking. For this reason, Searle defines the collective feature as an essential character of intentionality, meaning that it does not depend on (or derive from) empirical circumstances (Searle 2007). This is also the reason why Searle's position is not counted here among those considering the network as a precondition of collective intentionality. See Section 2.1.

[8] See Introduction, Section 3.

Using obvious abbreviations, 'p.i.' for prior intention, 'i.a.' for intention-in-action, 'b.m.' for bodily movement, and 'a' for action, we can say that the general form of these relations is given by the following schemata.

p.i. (this p.i. causes a)

i.a. (this i.a. causes b.m.)

a = i.a.+b.m., where i.a. causes b.m. (Searle 2007, p. 18)

To better delineate Searle's description of agency, it is necessary to mention the case in which an individual accomplishes a certain action by doing something else. For example, if someone intends to turn the light on, the goal is generally fulfilled *by means of* pressing the switch. Whereas the second part of the relation (that is not the main action meant by the intention to turn the light on) is assumed to be what causes the action represented in the first. Another scenario occurs when one does something that contributes to bringing about some further action for the gesture it represents. An example might be a person who shows her appreciation after a performance *by way of* clapping her hands. In these sorts of events, the phrasing would be:

i.a. B by means of A (this i.a. causes A, which causes it to be the case that B)

i.a. B by way of A (this i.a. causes A, which constitutes B). (Searle 2007, p. 18)

Given this account of individual intentionality, it is reasonable to assume that the structure will also shape the event of collective intentionality. In fact, the only thing that has changed in the context of shared agency is the grammatical form of the attitude, not its framework.[9] Thus, we can keep the formula and reflect on how to adjust it. For instance, when the intentions have a plural form: 'we intend to prepare the sauce together'. For this purpose, it makes sense to imagine that the collective intention (i.e., to prepare the sauce) contains something akin to Bratman's sub-plans–intentions regarding the specific contribution given by each participant. As for the sauce preparation, the contributions may be (1) to weigh the ingredients and (2) to stir them homogeneously. According to Searle, shared intentions are attitudes

[9] Despite some divergences, the continuity of structure is a feature that Searle's (2010) and Bratman's (2014a) accounts have in common: both maintain that the study of complex individual actions (over time for Bratman and made of parts for Searle) provides tools for investigating actions done by many participants together.

referring to the specific act to which any single agent is committed and which, depending on the situation, represents a cause or component of the entire collective performance. The intention connected with each participant's specific contribution is not part of the intentional content of the others. To represent it in a phrase: i.a. collective B *by means of/by way of* singular A (this i.a. causes A, causes/constitutes B), (Searle 2010, pp. 52–55).[10] A fundamental feature has to be emphasized: although the phrasing shows both collective and individual goals, Searle maintains that the only intention causally effective on the individual action consists in the singular attitude, A. This means that each participant's body is moved by the mental state connected with A, which is part of a wider plan that has no direct influence on the action. A only represents an assumption and a complex horizon within which each contribution acquires a meaning. Moreover, the formula does not involve any specification about what the other partners intend to do in view of B. Rephrasing, each agent is only informed about her own A, while ignoring the A' (if any) pursued by others. Reference to the others' intending can still be found in the content of beliefs parallel to intentions, which are about the action's context though not directly connected to it. Such mental states are not part of the intentional event, and consequently, the content they represent has no causal role in determining the action. It follows that no one knows what the others are doing. So, it is impossible to formulate one's intention based on the others' intention. Instead, each participant acts on the assumption that everybody is disposed to do her part to reach the shared end with the belief that the others are doing the same.

Moreover, in Searle's view, the idea that there are some others with whom one might believe to cooperate (and actually cooperate) is considered an aspect not grasped through intentional capacities. Rather, the presence of the other has to do with a *background* understanding of the context, which represents an acquired/embedded knowledge set established prior to the intentional attitude.[11] Searle profiles "a background sense of the others as possible agents" (Searle 1990, p. 415) that has its roots in basic human skills, enabling the exercise of both individual and collective intentionality and agency. The fact that some other agents are part of the same effort one is intentionally performing constitutes, at most, the content of a belief

---

[10] The intention relative to the individual contribution is identified with A, while the collective action is called B. B is the goal that can be caused or constituted by all As, since each A makes a specific contribution conducive to B.

[11] On the notion of background and conscious/unconscious, conceptual/non-conceptual attitudes related to it, see Schmitz 2013, Stahl 2013.

associated with one's collective intention for the action. This reference is external to the collective intention itself, and according to Searle's perspective, it represents the only actual connection between the we-attitude of each individual and the others' we-intending. Recalling the beginning of the brief introduction to Searle's thought, the 'we' is just a formal aspect of the intentional event, and it is more an epistemic feature or a mode rather than a term with an actual (ontological) counterpart in the world.[12] This means, in Searle's account, the 'we' is not the subject of intentions.

2.3 We-mode we-attitudes: Tuomela's proposal

Tuomela was a pioneer in the field of collective actions, and his contributions have become an essential benchmark for the debate in social ontology (Tuomela 1991, 1995, 2000, 2002, 2003, 2007, 2008, 2013a). In line with Searle, Tuomela conceptualizes we-attitudes for the action as internal, individual mental states, oriented towards some collective behavior. Despite the analogy, Tuomela's perspective differs from Searle's: the former has explicitly enriched the explanation of intentional agency by theorizing the mode of attitudes, which can occur either as an I-mode or as a we-mode (Tuomela 2003).[13] Assuming that the attitudes under investigation are group-oriented intentions for the action, i.e., we-intentions, it is thus possible to distinguish between I-mode we-intentions and we-mode we-intentions. The mode an intention correlates with depends upon how the agent approached the object represented in the content as a reason for the action. In the context of shared agency, the I-mode maintains that each of the agents involved has committed

---

[12] Although Searle does not refer to collective attitudes as we-mode attitudes, the way he talks of collective intentions as genuinely collective intentions, thought by the subject in the plural grammatical form, leaves room to rephrase his we-intentions in terms of we-mode intentions (Schmitz 2017, Wilby 2012).

[13] The difference between the form and the mode of the attitude is not a clear separation since both aspects identify the collective nature of the intention. However, Tuomela's notion of mode adds some conditions that are not present in Searle's concept of form, because the mode has strict connections with the social context and with the way in which the subject participates in it. Features like collective commitment, collective acceptance, and for-groupness make the we-mode a thicker notion than Searle's concept of form. In fact, the form is an original characteristic of mental attitudes: the plural form is typical of mental states produced by the collective intentionality of individual subjects who might be even brains in a vat (Searle 1990). Still, there are reasons to treat Searle's account as a mode-account of collective intentionality, locating the collective dimension in the kind of attitudes rather than in the content or subject of attitudes.

herself to the goal in a *private* way[14] –the dominant reason for pursuing the goal has been an individual one. Individual reasons for the action might be associated with the belief that other agents are cooperating with the same aim in mind, making the goal a common objective among the participants and not merely a private goal. By using the example of people painting the house together, Tuomela observes

> In the I-mode case, there can be a shared plan, roughly in the sense of each of the participants forming the intention to paint the house "together" with the other agent, in the sense that each is going to do a certain part such that the aggregation of the parts results in the full action. (Tuomela 2007, p. 71)

This sense of 'together' refers to a weak usage of the term. It requires the participation of the agents in a collective endeavor mainly for their own interest whereas, the stronger approach of the we-mode would require the agents to act as group members and pursue group reasons. The we-mode implies that people function fully as group members and seek to obtain, instead of their personal success, a collective task in support of the group benefit (*forgroupness*).

> Agents A1, . . . , Am forming a group, g, share the intention to satisfy a content p [...] in the we-mode if and only if p is collectively accepted by them qua group members as the content of their collective intention and they are collectively committed to satisfying p for g. (Tuomela 2005, p. 332)[15]

Since content *p* is the representation of the goal, all agents seeking to realize some group-oriented reason can be regarded as acting in the we-mode if and only if two further attitudes are in place: collective acceptance and commitment. Collective acceptance secures that, for an attitude to be properly collective, it is necessary that the group members have accepted the content of the mental state as a reason "true or correctly assertable" for the group (Tuomela 2013a, p. 128). A collective intention happens in the we-

---

[14] In Tuomela's account, the expressions 'private' and 'privately' refer to I-mode attitudes (Tuomela 2007, p. 14).

[15] The definition of we-mode intentional agency is implemented with the *collectivity condition*, establishing that, it is necessarily true that a content, *p*, is satisfied for a member of *g* if and only if it is satisfied for any other member of *g* (cf., Tuomela 2013a, pp. 40–42).

mode, just in case its content has been the object of an act of collective acceptance exerted by the participants all together. Actually, the acceptance in question represents an activity done in the we-mode, too, namely through an act of collective commitment.[16] Collective commitment can be viewed as another kind of we-attitude: each individual collectively commits herself to the common purpose insofar as this engagement is fulfilled with the group benefit in view. More precisely, the collective commitment associated with the we-mode can be described as an attitude with a double direction. On the one hand, collective commitment has as its object the content of we-intentions; on the other hand, collective commitment encompasses the act of committing oneself to being a member of the group. While the former meaning suggests an *intention-relative and non-normative* sense of the attitude (Tuomela 2005, p. 332), the latter creates the basis for a normative bond among the agents. In this sense, "collective commitment also involves that the members have group-based normative rights and obligations towards one another, which glue them together more strongly" (Tuomela 2013a, p. 43). Such a connection is relative to being part of the group, no matter if any intention for the action has ever been formulated.[17]

---

[16] In Tuomela's approach, the totality of all intentional contents that have been collectively accepted by the group members forms a shared cognitive background called *ethos*. The *ethos* contains all values, goals, reasons, and concepts that the members of the group have found the right contents to embrace. To put it otherwise, the *ethos* represents the 'common good' of the group (Tuomela 2007): it is a selection of motives for the action suitable for promoting the benefit of the collective. Despite the essential cognitive nature of the *ethos*, as a set of contents, it might be worth mentioning that all the elements in it also have normative value, as they coincide with what has been considered good or suitable for the group by its members over time.

[17] Since agents are kept together by virtue of their membership, none of them can leave the group as she pleases without facing the risk of being (legitimately) blamed by the other members. The group can properly dissolve only through a we-mode we-attitude of disbanding and the same can be said about the dissolution of a collective intention. Only the entire group can change something about the 'we' by preventing this change from causing tension between the parties. In fact, the way in which Tuomela presents the notion of shared agency in the full-blown sense, i.e., in the we-mode, depicts an image of the group that is particularly robust. Individual agents can act in the we-mode if and only if they collectively accept a group reason, collectively commit themselves with that reason (*ethos*) and with their status of group members. One might find the view shows some sort of circularity, as shared agency is presented in a way that the formation of a group attitude requires at least to mention the group *ethos* or membership relations: shared agency necessitates the agents being already part of the group to which the action refers. Faced with such criticism, Tuomela emphasizes that

2.4 Gilbert on joint actions

Gilbert approaches the notion of shared agency by adopting the discontinuity-thesis account of intentionality. Fundamentally, she argues that in order to understand shared agency, one needs to resort to the idea of people acting together as a group or as a body (Gilbert 1989, 1997, 2003, 2007a, 2009, 2011). In particular, according to Gilbert, the essential feature of collective action is the notion of joint commitment, which represents the condition *sine qua non* a number of agents can form a group and have collective attitudes toward the action. By virtue of the normative bond created through the act of commitment, two or more individuals give rise to a group and act as if they were one. This interpretation mainly implies that in the organization of any shared action, shared intentions for the action, though important, are secondary to the role played by commitment. Commitment enables the shift from an individual perspective to a collective one.[18] As the fundamental character of shared agency, joint commitment is the act through which each individual forms a group with others and acts with them jointly.

Although Gilbert approaches joint commitment as the fundamental aspect of the notion of shared agency, that feature has been further described as being a conditional attitude. Indeed, it is assumed to happen if and only if, among the agents involved in the context, there is common knowledge concerning the fact that the other participants are co-present and ready to commit themselves to the common purpose (Gilbert 2013, pp. 47–48). Insofar as each participant has such mutual beliefs, the conditions for joint commitment are satisfied, and the agents can form a group by expressing

---

the pattern based on collective acceptance and commitment can work only for those cases in which the group perspective has been already established. When a group intentional horizon is still lacking, pro-group reasons for the action could only be obtained through an agreement, as "there need to be not a joint intention to make the agreement", (Tuomela 2013a, p. 129). In response to this counter-objection, some might still question the possibility of generating fully-fledged we-mode thinking and stable collective commitment by starting from an agreement that was made by means of I-mode we-attitudes, allowing the agents to pursue some group goal based on self-interested reasons. In fact, I-mode we-attitudes only need shared purposes achieved for private reasons. Such a concern could be dispelled by taking a communitarian view of the individual, whereby every human being is prone to be in solidarity with others.

[18] This kind of engagement is like an agreement, and it is prior to the establishment of any shared goal. In fact, it only needs the presence of other individuals and their willingness to be part of the group. To find more of Gilbert's critique to we-intentions as fundamental features of shared agency, see Gilbert 2007b, 2010.

(either with words or gestures) their willingness to be part of the 'we' (Gilbert 1989, pp. 167–203).

Once individuals have mutually recognized themselves as part of the same group, they are in the right position to engage themselves as one in the action and collectively pursue some common goal. In this sense, "people may jointly commit to accepting, as a body, a certain goal" (Gilbert 2006, p. 136). In other words, accepting an end based on joint commitment has relevant consequences for the perspective from which the agents are holding the intention to obtain it. According to Gilbert's theory of shared intentions, when a certain number of individuals assume an attitude as group members, they will hold the attitude from a group perspective. This group perspective is a psychological level concerned with the individual acting as part of a group, distinct from the perspective in which individual intentions belong as personal attitudes. To support such psychological fragmentation, Gilbert postulates the existence of two intentional levels in the individual's mind, both generated by the kind of commitment and perspective (personal or joint) adopted by the agent when formulating the attitude. When planning individual activities, an agent has intentions on a personal level; in collective contexts, the intention belongs to another intentional domain. The split between individual-level and group-level psychological spheres creates a discontinuity that is at the core of Gilbert's version of the discontinuity thesis. This variation of the thesis does not pertain to the intentional faculty straightforwardly (as it was for Searle and Tuomela)[19]. Instead, it is defined by the commitment determining the particular standpoint in the mind of each individual.

By focusing exclusively on the group perspective, it is possible to think of shared intentions for the action as reasons through which the agents are jointly committed as one due to their being part of the same collective. In investigating these kinds of attitudes, Gilbert has identified three principles as the main features of collective agency. The principles in question are the *disjunction, concurrence,* and *obligation criteria* (Gilbert 2006, 2009, 2013). The *disjunction criterion* concerns the relationship between shared and personal attitudes of the participants. Since collective and individual intentionality rest on two different levels, mental states related to the former domain have no direct influence on the attitudes belonging to the latter and *vice versa.* Consequently, the two intentional stances can be treated

---

[19] Chapter Three will make Gilbert's and Tuomela's approaches closer to one another by considering the fundamental role that the notion of commitment has in both theories. We will be observing that in both accounts the notion of commitment is the keystone of the difference between individual and group perspective (Section 3.4).

separately—i.e., can be disjointed—so, it is possible to imagine a situation in which personal attitudes could even be in contrast with the collective aim without representing a relevant obstacle for the satisfaction of the group goal. More concretely, consider the situation in which *a*, *b*, *c*, and *d* intend as a body to go to work by car sharing. In addition to this shared plan, *a* would like to be more autonomous, while *b* would prefer to leave later in the morning. Even though two members have divergent individual inclinations characterizing the personal level of intentionality, the group keeps going to work together. The ride-sharing continues because collective and individual intentions run on different tracks. Under this disjunction, it is possible to ascribe shared intentions also in cases where some individual attitudes are not aligned with the collective aim (Gilbert 2009, pp. 171–173).

Apart from being separable from personal attitudes, shared intentions are characterized by the *concurrence criterion*. The concurrence criterion states that these shared attitudes require engagement from all of the parties in the action. This assumption has, at least, two meanings: first, it implies that shared intentions are properly formulated and realized only when each member of the group plays her role in fulfilling the entire performance. According to this, car-sharing is possible just in case *a*, *b*, *c*, and *d*, dividing the costs, are disposed to drive taking turns and adjusting their own schedule to each other's needs. Furthermore, the *concurrence criterion* has another meaning: shared intentions can be changed or rescinded only in a collective way, i.e., when the parties change or rescind the plan together. Meaning, nobody is in the position to break the shared intention unilaterally; at most, one might violate the collective intention by acting in opposition to the common effort without suspending the shared intention in question. The outcome would be the transgression of the collective attitude, which the other group members might rebuke as a betrayal. For instance, driver *a* cannot make her choice and decide that the commuter group will not rideshare anymore. She is not in the right position to attempt this solution because the intention from which she is trying to disassociate herself is not an individual attitude. As it has been taken by *a*, *b*, *c*, and *d* together, *as a body*, it can be changed or stopped only by a decision taken by the group who created it. Otherwise, the other members would have the right to condemn the conduct of *a* as an unfair performance.[20]

---

[20] In Gilbert's proposal, *a* has the possibility to interrupt her participation to the joint activity only through a collective decision regarding her exit. In view of this, Gilbert has introduced a *concurrence condition on exit* (Gilbert 2009, pp. 173–175).

The fact that the agents who share the intention are entitled to rebuke another member of the group is also connected with the third principle Gilbert identified, the *obligation criterion*. The idea is that "each participant has obligations towards the other participants to behave in a way appropriate to the activity in question", and such obligations are "grounded in the joint activity itself" (Gilbert 2006, p. 106). Any commuter joining in carpooling cannot abstain from paying part of the costs, nor can she decide not to drive on the day she was supposed to. More specifically, no one can engage in such behaviors without legitimizing blame from other members with whom the 'dissident' agent is bound by the constraints of joint commitment. The point being, behaviors such as not sharing expenses are not appropriate ways to act related to the shared intention 'to go to work by sharing the ride', which is a goal imposing duties and rights on the participants. Each party is bound by certain duties because sharing in a collective intention (and action) requires behaving in a way that is appropriate to the fulfillment of any personal contribution as constitutive of the entire shared intention (and action). Besides, the activity is a joint interplay among different participants that gives each member the standing to demand from the others the same fairness claimed from her by them. Indeed, bearing a shared intention means being collectively committed to a certain common goal, which is different from being personally committed to that goal (Gilbert 2009). Therefore, violating the bonds of joint commitment undermines the social unity of the entire group and generates attitudes of blame among the members.

To recap, according to Gilbert's interpretation of joint activities, the unique feature of shared agency is the joint commitment that turns a set of individuals into a plural subject. On this basis, shared actions follow three main principles: *disjunction, concurrence,* and *obligation criteria.* While the *disjunction criterion* secures the genuine collective nature of shared attitudes, the requirement of concurrence establishes the interdependence of roles and functions realized by each individual, and then the presence of obligations among the agents strengthens and improves the normative bonds firstly grounded on the basic principle of joint commitment. Gilbert writes:

> Persons A and B are collectively doing A if and only if they collectively intend to do A and each is effectively acting, in light of the associated joint commitment, so as to bring about the fulfillment of this intention. (Gilbert 2013, p. 89)

Gilbert's proposal, along with those of Searle and Tuomela, offers an account of shared agency based on the idea that shared actions correspond to collective intentions and that neither of these two aspects is translatable in terms of individual actions and intentions. In contrast, Bratman finds continuity between individual and shared action and believes that the latter is an intersubjective implementation of the former. Chapter Three delves further into this difference and acknowledges important conjunctions between the member-level accounts considered so far.

Chapter 3

Shared agency and the member-level account (MLA)

3.1 A distributive interpretation

Chapter One and Chapter Two outlined some of the key accounts of shared agency, all endorsing the premise that the "interpretation of an individual's behavior has to be given in terms of individual intentional states" (Schmid 2009, p. 23). This approach to shared agency is typical of the view that I have referred to as the member-level account (MLA), which focuses on the explanation of shared intentional behavior, considered from the perspective of those who participate in the action—or those who have the intention to participate in it. Aside from any specific commitment to the collective dimension, all MLAs pursue a common image of shared agency based on mental attitudes which plan each participant's contribution. Since mental attitudes are episodes of a mind, and groups do not have minds in any ordinary sense, the understanding of shared agency has relied on the following two assumptions:

1. all intentionality happens in individuals' minds,

2. individual intentions refer to individual actions while shared intentions refer to shared actions.

The apparent inconsistency of the claims takes root in the understanding that any attitude is located in the mind of each individual and, in the case of shared agency, attitudes are meant to be fulfilled by actions concerning the entire collective, without losing the intentional nature of the phenomenon. The challenge is to figure out how a state of mind located in the individuals' heads might relate to some shared action, which counts as the condition of satisfaction of that attitude. So far, the problem has been approached by conceiving collective actions from the individuals' side by assuming that shared intentions consist of the contribution each individual is ready to make to obtain the goal. Hence, the relation between shared intentions and actions has been characterized as a bond between the state of mind of each group member and the contribution one wants to provide towards satisfying the common goal. To explain contexts of shared agency, I have already introduced the continuity-thesis account—a position that wants to understand phenomena of the kind through concepts and descriptions involved in the study of individual intentional agency. In this sense, a plurality of agents can act together (in the relevant sense) because each participant has her own intention that 'the collective does something' by way of each sharing an intention. What makes the attitude a shared mental state is the content of the intention, which refers to the 'we', namely the plurality of individuals sharing the plan state. According to Bratman's theory, the continuity sustained depends upon— when compared to the case of individual intentional action—no further concept being needed, and the content being implemented by the network of all individual attitudes meshing towards the overall goal. Therefore, Bratman's proposal can be understood as a distributive conception of shared agency, maintaining that the jointness of the mental state is based upon each individual having her own intention for the action and that no intentional state is shared by the participants straightforwardly as if they had a common mind (Pettit 1996). To be shared by many individuals is, rather, a matter of content and organization among the plans (Ludwig 2016).

Per the distributive reading, Tollefsen (Tollefsen 2002a, 2015) defines Bratman's MLA as a non-summative approach: the shared intention, though located in the mind of each, is, indeed, something more than the mere aggregation of all the individual attitudes for the activities involved in the context.[1] In this sense, Bratman's theory is a case of difference between individual and shared intentionality due to the content of attitudes, which, in the case of collective performance, show the connection with the 'we' in the mental representation of the goal (Alonso 2018). Nevertheless, shared intentions—Tollefsen claims—could differ from individual intentions also in kind, as advocated by the proponents of the discontinuity-thesis. Philosophers such as Searle, Tuomela, and Gilbert appeal to a new theoretical kind, peculiar to cases of shared agency and not wholly reducible to the premises regarding

---

[1] Summative explanations account for activities done by two or more individuals 'together' by gathering all the intentions-that-I of each. Those attitudes are brought together just because they are oriented towards a common end about which there might be (though it does not have to) some mutual beliefs among the parties (Kutz 2000). Still, converging on some goal does not equal shared intentions: anyone in the context might be pursuing the same goal as the others only by chance and the addition of mutual beliefs is not enough to secure the sharedness of the activity. To know that other persons are trying to obtain the same result one is trying to obtain, and to know that this knowledge is common among all agents, does not mean that the individuals are cooperating with one another. There must be some connection, be it epistemic or normative, between the agents.

individual agency. The idea of a discontinuity between the two explanations (concerning individual and group intentional actions) lies in the assumption of genuine we-attitudes for the action that, ontologically speaking, are radically different from the attitudes involved in the theorization of individual intentional agency. Consequently, accounting for shared phenomena implies concepts that were not required to reflect upon individual intentional action. Even though different accounts have interpreted the distinctive aspect of shared agency extensively, it is possible to find a common way of approaching intentional shared actions. Tuomela makes this point in a way that clearly shows the contrast with Bratman's perspective:

> The social world can be adequately understood and rationally explained only with the help of we-mode concepts expressing the full-blown collective intentionality and sociality in addition to I-mode concepts. We-mode reasoning is not conceptually reducible to I-mode reasoning. (Tuomela 2013a, p. 15)

Despite specific variations in conceiving we-mode concepts, it is important to underline that all those concepts are originally collective because they do not derive from a combination of the concepts employed in the study of individual agency. Similarly, we-mode notions pinpoint attitudes that are not at stake unless the action is a shared one. The we-intention represents an element of discontinuity between individual and shared agency. As Tuomela says, we-intentions imply a thesis of irreducibility (epistemic and descriptive), which does not allow the construction of shared intentional phenomena through assembling the building blocks gathered from the description of individual agency. On the contrary, for collective intentional phenomena, the addition of new bricks is required (Tuomela 2018).

Therefore, Bratman's categorization offers a perspective from which one can approach the debate in social ontology and find a rift between two ways of theorizing shared intentions: reductive, in the case of continuity, and non-reductive, in the case of discontinuity.[2] Although this interpretation represents a

---

[2] The comparison between reductive and non-reductive approaches here is about the shared intentions that guide shared actions. Reductive are the theories that interpret shared intentions as re-describable in terms of (interrelated) individual intentions. Non-reductive are the theories that admit collective intentionality as an indispensable phenomenon. When, in Part Two and Part Three, we will be discussing group agency, that is, the ability of some groups to perform intentional actions, we will see that those who admit collective intentionality as well as those that reduce it to individual intentionality may want to be either reductionist or anti-reductionist with respect to the

fruitful way to organize the debate, it is also possible to bridge the gap between the two positions by analyzing how the notion of we-attitude has been generally (though variously) conceived. The assumption that individuals, when acting together, follow mental states of a particular nature, genuinely collective, is not necessarily in conflict with the distributive and non-summative perspective found in Bratman's proposal. As Tollefsen points out, if compared to personal plans, shared intentions *differ either in kind or content,* meaning that collective actions can be guided either by intentions in the individuals' mind recalling the 'we' in the content (Bratman 2014a) or by intentions held by individuals and otherwise connected to the 'we'. As far as the latter is concerned, the different way of having shared intentions creates a discontinuity due to the introduction of specific kinds of attitudes in the explanation of shared activities, but such an attitude is still a mental state located in the mind of each individual agent.

On the issue, Schmid suggests an understanding of we-intentions that brings the discontinuity-thesis account closer to Bratman's position:

> According to authors such as Raimo Tuomela [...], John Searle himself, and Michael Bratman, there is no single (token) shared intentional state that is behind the joint intentional activity, but many intentional states instead, individual intentional states that are marked out from those involved in the case of solitary or singular agency in that they are either of a special *form* (Searle), *mode* (Tuomela), or *content* (Bratman), providing the "glue" for collective intentionality. In other words, the existing accounts of collective intentionality tend to be of a *distributive* kind. (Schmid 2009, p. 23)

---

subject of group agency. Being reductionist about collective intentionality and anti-reductionist about group agency means recognizing some groups as subjects of intentional action without taking the members to have collective intentions. In this case, group intentions may be the result of the I-mode intentions of each combined in the appropriate way (List & Pettit 2011). As opposed to this, someone could be both anti-reductionist about collective intentionality and anti-reductionist about group agency. Group agency will then be planned by we-mode intentions in the mind of each (Gilbert 1989). Then, it can be the case that someone supports non-reductionism when it comes to collective intentionality and yet takes a reductionist stance toward group agency (Searle 2010). This means that collective intentions and actions are irreducible to individual ones, but that there are no subjects of action beyond individual agents. Finally, one can be a firm reductionist and admit neither that there are collective intentions nor that groups can be intentional agents (Ludwig 2016). Meaning, both collective and group intentional actions are entirely re-describable based on individual intentions and actions.

Thus, all approaches connected to individual and collective intentionality seem to be compatible with a distributive interpretation of shared intentionality, which is about the priority of individuals' attitudes in the explanation of any form of agency.

> This priority given to individual agency is taken by some to require showing that social actions or attitudes can be reduced to individual actions or attitudes. Others reject reductionism, claiming that social attitudes cannot be defined in terms of individual attitudes since the content of social attitudes must be mutually referring in distinctive ways. But the anti-social bias remains because even when the content of the attitudes is social, the attitudes themselves are ascribed not to social groups per se but to their members. (Stoutland 1997, p. 46)

In other words, all MLAs based on intentional agency establish the possibility of shared agency on the distributive principle that "(f)acts about a group are exhaustively determined by facts about the people who constitute it" (Epstein 2014a, p. 150).[3]

3.2 Four dimensions of shared agency

There is (at least) one point on which the Big Four of shared agency all agree: intentionality belongs to individuals. This is not the same as reducing collective intentionality to individual intentionality; it rather implies that both collective and individual intentionality are expressions of the individuals'

---

[3] As opposed to Schmid's interpretation, Laitinen (Laitinen 2017) has defined Tuomela's approach as a non-distributive account. According to Laitinen, Tuomela has assumed that in contexts of shared agency a collective group perspective is at stake because the group perspective has an influence on individual psychology, to the extent that it would be misleading to consider Tuomela's account as a distributive model of shared agency. Schmid contrasts this reading of Tuomela's position with an ontological argument by saying that: "Raimo Tuomela virtually treats groups as ontological non-entities because in his view, 'groupness' is, as he puts it, 'in the last analysis attributed to individuals' (Tuomela 1995, p. 199). It seems that in his account, the basic structure of we-intentionality does not per se presuppose collective entities such as 'groups' or 'communities'" (Schmid 2009, p. 31). Schmid considers Tuomela's theory as a distributive account, focused on individual psychology and experience. According to Schmid, a non-distributive theory would rather imply the recognition of a plural subject, who is taken to be the ultimate subject of we-intentions. Tuomela rejects such view though he explicitly endorses the possibility of an authentic and epistemically salient group perspective in the mind of each: this explains Laitinen's claim about Tuomela's non-distributive theory of shared agency.

intentional faculty. The genitive case here makes all the difference. Insofar as the intentional faculty is a mental capacity of rational (human) beings, the expression 'individuals' intentionality' emphasizes the ownership-relation, according to which individuals own intentionality. Then, the theory can treat intentionality either as happening only in just one mode, namely as individual intentionality or in association with various modes, as in the case of accounts assuming both I-mode and we-mode intentionality. What remains stable is the subject of those mental episodes: i.e., the individual agent and mind. Thus, all MLAs can be seen as distributive and reductive accounts of shared agency for what concerns the subject.

According to this interpretation, the MLA captures the structure of shared intentional actions based on intentions planning individual contributions. Thus, the theory seeks to describe how two or more individual agents do something together intentionally by analyzing how each participant's contribution to the collective performance connects to the relevant plan state. It is indeed by doing her part that a group member helps to bring about the shared plan.

As in individual intentional behaviors, the agent intends to do—and often does—something by doing something else (for instance, greeting a friend by waving the hand). Shared agency has similar characteristics, as it is composed of both primitive and consequent actions. Primitive actions are events planned by the agent with her intention-in-action and straightforwardly realized by the satisfaction of the relevant attitude. For example, the agent moves her hand by following the intention of waving it. Then, waving the hand, along with smiling, hugging, and saying something nice, plays a role in obtaining the wider objective of greeting an old friend with love. In fact, the wider objective can be satisfied in most cases only through the realization of many primitive actions. If the intentional action is a shared event, primitive actions are individual contributions—namely, actions planned by each individual working towards a broader goal somehow shared by all participants. Then, the consequent action coincides with the achievement of the common goal. Ludwig makes the point plainly:

> For a group to do something together intentionally is for each of them to contribute to bringing some event about (in the right way) by way of each executing intentions-in-action directed de re at primitive actions of theirs which bring it about in accordance with a plan each has at the time of acting that they bring about the event in accordance with a shared plan at the times of their acting. (Ludwig 2016, p. 228)

Consider the example of a familiar scene at Christmas: a family plans to decorate the tree by hanging colorful balls, little wreaths, and shimmering snowflakes upon it. To make the Christmas tree look pretty, each family member makes their personal contribution. Perhaps the children put up the balls and hang all the trinkets creatively, while the parents decorate the top of the tree and place the twinkly lights all around it. In doing their part, each family member executes the intention-in-action directed at the specific contribution each wants to make. In this sense, *each family member contributes to* decorating the tree *by way of each individual executing intentions-in-action directed de re at primitive actions* brought about *by a plan each has at the time of acting* (cf., *Ivi*). The general plan that they all have in mind while planning their specific individual contribution is about decorating the Christmas tree with family, which is a goal that can be obtained only by each working on it by way of contributive individual actions.

The Christmas tree example is simple, and it helps us to bring into focus the issue of shared agency when approached from the member-level perspective. The member-level perspective considers collective intentional behavior as an event brought about through each participant planning her own contribution in view of the event. With this in mind, the main issues for the MLA are: (1) understanding how the wider plan, shared by the participants, can become a shared feature for all and (2) how to account for the relation between that broader plan and the sub-plan of each participant. This chapter aims to show how the Big Four of collective intentionality have interpreted shared agency. In particular, I will focus on how each scholar has conceptualized the relation between intention and action. The analysis is meant to follow the same framework applied in the introduction to individual agency: for a subject to act intentionally is for her to bring something about by fulfilling a mental attitude. Specifically, an intention for the action, that is, the plan state motivating the subject to be the agent who realizes the plan. The plan state shows a multifaceted influence on individual behavior that can be captured by the combination of constitutive, structural, normative, and causal dimensions. More directly, following Searle (2010), I will take agency to be a composition of intentions and actions, about which it can be said that intentions (and actions) constitute agency in that they are essential parts of it. Then, considering the structural relation, intentions are connected to actions because they draw the direction of the activity. Such an orientation shapes human behavior partly due to a normative force that binds the agent to realize the plan state in practice. Finally, intentions are causally effective on action by triggering a performance that is the intentional object represented in the content of the attitude.

A 'shared action' refers to actions carried out by individuals acting together based on the type of relationships and intentions that keep them together in the performance. The investigation proposed here focuses on the members' level and thus features member-level accounts of shared agency.

3.3 A few points on the four dimensions

Before beginning with the in-depth analysis of MLAs, some aspects deserve additional commentary. Most importantly, we find that not all shared agency descriptions show relevant traits belonging to each dimension investigated in this book.[4] In fact, as ordinary intentional behaviors can prove, different kinds of action may involve some intentional relations and not others. Take the case of me wanting to turn on a laptop: because I have the intention to turn on the laptop, I can fulfill it by pressing the 'on' switch. This gesture causes the laptop to start. Hence, moving on to shared agency, it could happen that, this time, the device to be started is my car, which is parked on the lot and has a dead battery. So, I need someone to help me. If you agree to give me a hand, we will start the car together and the agency relationship between our shared plan of doing this together—by means of you doing your part and me doing my part—and the performance realizing it will be a causal connection (Searle 2010, p. 52). The case is different if I have the intention to wish my sister a happy birthday. I can fulfill my plan state by way of me saying 'Happy Birthday' to her. This by-way relation is a constitutive rather than a causal link because it is by me saying 'Happy Birthday' that I give my best to her. Looking at collective events, an example of a constitutive relation is the connection between citizens who vote for some political party by way of each putting a cross in the box of the right candidate. Each expression of preference counts as each individual's personal contribution to the wider plan to choose the

---

[4] This section extends some insights found in Section 1.1 about descriptive, conceptual, and micro-macro dimensions of shared agency. The four agency relations studied in this chapter belong to the descriptive dimension mentioned in Chapter One, which is about the distinctive components of shared agency. Then, variations depending on the endorsement of the continuity/discontinuity thesis account regard the conceptual dimension and so the theoretical model adopted in the investigation. The micro-macro perspective is instead common to all approaches, as Part One only considers the MLA that is the (micro) perspective of the members. A change in perspective will be considered in Part Two and Part Three engaged with group-level accounts (GLAs).

next government, but none of the crosses on ballots could trigger the voting process in causal terms.[5]

Thus, some variations in the four-agency-relations explanation might derive from the kind of object in focus. It is the opposite case when, having set the object of study (e.g., a certain intentional behavior), differences in the explanation emerge from specific theoretical choices. Upon investigation, the MLA selected yields some considerable variations on the emerging patterns between the discontinuity and the continuity thesis of intentionality. This becomes evident if we consider the role attributed to the shared plan. I will maintain that, according to the continuity thesis account, shared plans enter individuals' intentionality as part of the intentional content. In contrast, theorists of the discontinuity thesis assume that shared plans are not just part of the content of each individual contributory intention. Instead, the collective nature of the event affects the mode of intentionality, becoming a filter through which the agent perceives—and represents—herself as a group member (Schmitz 2017, 2018). The way the agent thinks of the shared plan as a collective occasion influences the account by privileging some agency relations over others, depending on the features involved in the explanation. For example, suppose Bratman's account is mainly concerned with the structural role played by the plan state in orienting the action. Gilbert's theory, in contrast, represents a normativistic account, where the normative dimension of intentionality and the function of notions such as commitment, rights, and demands are more crucial components than structural features (Gilbert 1989, 2003, 2013). Such a difference originates from Bratman's and Gilbert's endorsement of continuity thesis and the discontinuity thesis, respectively. Despite the inclusion of specific normative principles in Bratman's view, the normative dimension is more fundamental in Gilbert's perspective on collective intentionality. Normative attitudes of commitments between the agents are the *conditio sine qua non* those agents can have collective intentions for the action and act cooperatively as a body (Section 3.4.3).

In addition to the consequences that defending a continuous/discontinuous account might have on the theory, the focus on the four descriptive dimensions is further mediated by the importance each MLA attributes to intentions-in-action and prior intentions specifically. As introduced already, intentions for the action can be intention-in-action or prior intention; the former is an

---

[5] One could consider many other examples of intentional behaviors that refer especially to one of the agency relations. The choice of focusing on the constitutive-causal couple is motivated by the huge attention it has received in the debate on individual and collective intentionality (Ludwig 2016, Meijers 2000, Searle 2010).

attitude that comes with each intentional act, and the latter is an attitude that may come with more complex intentional actions. Particularly in the case of shared agency, intentions-in-action refer to the contribution of each participant. Simultaneously, prior intentions reference the wider plan, shared by all participants in the context and represented in the content of each individual's intention. On one side, when the theory endorses an MLA that is mainly concerned with intentions-in-action, as is the case of Searle's proposal, constitutive and causal dimensions become increasingly important, as this special kind of attitude is directly connected to action. On the other side, particular attention to prior intentions means considerable interest in the structural and normative sort of influence, which is highly involved in the explanation of how shared plans for the action might affect the intentions planning individual behavior by making it a form of contributory/pro-group activity.

3.4 Agency relations in member-level accounts

The attempt to investigate the MLAs of the Big Four based on four relations between intending and acting should not be considered a flattering interpretation, convenient for bringing all interpretations under one single theoretical framework. On the contrary, the analysis should point out some threads of the investigation that might be important in approaching the various member-level accounts of shared agency.

3.4.1 Constitutive relation

The introduction postulated that intentions and actions are constitutive parts of agency, meaning that actions and intentions are "interlocking components of a system of practical activity" (Epstein 2015, p. 218). According to this definition, intentions are components of agency, happening together with the physical movement (or speech act) and representing its psychological counterpart, and *vice versa*. Especially in Searle's proposal, an explicit reflection on the constitutive role of the intention in its plural form concerning the realization of shared performance can be found. Searle suggests that the action is the outcome of the intention-in-action added to the bodily movement: 'a = i.a. + b.m.', where the distinction between intention-in-action and prior intention is noted as a fundamental feature (Searle 2007, p. 18). The entire plan represented in the content of the prior intention is neither an essential nor a constitutive feature of the activity: it may be rational guidance but what is built in the performance is the attitude directly connected with the gesture. Thus, in the case of a shared intention, the attitude that is effectively part of the action performed by everyone as a group member is the intention-in-action. This kind of intention coincides with the mental state representing, in its content, the goal that the individual contribution should realize to fulfill the entire collective plan. For instance, it is the intention-in-action to buy the paint that can be considered as part of the activity played by an agent because of the collective plan of painting the house together. The reference to the collective dimension in which (and by virtue of which) the contribution takes place enters the picture only as a background assumption that, though relevant, is not considered to be a constitutive element of the performance. Therefore, it seems plausible to infer that the constitutive relation is a feature that concerns the intention-in-action relative to the individual contribution rather than the mental state planning for the entire endeavor.

Apart from Searle, none of the other Big Four provides deep attention to the distinction between intention-in-action and prior intention, neither in the individual nor in the collective form of intentionality. Instead, Bratman, Gilbert, and Tuomela generally speak of intentions as plans for the action, namely as prior intentions, which, according to Searle, are not constitutive parts of the activity.[6] However, it must be recognized that if a constitutive relation between intentionality and agency can be assumed, it refers to the intention of planning the individual contribution rather than the general plan regarding the whole group. In fact, if we consider Bratman's explanation, the

---

[6] Assuming that no one else among the Big Four has given fundamental importance to intentions-in-action does not mean that the concept of intention-in-action has been excluded from analysis. In fact, it should be said that Tuomela has proposed something similar to Searle's distinction between intention-in-action and prior intention (Tuomela 2007). Tuomela differentiates between action-intention and aim-intention: the former kind of intention corresponds to Searle's intentions-in-action, i.e., mental states relative to single gestures and satisfied by relevant single acts. Then, aim-intentions are close to prior intentions, representing complex plans that can be composed of many action-intentions held by the same individual over time or by different subjects at a time. With a difference from Searle's position, Tuomela assumes that aim-intentions do not occur when "the agent believes that he with nonzero probability can alone bring about or see to it that the action or its result event comes about. Rather the agent is assumed by his actions to contribute to the aimed result" (Tuomela 2007, p. 84). Thus, aim-intentions are the main expression of collective intentionality, which—in Tuomela's account— makes the subject think in view of the benefit of the group, i.e., as a group member. This means that action-intentions can be seen as attitudes of any group member, who is applying a kind of psychological filter to the way of representing the context (Schmitz 2017). As seen in Section 2.3, conditions such as collective commitment, membership, and for-groupness are essential for the occurrence of collective intentionality and genuine collective aim-intentions. Accordingly, all those requirements make Tuomela's view not completely match Searle's notion of prior intention, which could happen even in the absence of any social relationship among the parties.

structure of shared agency depicted by the building blocks approach is, to a certain extent, similar to Searle's formulation. Differences left aside, the shared intention is described as an attitude realized by way of the intention of each that x (second building block) and by way of meshing individual sub-plans (fifth building block).[7] More directly, the feature involved in each individual's performance promoting the shared intention (in the sense of prior intention) is the attitude (intention-in-action) related to the individual contribution rather than the plan concerning the entire activity. Also, in Gilbert's and Tuomela's versions of we-attitudes, it is the intention aimed at the personal activity—and not regarding the entire collective effort—that can be considered part of the agent's acting as a group member.[8]

3.4.2 Structural relation

As is for individual agency, a shared action is a behavior shaped by an intentional plan for the action, fixing the objective towards which the activity is oriented. This kind of relation is easy to find in every explanation of agency based on the intentional pattern: for this reason, it pertains to the totality of the approaches proposed by the Big Four. If we consider Searle's formulation, we find that all shared intentions refer to the collective goal realized *by way/by means* of individual actions conducive to it. In this sense, the collective intention provides a double rational guidance: on the one hand, it makes clear which is the specific goal of the performance attempted by each participant. On the other hand, collective intention provides the end of the collective activity. Thus, each intention gives a structure to the individual contribution in view of the shared objective and to the system of contributions by arranging some sort of coordination among the parts. Bratman clearly describes such control through the introduction of the *means-end coherence principle* that requires a balance between the end of the entire shared plan and the means, namely the individual sub-plans, employed in obtaining it. According to this claim, the intention planning for the activity gives a rational control on the entire performance, ensuring that all of the contributions involved are coherent with the final shared aim and consistent with one

---

[7] See Section 1.2 and 1.3.

[8] The point is difficult especially because the we-mode intention thought by Tuomela and the joint intention introduced by Gilbert are two kinds of attitudes taken by the agent through an act of collective/joint commitment. This means that the intention-in-action composing the activity, although relative to individual participation, still refers to the group dimension and is committed to it. This fact makes the constitutive role of the intention strictly intertwined with the normative agency relation in a way that is not part of Searle's and Bratman's account (Section 3.4.3).

another. In the spirit of the building-block perspective, the tenet regulates the coherence between the plan for the individual contribution and the activity done to perform it; then, the coordination among the various sub-plans held by different individuals will be established.[9] Analogous to the structural role covered by Bratman's normative principles are the three criteria proposed by Gilbert: *disjunction, concurrence,* and *obligation criteria.* We have seen that while the *disjunction criterion* concerns the collective psychological nature of shared attitudes, the *concurrence* principle makes the interdependence of roles and functions a stable structure, which is further enriched by mutual obligations among the agents (Gilbert 2006, 2009, 2013).

3.4.3 Normative relation

The presence of a normative feature within the characterization of shared agency opens the question of whether the explanation of the phenomenon embraces a normativistic perspective, which would imply the identification of the normative aspect as an essential element of the concept. Along this thought line, shared agency would be grounded on some normative bond between intending and acting. Only Gilbert openly accepts a kind of normativism in the theory (Gilbert 1989, 1990, 2007b, 2013). The issue then becomes if Bratman's, Searle's, and Tuomela's perspectives can endorse the normative relation as an inner aspect of shared agency as well. As previously discussed, Gilbert introduces the intrinsic normative connection binding the shared action with the intention planning for it by referring to the principle of joint commitment as the condition *sine qua non* any collective intentional attitude can occur. Joint commitment is a kind of commitment—opposed to the personal one—through which the agents engage themselves in the action by (1) taking on the status of partner and (2) embracing the content of the attitude as a goal that each of them as a group member is willing to realize. The core of the approach is that normative constraints do not derive from the endorsement of the attitude. Instead, it is the intentional attitude grounded in joint commitment: once the agents have adopted a group perspective by committing themselves to being partners, they can accept that the intentional content could become the object of a further commitment jointly exerted

---

[9] The sequence that goes from individual to shared phenomena follows a logical order. In analyzing Bratman's perspective, I argued that the explanation and the metaphysical status of events happening in time or among individuals are based on the explanation and on the metaphysics of phenomena concerning individual agency (Bratman 2014a). In this sense, the relation between the two levels—individual and social—does not consist in a temporal order. It is a kind of logical dependence.

concerning the goal. First, the intention has a normative influence on the performance because having a shared intention requires the subjects to be committed to the status of partner and to pursue the intention as if they were one. Second, the normative relation binds the agents to the realization of the goal represented in the content of the attitude, under the condition that the first normative relation—the one that serves to attribute the status of partner to all the participants—is satisfied. While the first kind of normativity depends on being partners, the second kind of normativity finds its source in mental attitude, and it is based on the normativity that emanates from having assumed the status of group member. As for the obligation criterion, Gilbert maintains that each individual must fulfill her role in the entire performance firstly, because of her commitment to the status of group member and, secondly, because of her engagement towards the common end.[10] Shared intention and joint commitment bind the agent to carry out the action—particularly the individual contribution conducive to it—and to do so from a group perspective. No one can rescind such a double constraint personally.

There is a difference between how Gilbert understands the normative agency relation and the viewpoint embraced by the other Big Four. While Gilbert draws the sharedness of the intentional attitude from the normative connection among the participants as partners, the other theorists are inclined to consider the intention as the source of the normative relation that keeps the agents together in the performance. In this sense, the plan state—and the acceptance of its content—sets the constraints that guarantee the realization of the shared action and that such an activity happens as a collective event. Hence, Bratman connects the normativity of the intentional stance with the *consistency* it shows with the system of beliefs held by the agents and with the *coherence* it has regarding the means adopted in pursuing the goal (Bratman 2014a). Such a kind of normativity expressed by the two principles (consistency and means-end coherence) finds its source in the cognitive nature of the intention: it is by recognizing some specific content as a suitable reason for the action that the intention is then taken as a task to be fulfilled. Similarly, if the strategies adopted for realizing the plan offer valid means towards the end, the performance can be described as a coherent event carried out under rational control. The normative connection between intending and acting—more than the background relationship among the

---

[10] Gilbert offers an account of shared intentions as attitudes grounded on basic forms of agreement (explicit or tacit) that enable the formation of the group perspective. Without basic agreements establishing the group level, no collective attitude could arise, because no group viewpoint could emerge (Gilbert 1989, 1997, 2009, 2013).

participants—seems to involve beliefs, reasons, and cognitive features that occur in association with and in support of the agents' shared plan state.

The cognitive aspect is noteworthy for Searle's view on the sharedness of the performance occasioned by the realization of a collective intention that, though having a plural grammatical form (we-intentionality), contains the reference to the group and to the contribution given by the other fellows, only as an assumption. This means that the relation with the others, and considering them partners in the action, is just a matter of belief and, as such, could lead the agent to a failure without implying the vanishing of the collective intention she holds in mind.[11]

Tuomela's interpretation deserves a special mention here, as it presents the normative relation between intending and acting as a problematic issue. Tuomela regards such normativity as generated by collective commitment and we-mode attitudes (Tuomela 2002, 2007, 2013a). Even if it is true that we-attitudes generally occur in the assumption (i.e., in the belief) that all individuals in the context are having an intention that is conducive to the same general goal—as Searle maintains—the we-mode also adds something new to the case. The we-mode emphasizes a way of bearing we-attitudes in mind that goes beyond any belief about the others' presence and cooperation: it requires a collective commitment to the fact of being partners in the action and pursuing goals in favor of the group. Thus, we-mode we-attitudes are normatively related to shared actions. Regarding attitude, the normative bond comes from the collective commitment to the goal. Regarding the mode, the bond derives from the collective commitment assumed by membership in the group. The normativity generated by the intentional state of mind is what Tuomela calls *instrumental normativity*, whereas the normative bond generated by being a group member is what falls under the description of *social normativity* (Tuomela 2003). This makes Tuomela's position closer to the normativism adopted by Gilbert, who effectively distinguishes, as Tuomela does, between (1) a normative relation, regarding the participants as

---

[11] Searle postulates a condition of adequacy, saying that anything we assume about collective intentionality "must be consistent with the fact that the structure of any individual's intentionality has to be independent of the fact of whether or not he is getting things right, whether or not he is radically mistaken about what is actually occurring. And this constraint applies as much to collective intentionality as it does to individual intentionality. One way to put this constraint is to say that the account must be consistent with the fact that all intentionality, whether collective or individual, could be had by a brain in a vat or by a set of brains in vats" (Searle 1990, pp. 406–407).

partners, which is prior to any shared intentional action, and (2) a normative relation arising from endorsing some specific intention for the action.[12]

3.4.4 Causal relation

The chance for shared intentions to have a causal power on some shared performance is inversely proportional to the cogency of the normative relation that connects the mental state to the action.[13] Now that we have identified a double meaning of the normative relation, it is arguable that the normative issue is distinguishable from the causal issue in two ways. Firstly, when normativity refers to the mutual commitment among the agents as partners, the causal power of the intentional state takes second place. To rephrase, the causal influence is indirect because it is mediated by the commitment necessary for the collective intention to arise. In fact, the normative source, depending on the relationship among the participants, has been introduced as an aspect that comes before the possibility of having fully-fledged, we-mode attitudes. Collective intentions could exert a causal power on agency only under the condition that some collective viewpoint has already been established. Secondly, once the unity of the parties has been secured based on normative relationships, the focus is brought to the shared intention for the action—the prior intention/aim-intention. This kind of attitude provides the general goal towards which each individual contribution is supposed to be directed. Because prior intentions only have indirect causal power over action, any account based primarily on normative constraints will

---

[12] The identification of two normative levels applies only to shared actions based on we-mode we-attitudes. Weaker forms of collective action do not require such double link as it would put the account at risk of circularity.

[13] This is not to say that, when normativity is assumed as a fundamental feature, the causal relation between intending and acting is completely overlooked; instead, the point is that privileging a certain kind of relation has entailed focusing either on prior intentions or on intentions-in-action. Indeed, those who have studied more deeply the normative side of intentionality have generally focused on prior intentions by leaving aside the investigation of intentions-in-action qua attitudes directly connected with the activity and, for this reason, specifically involved in the study of causality. If one maintains that to be causally effective an intention should directly refer to the phenomena on which it exerts its power, the case of prior intentions could not satisfy such a condition (Tuomela 2013a). Searle's account is an exception ascribing some sort of causal power to prior intentions, too. Prior intentions are taken to have causal power on individual intentional action (intention-in-action + movement) without being the direct cause of any bodily movement (Searle 2010).

likely be less interested in causality and more focused on how people make joint commitments to common goals.

Far from the normativistic characterization of agency, Searle offers a clear formulation of causality in the case of collective intentionality. He describes the relationship between the intention-in-action and the respective act as a causal relation. The intention-in-action is the effective cause of the act, which—in the case of a collective performance—can be found in the realization of each individual contribution. A way to put it formally is: i.a. (this i.a. causes b.m.), which means that the intention-in-action causes the bodily movement done by the subject. Passing to collective intentions, the phrasing becomes more complex because the intention-in-action, although referring to the collective dimension of the activity (the B term), contains, in its content only, the representation of the goal of the individual contribution (the A term). Therefore, the intention-in-action bears a causal power only in relation to the action aimed at fulfilling the individual goal. Searle puts the issue as follows: i.a. B by means of/by way of A (this i.a. causes A) (Searle 2007). While the relation between the collective intention and the action is causal just by reference to A, the individual sub-goal, the relation between the B term, i.e., the collective goal, and the performance can be either an instrumental (*by means of*) or a constitutive (*by way of*) one. The final goal is the outcome of the action done by each individual, under the assumption that the others are also contributing. Nonetheless, this cognitive endorsement does not have any causal influence on the action.

Thus, we can observe that even prior intentions for the action (when present) might generate some sort of causal power. In particular, prior-intentions are described by Searle to be causally effective not on the action (individual contribution) but on agency, namely on the entire phenomenon, including both the intention-in-action and the action itself. In this sense, the prior intention might have a causal impact on intentional agency and spark the realization of the plan, which consists in the formulation of proper intentions-in-action and the happening of the respective physical (or verbal) counterpart of such attitudes. In other words, prior intentions cannot move anybody; at most, they might lead the individuals to engage in the activity by making sub-plans conducive to the shared goal. The formulation of suitable intentions-in-action can thus be considered as the outcome of prior intentions (Searle 2010).

Looking back, Chapter One and Chapter Two outlined the MLA of the Big Four. In this chapter, we have analyzed how those accounts have interpreted the four agency relations between intention and action in the context of shared agency. So far, the focus has been on shared agency, understood as the ability of two or more individuals to act together intentionally. Part Two will ask whether and how the debate in social ontology has considered the group of individuals acting together as a proper subject of intention and action.

Part Two.
From member-level
to group-level accounts

Chapter 4

The subject of shared agency

4.1 Survey of Part Two

Current member-level accounts in social ontology differ widely from one another. However, it seems to be generally accepted that intentions in the case of shared agency are distinct from intentions planning individual agency either in kind or content (Tollefsen 2002a). Part One aimed to show that when the discrepancy between attitudes is located in the content of the mental state, each individual who takes part in the action is considered to have an attitude that expresses its shared nature by representing the collective dimension in the content: 'I intend that we do x together'. In contrast, in shared agency, intentionality can be different from intentionality in individual action due to a change in kind. According to this kind-account—which I have been calling discontinuity-thesis account—shared agency involves intentions that are typical of collective contexts of agency, in which the individuals have collective thoughts and conceive themselves as a 'we'—having intentions for the action in a plural grammatical form. The phrase for we-intentions (collective intentions) is 'We intend to do x together'. This phrase is the product of a special rational capacity that is collective intentionality instead of individual intentionality. Differences aside, no group mind is assumed over and above the individual minds, and all intentionality can be read as a special product of individuals' rationality. The distributive interpretation of shared agency has emerged on that basis. The distributive interpretation holds that the explanation of shared agency must be given in terms of each one's intentions and actions.

Part One argued that the purpose of MLA is investigating aspects of individual psychology, behavior, and interaction that are characteristic of collective contexts. In this sense, the focus on the collective features of shared agency is on individual-level features that are predominantly involved in fulfilling the wider collective plan. In regard to the subject, the member-level account follows a different distributive method. The MLA views shared intention for the action as an attitude held by the group considered as a whole. In the case of a group intention, the attitude would, in fact, refer to the collective as the effective subject of intentionality, in a way that the 'we' of shared agency would go from being a feature of individual psychology to being the subject of intention and action. Thus, shared agency would be group agency, and the account engaged in its explanation would be a group-level account (GLA).

Proposing the shift in perspective is very contemporary. Group agency has become a current issue, arguing that some social groups could be agents in their own right. In societies with high degrees of complexity, it has emerged as a commonsense view that political assemblies make decisions, courts pronounce their sentences, and big corporations drive the market. In light of these views, part of the philosophical debate in the social sciences has developed an interest in the possibility of considering certain social groups as agents having rights, duties, and responsibilities over and above their individual members (Copp 2006, 2007, French 1984, Haji 2006, Hess 2013, Hindriks 2014, Orts & Smith 2017). Contrary to this non-reductive reading of group agency, the possibility of considering some groups as fully-fledged centers of agency conflicts with the prevailing view endorsed by the MLA, according to which "(f)acts about a group are exhaustively determined by facts about the people who constitute it" (Epstein 2014a, p. 150). As a dominant piece of the debate dismisses group agents and group minds, the MLA remains the most popular view—rendering the defense of group agency a challenging goal to pursue (Tuomela 2013b). As the notion of agency has been shaped based on the idea that the subject of agency, namely the agent, has (or has the capacity to have) mental states planning the action, the challenge addressed by the group-level account (GLA) is finding *the subject of 'we intend'* (Schmid 2017a). In other words, the issue is to find a meaning according to which dimensions of shared agency allow some social groups to be considered potential subjects of intentional agency.

Revisiting the categorizations proposed in Section 1.1, dimensions of shared agency can be sorted as follows:

1. descriptive dimensions:
    (1a) intentional behavior: intention (subject-mode-content) + action,
    (1b) agency relations: constitutive, structural, normative, and causal relation.

2. Conceptual dimensions:
    (2a) continuity-thesis account,
    (2b) discontinuity-thesis account.

3. Micro-macro dimensions:
    (3a) member-level account,
    (3b) group-level account.

Part Two explores the dimensions of shared agency when viewed from a macro/group-level perspective (3b). The difficulty is questioning whether, in response to the demands of the social sciences, the Big Four have found a way to conceptualize the 'we' and to profile a group-level account of shared agency, capable of grasping the collective as a subject, not reducible to its individual components. This investigation will be the object of Chapter Five. Then, Chapter Six will consider whether current interpretations of the GLA have succeeded in providing stable high-level explanations of the descriptive dimensions of shared agency (1a and 1b) independently of how those descriptive dimensions have been conceived in the MLA (2a and 2b).

The following sections show three interpretations proposed in social ontology and conceptualized by Frank Hindriks (2008). All of these interpretations aim to grasp the 'we' from a high-level perspective, rather than considering it as a feature of individual (epistemological/phenomenological) experience (3b). The purpose is to understand how to set up the transition from the MLA to the GLA, namely from an explanation based on facts about the members (or seen from the members' perspective) to an explanation also concerned with groups (or experienced from a group viewpoint). As the focus shifts from shared agency as collective agency to shared agency as group agency, the survey will concentrate not only on the accounts proposed by the Big Four but also on List and Pettit's theory of group agency. Therefore, in Part Two (and Part Three), we will be mainly referring to the approaches developed by the Big Five.[1]

4.2 The intrinsic account

In order to profile a group-level account focused on the macro dimension of shared agency, the notion should be better investigated. This investigation begins by starting from the premise that shared agency is a kind of intentional agency. The intentionalistic nature of action binds it to the intentional faculty, comprised by a (representational) mental state and held by a subject and oriented towards an object (the action). On this basis, one might want to identify the subject of 'we intend' with the group of participants and take the mental state to coincide with the entire plan for the action, which is the group-scale performance. Therefore, it is noteworthy to dwell a little longer upon the first feature, namely the notion of group-scale subject, and better delineate the kind of issues it addresses. The notion must be characterized by

---

[1] As specified in the Introduction, the expression 'Big Five' here refers to Bratman, Gilbert, Searle, Tuomela, and the duo formed by List and Pettit. In the original formulation, List is not included in the group (Chant, Hindriks & Preyer 2014).

considering that the MLA—in both its versions—has been formulated based
on two main assumptions related to the model of intentional agency:

1. all intentionality happens in the individual's mind,

2. individual intentions refer to individual actions while shared
    intentions refer to shared actions.

Primarily due to the first condition, the most difficult point encountered by
the Big Four has been extending the intentionalistic pattern endorsed by the
MLA to the GLA. Moreover, the GLA—being aimed at providing a non-
redundant perspective—should be somehow irreducible to the MLA.
Otherwise, there would be no point in proposing high-level concepts and
descriptions aimed to hold some groups as subjects of we-intentions, as the
GLA is meant to do.

   There are various ways to regard a group of individuals as a group agent.
One way is to consider that a bunch of individuals together might form a
group agent by conceiving themselves as group members and thinking as if
they were part of a plural subject. Another way is to think that a group agent is
identified as such due to features that are not strictly intentional or
psychological. Thus, taking the intentional faculty as a parameter, a group
might be either intrinsically or extrinsically determined (Hindriks 2008,
Tuomela 2013a, 2013b). Considering the intrinsic view, a certain number of
individuals form a group agent insofar as their sharing of an intentional
standpoint makes them (and the observer) see the set of participants as a
plural subject. In this sense, the shared attitude is the feature that grounds the
chance of recognizing and treating the collective as the subject of shared
intentionality. The kind of reference that attaches the shared attitude to the
group can be interpreted in two different ways: (1a) the intention can be a we-
mode attitude, representing the subject of intentionality in the mode, or (1b)
the plan for the action can be the result of an agreement-making procedure,
which combines individual intentions for the action into a group-scale
attitude. Consequently, we may take the intrinsic account to say either (1a)
that the group arises directly from plural states of mind occurring in the mind
of each, or (1b) that the collective is the byproduct of some mechanism that
processes and combines all individual intentional plans into a single output.

   Regarding the first option, Searle's proposal suggests a fruitful guideline,
observing that the form—i.e., the original collective form—of the attitude
allows the identification of the 'we' as the term to which one should ascribe
collective intentions. Searle claims: "the collective arises from the fact that
collective intentionality is in the individual heads of individual organisms"
(Searle 1997, p. 449). In support of this interpretation, Schmid's view presents

the plural subject as a feature deriving directly from the intentional event (Schmid 2009, 2017a, 2017b). In particular, Schmid assumes that perceiving agency related to the group is what turns the collective into an agent, or better, into the subject of collective intentionality. By focusing on the mode of the attitude, the philosopher is able to direct their attention to the 'we', that is the mode (for instance, Tuomela's we-mode)[2] through which each individual perceives the attitude as the attitude of a group. Thus, attributing the intentional stance to a plural subject is part of the experience of the individuals who think in the we-mode by virtue of being intrinsic components of a 'we', phenomenologically speaking. Such an understanding of the collective dimension does not threaten the fundamental assumption in social ontology that only individuals exist as substances. Indeed, behind Schmid's conception, there is no metaphysical commitment because the subject is considered a term to which a certain phenomenon is referred, not as a substance. The plural subject is an intrinsic part of experience; it is part of how each (single) agent feels or conceptualizes the intention rather than an essence existing as a premise (cf., Schmid 2017b, p. 12). Thus, taking the group as the subject of intentionality should not be a problematic choice. It does not imply characterizing the group as a substance: the 'we' is part of the intentional pattern in the sense that it is the we-intention itself that requires the postulation of a plural term to which it is being referred.[3]

---

[2] Schmid and Tuomela discuss how to understand the we-mode in Schmid 2017b and Tuomela 2017.

[3] More generally, Schmid contends that the idea of subjectivity might be related both to singular and plural perspectives, meaning that the 'we' as much as the 'I' can be the subject of intentionality. Without claiming to be exhaustive, we can mention that Schmid firstly identifies four features that, in the case of I-intentionality, make an I-intention a self-referential mental state. Then Schmid extends the reflection to events of we-intentionality by proving the self-referential character of these attitudes through the identification of the 'self' with the plural subject, namely the 'we'. The four features characterizing any we-attitude as a self-referential mental state of the group are self-identification, self-validation, self-commitment, and self-authorization. Self-identification happens when a certain agent has in her mind a we-intention for which the question of who she takes to be the 'we' is a fundamental issue. In order to know what the 'we' represents, it seems necessary to have a mental representation of the other members participating in the activity. Yet, the point could be (and has been) formulated otherwise. If we recall how Searle, Tuomela, and Gilbert deal with the issue, the representation of the partners loses its salience and leaves room for another kind of solution that considers the group straightforwardly. The representation of the group does not rely on the individuation of the members. For example, Searle thinks about a pre-intentional sense of us (Searle 1990) that is part of the background skills of the

Then, regarding the second intrinsic view, the group might be identified as the subject of intentionality for its holding attitudes—the outcome of an agreement-making procedure. Hindriks clearly affirms, in line with this version of the intrinsic account, that it could be that "establishing a way of making decisions together or of forming joint intentions is the mark of collective agency as characterized from the internal perspective" (Hindriks 2008, p. 126). Meaning, the group can be assumed as such based on the process through which the members establish a shared and unique plan state. In this respect, the theory proposed by List and Pettit (List & Pettit 2011) illustrates the point clearly. The authors maintain that the formation of group attitudes needs some mechanism, which ensures that individual attitudes will merge into a proper group perspective, functioning as the point of view of a single agent. Such a viewpoint can be obtained in various ways: the group perspective can be the outcome of an organizational structure imposed on

---

agents besides the actual exercise of their intentional faculty and cooperation. Similarly, Gilbert (Gilbert 1989, 1997, 2009, 2013) and Tuomela (Tuomela 2003, 2007, 2013a, R. Tuomela & M. Tuomela 2003) introduce the group perspective under the condition that the individuals have undertaken a particular kind of commitment (joint/collective) to being group members that is established no matter who the other participants might be. Therefore, it can be argued that the representation of the 'we' does not come from the representation of any other singular individual. The condition of self-validation is spelt out by observing that the individuals having we-intentions do not need to observe the other participants to make sure of their collective attitude. Each agent has a direct access to the content of the collective attitude. As Searle vindicates, individuals may be brains in a vat (Searle 1990). As for self-commitment, it can be observed that we-intentions commit the agents to some sort of collective deliberation through which all participants find an agreement about what is to be intended from the shared viewpoint. This kind of commitment is the one Gilbert describes as the commitment to being partners in the action and that Tuomela identifies in terms of 'social commitment'. Once this kind of commitment is established, the rational standpoint is fixed, and it will be possible to make a decision and formulate the intention from a group perspective as if it were a first personal view. Finally, Schmid takes the idea that we-intentions exert some form of subjective authority on individual's intentionality. Being subjective in relation to the 'we' does not imply, however, being autocratic. Schmid explains: "'We intend' does not fail to come with some form of first-person authority: the authority is not the authority of the autocratic 'maker of the mind', but that of the democratic participants in the making up our mind about what we intend. This is first person plural authority: it is democratic rather than autocratic in nature" (Schmid 2017a, p. 240). In summary, Schmid accounts for how the collective could be the plural subject of shared intentions by focusing especially on the features that make an attitude a self-referential one and by showing how such features could apply to the case of we-intentions, concerning the entire group as a plural subject.

the members to arrange the contributions of each into a comprehensive system. It might be the by-product of a long-lasting, flattering, cultural evolution. It could be the consequence of the members' intentionally joining in the action. No matter how the group's rational perspective is achieved, it will consist in an autonomous action-guiding rational stance, which interacts with the environment thanks to the inputs provided by the members and their capacity to have preferences and form motivations for the action—as the continuity thesis of intentionality requires the case to be. The method through which the group processes and elaborates the individuals' (representational and motivational) inputs makes the group perspective different from the attitudes of its components (Pettit & Schweikard 2006). For the sake of simplicity, we can say that the procedure that turns the group of agents into a group agent consists of the aggregation of the individual states of mind into a single group-level attitude. The operation requires an 'aggregation function' that assigns to each input—i.e., to each configuration of attitudes at the member-level—a collective attitude as its output (List and Pettit 2011, pp. 42–58). It is primarily through that mechanism that the group formulates its own autonomous reasons. For the intrinsic account, that mechanism is the aspect that turns the set of individuals into the subject of intentionality.[4]

4.3 The extrinsic account

Alternatively to the intrinsic account, the extrinsic account identifies group intentions as non-essential characteristics of group-scale subjects. The group is thus individuated based on additional elements, beyond the psychological—such as a structural organization, norms, and functional roles—that make the shared attitude concretized through the cooperation of the members.

> The structure of a group can be represented with nodes (or places) and edges connecting nodes to other nodes. The edges of a structure capture the relations that hold between nodes. Since all members of a group are related to some degree, each node in structure S is connected to every

---

[4] Interesting insights regarding the notion of agent as a rational/computational system can be found in Huebner 2013, proposing a version of collective and distributed cognition. The account suggests that having a mind is a property coming in stages and that some groups can be held epistemically responsible for the things they carry out. Collective attitudes are the result of mechanisms processing the inputs of the components into a single output. I will further discuss frameworks of distributed cognition in Section 9.3.

other node in S. Functional relations connect nodes in group structures.
(Ritchie 2013, p. 268)

The distinctive aspect of connecting and organizing efforts into a single structure grants the group the agency status. Even though this view focuses on nodes, functional roles, and relationships among them, it does not deny the intentional nature of agency. Incidentally, it is the organization of the members' roles (i.e., the structure) that, for the extrinsic account, makes it reasonable to identify a certain group as an agent, no matter what kind of intentions (we-intentions, intentions-that-we or even I-mode pro-group attitudes) have been motivating the action of each.[5] As things stand, the capacity at the basis of each process of (group) agency is the (individual) intentional faculty. Tuomela elaborates by observing that, in the case of group agents as extrinsically intentional, "the group members form the group mind collective attitudes (wants, intentions, beliefs), by their collective acceptance (construction) or some related group-intentional process or mechanism" (Tuomela 2013b, p. 14). Thus, a group can be considered an agent due to its capacity, as a whole, to accomplish shared goals through underlying intentional processes, mechanisms, and patterns of behavior that make the members act as one. In this sense, a group is defined as an agent by appealing to its power of processing and enacting the inputs provided by the members.

The extrinsic account is not necessarily in contrast with the intrinsic approach. Although some theories could not represent suitable examples of both perspectives, there are, instead, approaches for which the two ways of identifying the group are right. For instance, on the side of the continuity thesis of intentionality, Bratman's approach matches only the extrinsic account. To deny—as Bratman does—that shared agency requires more than interlocking individual attitudes towards the action does not coincide with the rejection of a wider perspective, which attributes the performance of the action to the group as one (Bratman 2017). In fact, the group can be viewed as the by-product of individual agency, becoming the system to which the action can be functionally attributed:

---

[5] As Bratman suggests, the group can be defined as the proper subject of shared agency in the sense of being the executor of the common plan. The group intention is set by meshing sub-plans of all the contributors, which is not the same as the group intentional stance allowed by the intrinsic account. The separation of the group as subject of intentionality from the group as actor is addressed by treating the 'we' as a subject that is not intentional, in the intrinsic sense, but related to intentionality (Bratman 2017).

> if a group has a shared intention to bring about an untoward effect and succeeds in doing that, we may want in some sense to hold that group accountable. But then what we need is an interpretation of such accountability that does not require a group subject (though it may require a group agent in the weak sense we have been discussing). (Bratman 2017, p. 128)

Taking the group as the actor is in line with Bratman's position (augmented individualism) that, similarly to the case of individual action over time, agency in shared contexts is regulated by a network of intentions brought together in a consistent and coherent way by two normative principles (respectively, the consistency and means-end coherence principle). Such principles guarantee the realization of the entire plan under a strict and shared rational control of the participants. Each sub-plan relates to that of the others and acquires its function only under the condition of publicity and common knowledge among the parties. Even though none of these elements exceeds member-level descriptions, obtaining the final goal would require, apart from satisfying every single contributory intention, fulfilling the entire planning activity. Insofar as shared agency is constituted by contributory intentions that are mutually interlocked and interdependent, speaking of a group as the actor realizing shared intentions might have, at least, a weak explanatory meaning (Bratman 2017). Bratman's theory does not fit in with the intrinsic account, for the group is recognized only as the organizational design putting the individual contributions together. Nevertheless, it still offers support of a (weak) extrinsic approach.

Similarly, from the point of view of the discontinuity thesis, Tuomela states that the perspective he proposes represents an extrinsic account of groups as intentional agents: "group agents are intentional only in a *derived, extrinsic* sense in virtue of their members' collective construction of the group as the intentional entity they identify with" (Tuomela 2013a, p. 23). In this sense, the intentional properties of group agents are the properties of a collective, which consists of "interrelated individuals such that this system is, through them, capable of producing uniform actions and outcomes" (Tuomela 2013a, p. 21). Among the proponents of the discontinuity thesis, Searle's perspective seems to be closer to the intrinsic account, but not a proper case of extrinsic approach: the collective nature of shared behaviors is, indeed, identified by the philosopher based on the plural form of mental states (Searle 1997). In addition to this, no organizational structure among the participants seems to have a decisive role in determining the scope of collective actions. Then, approaches such as List and Pettit's theory of group agency might be examples of both identification processes. As far as the extrinsic strategy is concerned, their account holds that group attitudes might instantiate, in practice, a design, that is the set of roles, rules, and positions covered and followed by the individuals, and arranged so as to make the group function as an agent properly.[6] List and Pettit explain that the members "may relate to one another in a more or less coordinated manner, with each playing a similar role. Alternatively, they may be divided up into different subgroups, each with its distinctive tasks. In either case, their relations with one another may involve a hierarchy or a more or less egalitarian arrangement" (List & Pettit 2011, p. 32). It is due to such arrangement that individuals can act together and be recognized as one. At the same time, from an intentional point of view, List and Pettit maintain that the group is intrinsically determined by the fact of being an autonomous source of rationality. In particular, the intentional autonomy of the group derives from the outcome produced by the aggregative function, which associates a group attitude to a network of individual attitudes. As a complex mechanism, the process of decision/agreement-making provides outcomes that cannot be traced back to individual intentions anymore. In this sense, and through rational autonomy, the group is considered intrinsically intentional.

Before continuing, Gilbert's view deserves special mention here. As discussed in Chapter Two, Gilbert argues that, as a result of joint commitment, two or more individuals can act together as if they were a plural subject. This description may lead to two different interpretations. Gilbert herself observes that the first way to understand such unity of the wills is the so-called 'subjectivist stance', which focuses on "how these individuals see themselves and their relation to the other individuals" (Gilbert 2013, p. 342). The approach concerns personal and inter-subjective features of collective intentional action because it describes collective actions by assuming the perspective of the members and by looking at some definite aspects of their psychology, behavior, and interaction. Due to the centrality of individuals' perspectives, it seems reasonable to refer to the subjectivist stance as an example of MLA, reducing the subject of collective attitudes and behaviors to (the interaction of) the members. This form of reduction locates the collective dimension in the mind of each individual in a way that the notion of the plural subject appears just as a metaphorical concept, reducible to member-level attributes and relations. Gilbert then outlines another reading of collective agency: the 'objectivistic stance'. This account focuses on "one's thinking in terms of 'us' as opposed to 'me', 'you', and all the rest" (Gilbert 2013, p. 344). Unlike the subjectivist stance, the objectivist view involves a

---

[6] On the notion of organizational structure, see List & Pettit 2011, pp. 60–64. An extensive analysis of the structure of social groups can be found in Ritchie 2018.

kind of perspective-taking, through which the 'we' is somehow identified as the subject of collective attitudes. However, Gilbert's view seems inclined to reject the idea of groups as intrinsically intentional subjects:

> [I]n using this label I have never meant to refer to something that exists independently of individual human beings, their attitudes, and relationships. Nor have I meant to suggest that when there is a plural subject there is a stream of consciousness or sequence of subjective experiences that exist apart from any such streams or sequences associated with the individual human members of the plural subject (Gilbert 2018, p. 180).

Non-reducible, in this context, are some traits of individual experience, which can be considered similar to we-mode intentionality but closed to the claim of intrinsically intentional, plural subjects. The author has accounted for collectives in strict relation to the sequence of subjective experiences of the group members. Although the non-reducibility of collective attitudes to personal attitudes is a clear point of Gilbert's account (discontinuity thesis), it seems that the objectivist stance aims at assuming the non-reducibility of plural subjects while, psychologically speaking, it relies especially on distinctive member-level features rather than addressing the issue of a non-reducible plural subject straightforwardly, as the intrinsic interpretation would instead suggest.[7]

To conclude, a fundamental observation, underlining both intrinsic and extrinsic accounts, needs further specifications. Regardless of how one wants to identify groups as subjects of shared agency, either through intrinsic or extrinsic explanations, it is important to notice that the notion of group (i.e., the 'we') has been here limited to, and identified with, the concept of group agent. This narrow conceptualization highlights that, among the great variety of meanings that 'group' might assume in philosophy, the study of shared agency requires us to consider the concept in strict relation to intentionality and agency. Therefore, from here on, I will be taking the concept of 'group' to be co-extensive to that of 'group agent', to signify the subject to which the intentional action is ascribed, either in line with the intrinsic or extrinsic interpretation of the issue. This does not imply that other meanings of the notion are fully disregarded and rendered useless for the explanation of

---

[7] I discussed Gilbert's double interpretation of the plural-subject account in Lasagni (forthcoming).

shared agency.[8] On the contrary, a broader reflection upon the notion of group would benefit discussions concerning group agency. As Iris M. Young pointed out, as long as a theoretical clarification on the meaning of 'group' is needed, the risk of misinterpreting that notion is always around the corner (cf., Young 1990, p. 44). Without a clear distinction about whom/what can be an agent and whom/what cannot, faulty interpretations might arise, and inappropriate theoretical, practical, and moral expectations concerning group agency might derive.

4.4 The status account

The previous sections have shown different approaches one can endorse to consider a group as an agent. It could turn out to be the subject to whom intentionality is referred (intrinsic approach), or group agency could be recognized based on non-psychological features that depend on the individuals' intentional faculty (extrinsic approach). Accordingly, it seems that the issue concerning the definition of the group as the subject of shared agency can be seen as a question about the identification of the notion of agent implied by the theory. In fact, the group agent has been individuated, rather than being defined directly, depending on the main features that make a collective of individuals the subject of intentional action. This assumption is the equivalent of saying that defining the group as an agent has come as a consequence of defining shared agency as an intentional behavior. In this sense, I suggest, agency 'emerges' by establishing, in the first place, the kind of attitudes, relationships, and levels of organization required by the proper unfolding of agency, and then, the group can be identified as its bearer. Therefore, it seems reasonable to assume that the subject of shared agency has been individuated using *functional* definitions, namely by descriptions that have derived from the kind of phenomenon to which the theory wants to assign a subject. In particular, in the case of shared agency, the group has been individuated as the agent because it represents (and is recognized as) the ensemble of members,

---

[8] It is especially the notion of social group as institutional fact that deeply intertwines with the concept of group agent. In fact, the greatest part of groups that we commonly view as capable of agency also has an institutional status. For instance, corporations, universities, and parliaments are all kinds of groups with some normative status. However, normative powers of institutional collectives are not the same as the agentive properties of an organization. If it is true that deontic powers make the institution have effects on the world, that outcome is not the kind of effect that one could explain by asking 'why did you do *x*?'. In fact, it is generally accepted that an institutional fact "is not the kind of thing that acts" (Ware 1988, p. 61). For a deep investigation on group agency in institutional contexts, see Hindriks 2013 and Ludwig 2017a.

attitudes, actions, norms, and functions that puts the event in place. "Rather than start with a list of criteria that a subject has to meet in order to be an intentional agent" the theory starts with our practice, namely our way of accounting for shared agency: "It takes as its starting point the explanatory power of this practice" (Tollefsen 2015, p. 103).[9] Thus, how the debate has made sense of shared agency has determined the definition of 'agent'.

If assuming *functional* definitions of being an agent sounds convincing, we should be able to find that strategy laying behind both the extrinsic and the intrinsic accounts of the notion. First, in the intrinsic approach, it is by defining shared agency as a phenomenon taking place under the condition of individuals having we-attitudes in mind (perceiving themselves as a 'we', phenomenologically speaking) or producing autonomous group attitudes that the group can be identified as such. Second, in the extrinsic account, the group could be conceived based on the identification of the network of attitudes, norms, and functions that comprise the idea of acting in a shared way. Then, the group can be viewed as an agent, i.e., as the structured whole realizing the plan conceived by the members and pursued by the entire network.

Furthermore, it seems that *functional* definitions might be intertwined with some process of attribution, according to which something acquires the role of agent by having been recognized as such. In this line of thought, we find Frank Hindriks' status account (Hindriks 2008), according to which "a collective agent can come into existence by outsiders granting a collection of individuals some kind of status" (Hindriks 2008, p. 119). Thus, a group is an agent insofar as some outsider attributes to it such a status.

A few comments are important in this regard: first, Hindriks' proposal sheds light on the idea that the chance of considering a set of individuals as a group requires some form of recognition. By acknowledging there is a social group and that such a social group may count as an agent, it becomes reasonable to

---

[9] The quoted passage was originally meant by Tollefsen as a comment on interpretivism, a theoretical position according to which "propositional attitudes such as belief are not internal states of the mind or brain but states of whole systems. [...] When we attribute these dispositional states to groups, we are taking the intentional stance toward the group. We assume that the group has a unified perspective—a rational point of view— and that it shares our norms of rationality" (Tollefsen 2015, pp. 103–104). Another way of addressing the issue is considering the *functional* approach as a normativistic theory. In this sense, the definition of 'agent' would start with answering the question: who/what should we take to be the agent? My critical discussion of second-level normative individualism (NI2) is about an individualistic answer to that question, considering the individual human being as the standard instantiation of 'agent'. See Section 8.4, 9.1, and 9.2.

recognize that pool of individuals as an agent. Without the recognition of the fact that the group exists and can bear a particular function, no group agent exists to be recognized. Second, the concept of recognition recalls the notion of recognition as acceptance introduced by Searle to explain the creation of institutional facts.[10] According to Searle, recognizing something as something

---

[10] Laitinen (2011) brings into focus an interesting distinction between three meanings of the term 'recognition' that may be useful here to better understand the specific meaning of recognition found in Searle's theory. 'Recognition' might denote (a) horizontal recognition between persons, (b) acknowledgement of reasons, (c) acceptance of institutions. Inspired by the Hegelian tradition, the first meaning of 'recognition' refers to taking someone as a person. This form of recognition is a horizontal relationship between two or more subjects wherein each of the subjects involved is both capable of recognizing the other and being recognized: "both the recognizer and the recognized one are persons, who can mutually recognize each other horizontally" (Laitinen 2011, p. 311). Recognizing someone as a person means (1) believing that the other is a person, (2) appreciating the moral values embodied by that person, (3) being willing to observe those values, and (4) having unselfish recognitive attitudes of respect and solidarity. Laitinen endorses the view that this type of recognition fully applies only to human persons but not to groups, and this is for reasons concerning morality. In this book I am going to advance a different claim by arguing that groups can be recognized as persons, though by 'person' I mean performative person, i.e., an agent, which has rights and duties only to the extent granted by its being an agent. Next, Laitinen talks about recognition as acknowledgement of reasons, values, and principles. In this case, the relationship occurs between a subject capable of recognition and an object that can only be recognized. To acknowledge a reason/value/principle means (1) identifying its descriptive meaning, (2) noticing normative features, (3) taking charge of normative implications, and (4) forming intentions based on the reasons provided by those implications. Last, there is recognition in the form of acceptance, about which accepting does not mean approving the institution but simply acquiescing to its creation and existence. This is the meaning used by Searle in describing recognition as an act of accepting institutions as in force and valid. To Searle, accepting institutions as in force and valid is constitutive of their being in force and valid: "institutions are created by imposing status functions, and the statuses require collective acceptance and recognition" (Laitinen 2011, p. 333). Status functions bear deontic powers and therefore characterize the normative profile of institutions by specifying how each institution becomes part of the social and institutional context. Searle takes institutions to be constructed by the collective intention to acknowledge the validity of the statement that gives to some brute fact a specific status function. Accepting an institution is therefore related to the recognition of persons and to the acknowledgement of reasons. As for the recognition of persons and the acceptance of institutions, the correlation between the two is not only concerned with the fact that collective acceptance may in some cases require a relationship of recognition between the recognizers (as in group formation) but also concerns the possibilities and contexts

else means recognizing that X counts as Y in context C, which is the same as saying that X acquires the status Y in C (Searle 1995, 2007, 2010).[11] As it is in the case of status functions, we might assume that the idea of granting groups a certain status is a process involving the ascription of deontic powers to a certain X term: by recognizing X working as Y, we attribute to the X term tasks and duties associated with Y. Thus, as a piece of paper might bear the deontic powers connected with money. Similarly, insofar as a group of individual agents has acquired the status of agent, it comes to bear the duties and the rights usually ascribed to agents. In the absence of any recognitive process of this kind, the group agent would be unburdened from the normative implications of being an agent by losing its power to work (and be seen) as such. Third, concerning the possibility of considering groups as agents, 'performative person' is a notion connected with the capacity to establish meaningful relationships with other persons through the mediation of normative expectations and obligations (Hirvonen 2017). A definition of performative person is suggested by List and Pettit, assuming that being a performative person means having the capacity to perform as a person.[12]

> And to perform as a person is to be party to a system of accepted conventions, such as a system of law, under which one contracts obligations to others and, to add a point not explicit in Hobbes, derives entitlements from the reciprocal obligations of others. In particular, it is to be a knowledgeable and competent party to such a system of obligations. [...] In short, a person is an agent who can perform effectively in the space of obligations. (List & Pettit 2011, p. 173)

Fourth, it might be observed that the status account has something in common with Tuomela's argument that a group agent, in the extrinsic sense, depends on acceptance or construction (Tuomela 2013b). Even though the attention drawn to the process of attribution might seem similar, Hindriks' formulation is particularly (though not exclusively) focused on the fact that the process of ascription responsible for creating the 'we' should come from the outside. Thus, while Tuomela might be read as defending the idea that the (extrinsically

---

of recognition opened by the creation of new institutions. Regarding acknowledgement, we can see how the full-blown recognition of an institution is only achieved through the acknowledgement of the validity of the reasons supporting its creation. On the concept of recognition in social ontology see also Ikäheimo & Laitinen 2011, Laitinen 2014, Stahl 2011, Testa 2011.

[11] On free-standing Y terms, see Searle 2010, pp. 19–24. See Introduction, Section 2.

[12] The idea of performative person will be further developed in Section 8.3 and Section 9.2.

intentional) group is the product of the acceptance that the members exert on the collective to which they belong, Hindriks' version is rather inclined to attribute the status of agent based on a process of recognition exerted by people that are not part of the collective. In this sense, the 'outsiders' (Laitinen 2014) are those who attribute the normative status to the group.[13] This is not to say that recognition from outsiders is necessary for the construction of the group. I want to emphasize that being recognized by other agents qualifies the group as an agent that will then be able to participate in practices of social interaction. For example, it could be that there is a secret society based exclusively on the recognition of the members who form it. Yet, this society could not enter into agreements with other societies unless they recognized it as a subject. Finally, based on the introduction of the status account, the reflection leads us to reconsider the extrinsic account and to take it not to represent, at least not necessarily, an external perspective. As the extrinsic account is based on the recognition of structural, intentional-related features, the account could be developed both through the case in which the recognitive attitude is ascribable to the group members and in the event recognition comes from the outside. In this sense, not all extrinsic accounts are external perspectives. The opposite is also true: an externalist account, which assumes the viewpoint of the observer, does not necessarily have to recognize groups as agents by assuming an intentionally extrinsic perspective. The fact that an observer could grant the status of group agent to a set of individuals does not exclude that the ascription might have happened by looking at some intentional attitudes shared by them. Accordingly, the status account might be compatible with, and come in addition to, the intrinsic perspective, which rests the identification of the group agent on the ground of its being the subject to whom intentionality refers.

---

[13] Noticing that Tuomela gives more importance to the acceptance exerted by the members does not coincide with denying the role of recognition coming from the outside. Rather, the point is that the most important feature in the group's formation consists in the members having accepted the ethos through collective acceptance and commitment. This is what ensures the possibility of group agents. Then, the group could work as an agent for (and could be treated as an agent by) an observer in the proper way only in case the collective has been recognized as such from the inside. Similarly, considering the acceptance of outsiders to be a fundamental aspect in Hindriks' account does not mean that member-to-member recognition has no role. Indeed, Hindriks' proposal includes relations of recognition among the members who ascribe to one another the normative status of group members and partners in the action. This kind of attribution of a status is a process that establishes the construction of the group for the insiders, which is a relevant aspect for the functioning of group agents.

To sum up, the status account considers the identification of group agents based on the attribution of a status, which is a form of recognition close to Searle's notion of acceptance, meaning that the attitudes come with the ascription of deontic powers. In this sense, group agents are performative persons and can be recognized either from the inside, as is in Tuomela's approach (2013a), or from the outside, by agents who do not participate in it (Hindriks 2008). The status account is alternative, though not opposed, to both intrinsic and extrinsic views of group agents.

In Chapter Five, we will try to clarify how it can be that a theory might refer to group agents without undertaking to defend the ontological objectivity of such entities.

Chapter 5

Holistic individualism

5.1 The (apparent?) paradox

The goal of the GLA is to grasp shared agency straightforwardly. The troublesome part of the story is that, to describe shared actions, we are left with a notion of group-scale subject, which—for the sake of argument—has no objective, ontological reference in the world. The intentionalistic theory of shared agency supported by the Big Four of social ontology essentially assumes the individualistic claim that nothing exists apart from individuals and their properties.[1]

In order to face the (apparent?) paradox embedded within the possibility of conceiving non-substantial groups as sources of agency, it should be observed that Chapter Four's identification of 'we' is not in conflict—at least, not in principle—with the rejection of group-scale subjects populating the social world. The intrinsic, extrinsic, and status accounts denote the 'we' of shared agency without calling into question its ontological objectivity. As mentioned, the identification of the group hinges on determining how a system can be accountable for the performance of any action (Section 4.4). In one response, Tuomela states that although groups "exist relative to the framework of agency, yet these do not really exist" (Tuomela 1984, p. 3). Meaning the

---

[1] I take the claim of ontological individualism to be a fundamental premise of the Big Four of collective intentionality (Chant, Hindriks & Preyer 2014). However, a survey of other parts of the debate on the nature and structure of the social world would show how variously contemporary discussions regard the ontological status of social facts. An example is the social ontology endorsed by critical realism: a position in sociology that regards social facts as being ontologically emergent and objective. According to this interpretation, high-level facts are emergent components of social reality, a multi-layered structure made up of increasingly complex layers, ontologically autonomous from their foundations and characterized by novel properties (Archer 1998a, 1998b, Bhaskar 1998, Elder-Vass 2007). With a difference from critical realism, I will argue that the framework embraced in analytical social ontology does not allow a strict separation between levels of complexity, because the ontological relation between levels assumed in the debate is weaker than emergence as it does not introduce new properties into the higher level that are not present at the lower level already. Such a relation is a form of supervenience: a form of co-variation and dependence granting ontological objectivity only to individual-level facts (Kim 1984). Chapter Six discusses supervenience in detail.

expression does not have an objective connotation but, instead, its meaning derives from within the theory concerned. The reference of 'group' is an object defined *functionally*, not a metaphysical premise. Hence, the notion is stable only within the description provided by the theory. In this sense,

> [...] our concepts of agent, social action, group, and so on are functional. This means that they are specified in terms of their roles in our theories and in the uses to which we put our theories. (Tuomela 1984, p. 4)

Thus, the chance of taking a group as an agent seems to rely on a functionalist theory of agency: an agent is what functions as such for the theory (List and Pettit 2011, p. 75).[2] If the concept of group agent has a functional role within a certain approach (even without an ontological equivalent in the realm the theory wants to describe), it is because some division between the explanation and the ontological concern has been established. In particular, theorists such as Tuomela (2011, 2013a, 2013b), Pettit (2014), List (2018), and Gilbert (1989), among others, trace a line that clearly separates the explanation from the metaphysical reflection. Such separation stipulates that, on the one hand, the explanatory issue represents an epistemological and methodological stance, concerning to what extent social explanations should focus on individuals and social phenomena, respectively. On the other hand, the ontological perspective encapsulates what there is and what the ontological status of social phenomena is in relation to individuals (Zahle & Collin 2014). The idea behind this discernment concerns the two issues separately and assumes that the notion of group, although useful in the account of social phenomena, is not present among the elements composing the world in which we live. The widespread tendency resulting from this analytical strategy leans towards embracing an individualistic stance regarding the ontological issue and rejecting that perspective for the explanation. To grasp the complexity of shared agency, it is necessary—both in the MLA and in the GLA—to rely on concepts referring to social phenomena. As established by the MLA already, reflecting upon group performances from the side of the members (or from the side of the group as the GLA attempts to do) is an effort that requires higher-level descriptions and concepts such as collective intentionality, joint commitment or, at least, the representation of the network forming the 'we'.

---

[2] On functionalism in the social sciences, see Kincaid 1996, pp. 101–141.

As far as the necessity to introduce social or high-level concepts is concerned, the main hurdle is reconciling the explicative claim with the individualistic assumption at the heart of the intentionalistic approach, which prevents it from going beyond the existence of the individual's mind and properties. As it stands, the distinction between the explanatory and the ontological issue could provide a solution by making it feasible to speak of the 'we' and, at the same time, keep the premise that only individuals exist as a valid standpoint. In this sense, while the individualistic claim would be a thesis about what exists, the introduction of facts about groups could be considered an explicative move aimed at accounting for a phenomenon (namely shared agency as group agency) that has relevance only within the theoretical framework one is constructing. From this perspective, no group agent can be reasonably assumed to exist so that "we can be ontological individualists, and still debate explanatory individualism" (Epstein 2015, p. 22).

Within the framework of the MLA, the ontological nature of the 'we' does not represent an urgent issue because the features under investigation are the members in their being singular individuals (ontologically speaking). The point becomes a pressing problem as soon as we consider the GLA. The group-level account aims to describe shared agency as ascribable to the collective as a whole. Still, the ontological thesis underpinning the entire reflection defends an individualistic position:

> the basic social ontology consists solely of the activities and properties (including mental activities and properties) and interactions (including mental interactions and relations) between individuals and it may contain groups and group properties that are reducible to the individualistic (and possibly other nonsocial) basis [...]. (Tuomela 2013a, p. 10)

In line with such an ontological assumption, the group-level account can happen in two ways. First, the account can associate the individualistic ontological claim with an individualistic explanation of social facts, which "has as its explanatory basis the individual's own attitudes and motivating reasons" (Tuomela 2013a, p. 10). In this case, the result would be the reducibility of social explanations to descriptions focused at the lower level and the consequent redundancy of the high-level account to "a mere convenience of language" (Ludwig 2017a, p. 218). Alternatively, the explanation can (and actually does) take a holistic perspective and—without discarding what has been fixed at the ontological level—assume that the description of social phenomena must employ non-individualistic terms (List & Spiekermann 2013).[3] As it is, explanatory (or methodological)[4] holism "does not imply any more radical form of holism that gives some kind of metaphysical priority to social structures over and above the individuals living in them" (List & Spiekermann 2013, p. 629). This means "holist explanations involve holist theories which are distinguished by their use of holist terms such as 'university' or 'school'" (Zahle & Collin 2014, p. 8).

5.2 Traditional positions

The disjunction between the ontology of groups and the explanation about them conveys, at least, two different ways in which one might be an individualist in social ontology. On one side, one might be an ontological individualist and think that all elements composing the social world are reducible to individual subjects and facts related to them. On the other side, one could be a methodological individualist and try to explain social phenomena based on concepts, laws, and descriptions employing principles that should be deduced from "principles governing the behavior of participating individuals from analyses of their situations" (Watkins 1952, p. 186). To speak of shared agency as group agency, some accounts keep defending ontological individualism but reject the kind of individualism that pertains to the explanation. The outcome is the perspective called 'holistic individualism', where the first term 'holistic' refers to the methodological claim and 'individualism' is about ontology.[5] According to this view, shared

---

[3] On explanatory issues, see Lukes 1968, Sawyer 2002, 2003.

[4] On the meaning(s) of methodological individualism, see Hodgson 2007a.

[5] Among the Big Five, some version of holistic individualism can be found in Tuomela's and Gilbert's accounts, since both of them explicitly combine ontological individualism with high-level explanations of shared agency as group agency (Tuomela 2013a, Gilbert 1989). In addition, List and Pettit (2011) defend holistic individualism about group agency by proposing one of the most refined attempts of presenting social groups as ontologically reducible though epistemically irreducible subjects of agency. The theory develops Pettit's anti-singularism, based on which groups can be said to have a mind of their own (Pettit 2003). (Anti)singularism, will be discussed in Section 5.3. Perplexities arise regarding the possibility of conceiving Searle's view on social reality in terms of holistic individualism. On the one hand, in line with holistic individualism, Searle embraces the idea that social facts are epistemologically objective whilst they are ontologically subjective (Searle 2010). On the other hand, Searle does not extend the reflection on social facts to group-scale agents and actions. This means that, from the study of Searle's social ontology, we might obtain a theory of social institutions and yet it would be difficult to find some attribution of intentionality to subjects other than individuals. For this reason, I will treat Searle's GLA very cautiously. Then, concerning Bratman's account, it will be maintained that the kind of

agency as an intentional phenomenon is a proper group event, graspable through concepts such as 'collective intentionality' and 'group agency', which are not meant to contradict the claim that society is comprised of nothing more than individuals. Still, the notion of group agent, although valid in terms of description, depends on its members as the ultimate ontological components of the whole. In this sense, groups are ontologically reducible in a way that reductionism does not imply eliminativism: even though groups are (ontologically) reducible to their components or the network of attitudes, norms, and commitments in place at the members' level; the explanation of group phenomena still requires a holistic lexicon.[6]

For those familiar with the history of political philosophy and social theory, the phrase 'holistic individualism' might still suggest a paradoxical association, bringing together two terms that have been traditionally treated in opposition.[7] The issue, which is at the core of current discussions in social ontology, finds its roots in the social sciences of the nineteenth century with significant contributions including, among others, the works of Émile Durkheim (1895/1982, 1897/1951) and K. E. Maximilian Weber (1922/1978). The original dispute is rooted in whether it could be meaningful to admit the existence of social facts as *sui generis* phenomena, not reducible to events concerning individual agents and not predictable based on psychological principles. On the matter, Durkheim's view was in favor of the holistic claim that social facts do exist *sui generis* as special phenomena:

> A social fact is any way of acting, whether fixed or not, capable of exerting over the individual an external constraint; or: which is general over the whole of a given society whilst having an existence of its own. (Durkheim 1982, p. 59)

Furthermore,

> Sociological method as we practice it rests wholly on the basic principle that social facts must be studied as things, that is, as realities

---

methodological individualism he defends has been recently implemented with the increasingly important function of networking (Bratman 2017). Augmented individualism is, in this sense, open to functional high-level explanations of shared agency that take the group as the actor of the performance.

[6] On the features of collective agency that can be reduced to features of individual agency, see Schweikard 2008.

[7] Tollefsen (2018) has recently offered a thorough introduction to methodological individualism and methodological holism. On the issue, see also Zahle & Collin 2014.

external to the individual. There is no principle for which we have received more criticism; but none is more fundamental. Indubitably for sociology to be possible, it must above all have an object all its own. It must take cognizance of a reality which is not in the domain of other sciences. But if no reality exists outside of individual consciousness, it wholly lacks any material of its own. (Durkheim 1951, p. XXXVi)

If compared to the distinction between ontology and explanation—which was not an explicit acquisition at the time—the former quotation would put Durkheim's theory on the side of ontological holism, as it postulates the existence of facts that are not reducible to the laws governing their individual basis. Then, the latter passage could be a claim about the method of the social sciences.[8] The sociologist thus assumed that in order to study the social world, it would be necessary to make use of concepts and descriptions that understand social facts as such, namely as regularities happening in the world and having the power to modify what the individuals do concretely (Greenwood 2003). However, as Durkheim himself pointed out, "men's dignity is diminished whenever he is made to feel that he is not completely self-determinant" (Durkheim 1982, p. 4). So, the idea that social regularities might affect individual behavior could represent a bitter pill to swallow.

Moved by such perplexity, Weber insisted on the individualistic thesis that the main forces operating in the social world are those of individual rationality and psychology. Weber suggested a rational actor foundation for social sciences, claiming that the only way to grasp social phenomena is by studying events related to individual intentional actions.

> [...] collectives must be treated as solely the resultants and modes of organization of the particular acts of individual persons, since these alone can be treated as agents in a course of subjectively understandable action. (Weber 1978, p. 139)

---

[8] The kind of ontological holism held by Durkheim does not necessarily imply the assumption of social entities as *sui generis* objects. Durkheim's claim was about the existence of social facts—such as tendencies and rules—that exist independently of individual psychology and behavior. He did not mention groups as social facts but just phenomena concerning groups, among which the rate of suicide is the best-known example (Durkheim 1951). According to this, it might be reasonable to interpret Durkheim's ontological perspective as a form of holism about properties, which assumes that "a society can have properties that are irreducible to the properties of individuals" (List & Spiekermann 2013, p. 631).

Thus, it seems reasonable to argue that Weber embraced a form of individualism that holds both methodological and ontological assumptions. In fact, the claim that all events happening in the social world should be explained based on individual psychological laws is a suggestion that fully grasps the core of methodological individualism. Similarly, concerning ontology, the idea that only individuals can be agents is a remark that seems to exclude group agents from the list of what there is.

The debate between individualists and holists has developed over time, and during the 1950s, the defense of the individualistic perspective, especially in its methodological aspect, was greatly diffused. In particular, the debate rehashed focusing on methodological issues after Watkins' definition of methodological individualism as opposed to methodological holism (Watkins 1952, 1955); the classification was later adopted and sustained employing individualistic arguments by theorists such as Friedrich A. von Hayek (1942), Karl R. Popper (1944a, 1944b, 1945) and Steven M. Lukes (1968), among others. More recently, the holistic side of the diatribe has been reconsidered, and the increasing interest in social ontology has effectively played a role in such re-evaluation. Even though most theorists have accepted that social facts and events should be explained only by referring to individuals and their attitudes and actions, many philosophers have taken seriously the idea that, in accounting for what happens in society, it is necessary to adopt holistic terms and descriptions. For instance, shared agency has been regarded as irreducible to the agency of every single participant in connection with others: the 'we' involved in the phenomenon makes the difference. Such a gap created by the 'we' might be interpreted in two ways, both concerning the methodological side of the discipline: epistemological and descriptive. As an epistemological position, the assumption of a we-perspective allows the interpretation of collective phenomena as something that the individuals involved in the performance see as something they do as part of a whole[9] (List

---

[9] The divergence generated by holistic concepts concerns the way in which the subject of intentional action may think of, perceive, and feel herself as a member in relation to the group context. Such theoretical features concern the capacity to conceptualize oneself as an agent, as someone who acts as a group member (Ludwig 2017a). It is important to underline that representing oneself as a group member comes with different degrees of complexity, depending on the sort of group taken into consideration and on the way in which the characteristic traits of that specific group affect the members' experience. Those external/non-mental aspects are relevant for the MLA to the point that Schmitz has introduced the concept of role-mode intentionality, a way of bearing in mind intentions for the action by representing the subject of those attitudes as an individual agent fulfilling a specific function within a system. In this

2016, Pacherie 2018, Salice & Schmid 2016, Schmid 2014b, 2017b, Schmitz 2017, 2018, Tuomela 2013b). As a descriptive claim, the holistic account aims at comprehending events of shared agency through non-individualistic terms and principles (Bratman 1999, 2014a; Gilbert 1989, 2006; Jackson & Pettit 1992; Kincaid 1996; List & Pettit 2011; Pettit 1996, 2014; Tuomela 2007, 2013a, 2013b). In other words, while the epistemological account concerns the first-person perspective endorsed by the agent, the descriptive account is about the observer's point of view.[10] Instead, concerning the metaphysical issue, discussions in social ontology still revolve around social and group phenomena.(Bach 2016, Effingham 2010, Epstein 2014a, 2014b, 2017, Hauswald 2016, Hindriks 2012, 2013, 2017, Laitinen 2017, Ludwig 2003, 2007b, 2014, Ritchie 2015, Ruben 1985, Stoutland 2008, Thomasson 2002, 2009, 2016).

5.3 Three issues in social ontology[11]

Since its origin, the holism-individualism debate has established conflicting positions based on the radical opposition of the two terms. Philip Pettit is the one who has recently brought the dichotomy into focus within social ontology

---

sense, the subject of role-mode intentionality is not the individual agent as such, but the individual who brings herself under the concept of 'group member'. Schmitz explains that "role modifies the theoretical and practical vantage point of the role bearer, his or her perceptual and actional apparatus with regard to the 'world'" (Schmitz 2017, p. 63), so to make the experience of being part of a group a kind of filter for individual thinking and acting. This modification in the subject of intentionality should be what allows us to speak of the intentional mode as a subject-mode: instead of being part of representational content, the collective dimension of joint action is viewed as a filter, a feature that affects the subject to whom the attitude is attributed in experience. This means that the way in which any individual agent 'feels' the attitude determines the subject of that attitude, which could be the individual agent as such, a group of people taken as a 'we', and even the individual *qua* role-bearer.

[10] Chalmers makes the point, by stating that at the individual level "[W]hen a conscious system is observed from the third-person point of view, a range of specific behavioral and neural phenomena present themselves. When a conscious system is observed from the first-person point of view, a range of specific subjective phenomena present themselves" (Chalmers 2004, p. 1111). Chalmers' distinction of first- and third-person points of view spells out the meaning of the divergence between theoretical and explicative tasks plainly: theoretical tasks are about first-person issues, while the explicative side concerns third-person investigations. Since intentional agency has to do with a faculty of the mind, or to say it otherwise, since it regards rational systems of agency, it makes sense to extend Chalmers' reflection to our study of intentionality and agency, even when group-sized systems (e.g., social groups such as corporations) are at stake.

[11] The title of the section is inspired by Pettit (2014).

in an alternative interpretation. Pettit, a supporter of holistic individualism, has tried to avoid the paradoxical connection of holism and individualism by disaffirming the opposing character of the terms (Düber et al. 2016). According to Pettit, opting for an individualistic ontology and—at the same time—for a holistic methodology is feasible and consistent and not only because the questions (i.e., explanation and ontology) are assumed to be separated. The position's stability—he claims—stems from its combination of two perspectives that are not merely two sides of the same coin, as individualistic and holistic issues belong to different kinds of analysis in the social sciences, which regard different levels and subjects of interaction. Pettit explains:

> The first issue in social ontology has to do with how far individuals are compromised from on high, by aggregate or structural factors. It is a vertical issue, as we may put it. The second issue, by contrast, is of a horizontal character. It is the issue between what I call atomism and holism. The question bears, not on the relation between high-level factors and individual human beings, but on the relation between the individuals themselves. It is the question as to how far people's social relationships with one another are of significance in their constitution as subjects and agents. (Pettit 1996, p. 111)

Table 5.1. Methodological stances.

	INDIVIDUALISM	COLLECTIVISM
ATOMISM	1	2
HOLISM	3	4

According to Pettit, the point is to consider the relationship between individuals and society (between the members and the group) as a double question. This double question concerns the vertical relation between every single individual and the group to which she belongs and the horizontal interaction among the members. Thus, it falls on the vertical issue to discuss to what extent individual agency is affected or compromised by external non-psychological influences. It is a matter of horizontal relationships whether a subject might develop her skills and become an agent outside society. Each side of the debate can be addressed from—at least—two contrastive points of view: individualistic and collectivistic for the vertical stance; atomistic and holistic for the horizontal stance. In general, the advocates of individualism assume that individual agents, as the ultimate ontological components of the social world, are autonomous and free from (causal) forces from the environment. In opposition, collectivists argue that social facts exist and exert influence on individual psychology. Similarly, while atomists contend that basic individual skills flourish in the absence of any social interaction, holists argue in favor of the necessity for human beings to grow up and live with other individuals in order to develop their faculties, including rationality (Pettit 1996, 2014).[12] In addition to this classification, Pettit maintains that each way of interpreting a particular stance (be it horizontal or vertical) could be combined with any interpretation of the other.[13]

Table 5.1 above shows the four possible combinations, of which (1) and (4) represent opposite views, taking the agent's psychological autonomy as strictly connected with her self-sufficiency in developing full-blown skills. Therefore, atomistic individualism accepts, affirmatively, the conjunction of the two claims, while holistic collectivism refuses both. More problematic are the cases of (3) holistic individualism and (2) atomistic holism, which are based on the independence of the psychological determination question from the inter-relational one. As far as atomistic holism is concerned, Pettit says that the position can be found in Hobbes' account, which treated "the idea of solitary individual as a suitably coherent notion: the solitary individual never interacts socially with others, even if there are others around"; despite this, "human beings can display all distinctively human capacities" (Pettit 1996, p. 173). Independently of the mutual interaction among the subjects, on the psychological side, Hobbes maintained that individuals are indeed subject to the causal and normative power of the whole, even though—for the sake of argument—such a social unity is not the outcome of the interplay among the parts (Hobbes 1651). Then, holistic individualism could be antithetical to Hobbes' affirmation of psychological autonomy and rejection of the hypothesis of self-sufficiency:

> Imagine that someone is a holist, believing that as things are, human beings depend on their relations with one another for the realization of the capacity to think: with human beings the capacity to think, like the possession of power or status, involves the enjoyment of relations with other people. There is no reason why such a person cannot be an individualist, no reason why he cannot think that aggregate regularities that characterize social life leave the individual uncompromised in her

---

[12] Pettit's definition of 'atomism' overlaps with Gilbert's 'singularism' (Gilbert 1989). Later in this section we will be outlining Pettit's concept of singularism.
[13] Table 5.1 is inspired by Pettit 1996, p. 172. A conceptualization of the kind can be found also in Gilbert 1989, pp. 427–436.

autarchic status. The endorsement of holism is entirely consistent with
accepting the intentional-psychological picture of human beings [...].
(Pettit 1996, p. 173)

Thus, the point proposed by Pettit is that holistic individualism does not
represent an association between contrasting terms but rather a kind of
reconciliation between two positions concerning different aspects of the
relationship between individuals and society.

It is worth noting that, in addition to offering a reinterpretation of
individualism/collectivism and atomism/holism, Pettit has brought into focus
a third issue in social ontology: the question of singularism/anti-singularism.

It is the debate as to whether there are centers of intentional attitude
and action over and beyond singular agents; whether singular subjects
ever combine to form novel, plural centers of intentional life: minds of
their own [...]". (Pettit & Schweikard 2006, p. 36)

This debate concerns whether only individuals can be capable of intention
and action or whether groups can exhibit such properties too. Singularism
defends the idea that there can be only singular agents, therefore, coincident
with single human beings; anti-singularism considers instead that agents can
be composed of several individuals and yet be considered as single subjects of
intention and action. As Pettit and Schweikard observe (Pettit & Schweikard
2006, Pettit 2014), the issue of singularism is independent of the other two
dichotomies. On the individualism/collectivism side, one can be a singularist
and deny that groups can be agents either by believing that individual
psychology is not determined by social tendencies or by thinking that it is.
Likewise, some groups can be said to be subjects of agency by either denying
or affirming psychological determination in relation to each subject's
psychology. Moreover, recognizing oneself as a singularist does not affect the
idea that agency-related faculties develop socially or are bestowed by nature.
Regardless of whether the subject is singular or plural, it is legitimate to
consider either that its faculties have developed socially or, conversely, that
they are intrinsic. Therefore, singularism opens a third question in social
ontology that, it is argued, can be treated independently of the others.[14]

---

[14] Raising the issue of singularism as an additional problem to those already pointed out
in the debate certainly helps to shed light on the multiple relations between individual
and society. As I am going to show in Chapters Eight and Nine, I find that considering
singularism as an independent aspect other than individualism and atomism is

In the next section, we will further discuss individualism and holism so that we can better understand how the Big Five utilize them.

5.4 Holistic individualism and shared agency

The interpretation proposed by Pettit regarding 'holism' and 'individualism' in the social sciences represents an important remark for better understanding the traditional debate and the way to associate the two poles. Given that holistic individualism in social ontology applies the former perspective with reference to the explanatory issue and the latter in accounting for the ontology of the social world, such a dichotomy could now acquire an additional meaning when compared to Pettit's insight. Pettit suggests that, while individualism is concerned with vertical relationships, holism regards the horizontal interplay among individuals (Pettit 1996). According to this perspective, the ontological stance held by individualists would imply a claim about agency and intentionality. If one says that only individuals exist, one also means that individuals in society are autonomous in the sense that they have the power to decide and determine their intentions and actions. In opposition to the collectivistic approach, the individualistic view does not admit any external (causal) influence or determination of individual psychology from the outside; each singular agent, both in personal and in shared contexts of agency, is free to decide about her attitudes and thoughts.

---

appropriate and demanding. In fact, if we embrace the anti-singularist thesis that groups can also be subjects of agency, we should be willing to apply the same individualistic/collectivistic and atomistic/holistic theses to group-sized subjects as we do with respect to individuals. This means that if, concerning vertical influences, we think that the psychology of subjects is (or is not) determined by external social factors, then we should hold that to be true for group-sized subjects as well. Regarding horizontal influences, if we think that rational skills are (or are not) developed through interaction then groups should also be included in this network (or considered to have the skills necessary for agency intrinsically). By this I mean that while I recognize the specificity of the three issues, I feel that an effort must be made to ensure consistency relative to the definition of the subject, which will probably have a wider meaning once the anti-singularist position is affirmed. As for anti-singularism both individuals and groups can be agents, questions regarding rational autonomy and mental faculties should be viewed as processes that affect both kinds of subject by avoiding focusing only on agents of human proportions. We will examine how some assumptions in List and Pettit's theory might lead one to doubt that their anti-singularism has been supported by a full application of the notion of subject (performative person) to individuals as well as to groups.

According to individualism about the mind, the mental natures of all a person's or animal's states (and events) are such that there is no necessary or deep individuative relation between the individual's being in states of those kinds and the nature of the individual's physical or social environment. (Burge 1986, pp. 3–4)

Individualism does not imply that any individual who acts in a social context is exempt from restrictions and regulations; instead, for what concerns her mental states, the subject should always be accountable for the attitudes she bears. For the social environment or the group to which one belongs is not meant to determine the individual's mind, the ontological thesis supports some psychological autarchy of individual agents—at least, as Pettit puts it.[15] At the same time, observing that the issue related to holism is that of horizontal relationships among agents serves to point out an interesting aspect of the methodological question to which the holistic view is associated. In fact, by maintaining the worth of the individualistic ontological (and psychological) claim, the holistic concern finds that,

[L]iving in our society is a necessary condition of the development of rationality, in some sense of this property, or becoming a moral agent in the full sense of the term, or becoming fully a responsible, autonomous being. [...] the view (is) that outside society, or in some variants outside certain kinds of society, our distinctively human capacities could not develop. (Taylor 1985, p. 191)

Thus, the development of rationality as a faculty that any individual can exercise autonomously—with no causal determination from the social— requires the presence of other persons and formative (eventually affective)

---

[15] This interpretation might sound a bit rigid, as Pettit himself associates his ontological individualism with a form of realism about groups (Pettit 2007a, 2007b, List & Pettit 2011). Even assuming that that kind of realism is not an ontological position but just an epistemological assumption, considering groups as proper centers of rationality and intentional agency might address some doubts about individual intentional autonomy in connection with the ontological individualism of the theory. The point will be reconsidered later in the present book, when the critique of ontological individualism is further developed in relation to other forms of individualism such as intentional, metaphysical, and normative individualism (Section 8.3). To say it briefly, I will doubt that ontological individualism is a position concerned exclusively with the composition of society and maintain that ontological interpretations are rather shaped by the idea that individual agents, as rational creatures, have an undeniable (metaphysical and normative) priority over groups (Chapter Eight and Chapter Nine).

relationships with them. In this sense, our being intentional agents strictly depends upon our being grown up socially, as the interaction with others is the foundation of our autarchic attitudes and actions. As holistic explanations make it possible to spell out the development of individuals' mental skills, the explicative stance coming with the holistic position becomes noteworthy: even if social concepts are ontologically reducible to their individual bases, they seem to be indispensable for grasping how some facts belong to that individualistic foundation.

Since the individualistic ontological claim has some implications on the kind of psychological autarchy embraced by the theory and because holistic explanations tell something relevant about the relational nature of our capacities as agents, it appears quite clearly that the two levels (individual and social) should be kept separate. Mixing things up would confuse the issues by making it difficult to defend a complex and quasi-paradoxical position, like the one captured within holistic individualism. However, alongside this remark, it is necessary to bring ontological and methodological questions together to unearth the connection that might be established between the two levels, given the re-conciliation proposed by holistic individualism in the GLA. Assuming, as the GLA does, that social facts do not really exist, their usefulness in explaining what happens in society tells us that there should be something in the world allowing our usage of high-level concepts, such as group agent and group agency. Saying that groups are not ontologically primitive is not the same as affirming an eliminativistic stance about group-related phenomena. Moreover, describing group-level facts as facts that ontologically depend on individuals acknowledges the presence of some sort of relation between high-level and low-level facts.[16] Clarifying the meaning of dependency is crucial here: Chapter Six deals with just that.

---

[16] Assuming social phenomena (here, groups) can be better grasped through a holistic point of view does not equal denying the salience and effectiveness of explanations based on individual behavioral and psychological laws. In fact, one might acknowledge the necessary character of holistic explanations without standing for the dispensability of individualistic accounts. The dispensability debate in the social sciences can be approached from three different perspectives: "Methodological individualism: Individualist explanations should be advanced. Holist explanations may, and should, be dispensed with. Strong methodological holism: Holist explanations should be offered. Individualist explanations may, and should, be dispensed with. Weak methodological holism: Not only individualist but also holist explanations should be put forward. Neither individualist nor holist explanations may, and should be, dispensed with" (Zahle & Collin 2014, p. 5). The view proposed by holistic individualism follows the third option, assuming that holistic explanations are necessary while individual-level

considerations remain noteworthy. As it is, different levels of explanation describe kinds of phenomena, not reducible to one another—at least, they are not reducible from a methodological perspective. As said, while the MLA views group agency based on attributes of people, the GLA claims to offer a more comprehensive reading of the event, not limited to individuals' experience and jet anchored to member-level facts as basic ontological components. In other words, one can take the MLA and the GLA to be two sides of the same coin, namely two different ways of considering the case of group agency: the former view assumes the members' perspective and focuses on micro-level facts, whereas the latter (whenever suitable) takes the group's measure and studies macro-level events and regularities.

Chapter 6

The supervenience of group-level facts

6.1 Supervenience relation

The relation between the individual level and the social horizon could have various descriptions, depending upon the perspective from which one approaches the matter. The standpoint of this chapter concerns the ontological question: how can we think of group-scale subjects when they are considered dependent upon the lower level of reality, that is, the level of the members? Given that the individualistic ontology embraced by holistic individualism is grounded on the assumption that no group really exists as an ontological primitive; groups are ontologically determined on an individual basis. Accordingly, the question posed above revolves around the sense of determination at stake here.

Before providing an answer, it should be highlighted that the ontological problem cannot be treated as a univocal issue: dwelling upon the ontology of groups (and upon the status of any other social fact, generally) could be subject to different interpretations. In particular, the question might refer to group-level facts by considering the concept as signifying, respectively, objects (i.e., entities, events, or processes) or properties. Therefore, an ontological position could be to accept the existence of properties (including intentional and agentive properties) as related to groups without assuming groups to be objects.[1] Otherwise, one could admit the proper existence of groups as objects while refusing their capability to have attitudes for action. To clarify, one can embrace their objective ontological status whilst not considering them as bearers of agential properties.[2] Of course, another

---

[1] Ruben (1985) has named the position 'e-individualism', which has even been called 'token individualism'.

[2] The case represents an issue of 'p-individualism' or 'type individualism', according to which no high-level property exists as an irreducible feature (Ruben 1985). It could be interesting to observe that social groups might be social objects without agentive properties whilst having influence on the social world due to the normative status they have, as institutional facts (Searle 2010). In this case, although agentive properties are individual properties, some groups may interact with other parts of society, by exerting some normative power on them based on the rights and duties of the institution. Assuming agentive properties are individual properties, institutional groups could not

position could be denying that the notion of 'group' can refer to any social object or property at all by affirming the reducibility of both (Ludwig 2014). In opposition, considering groups as objects endowed with properties, most notably the property of being the subject of intentional actions, would imply the underpinning of a (ontological) realist perspective according to which the term 'group' (and 'social phenomenon' in general) might denote both objects and properties. For the sake of simplicity, the present reflection takes a less committed view, assuming issues concerning groups regard any high-level fact that propositions can express. In this sense, questioning the ontological relation between individuals and groups may be read as a question about the kind of determination in place between facts of the lower (individual) level and facts about the higher (social) level, no matter if they instantiate properties or objects (List & Spiekermann 2013).[3] The only requirement is that those facts can be suitable objects of linguistic expressions. To exemplify, the phrase 'Hannah and Martin want to visit Milan' concerns individual facts, and the proposition 'an increasing number of tourists have been visiting Milan' represents a social phenomenon. By following this interpretation, the ontological commitment required by the notion of fact does not necessarily lead to the assumption of groups being ontologically objective.

In an attempt to elucidate how holistic individualism accounts for the way in which individual-level facts determine group-level facts, we should now consider the kind of determination theorized in social ontology and, more precisely, by the Big Five. The connection in question has been defined as a supervenience relation, which states that "one set of facts, say B, 'supervenes' on another, say A, if and only if fixing the A-facts also fixes the B-facts" (List & Pettit

---

be intentionally intrinsic agents (Section 4.2) but have the power to modify human behavior due to the normative status they bear (Hindriks 2014, 2017; Ludwig 2007a, 2017b). Tuomela regards the influence that intentionally extrinsic social groups (Section 4.3) have on society as a kind of causal relation between the organizational structure of the group and the behavior of people, be they group members or outsiders (Tuomela 2013a). On the causal power of groups, see Section 6.4.4, 7.4, 10.4.

[3] The choice of this terminology and conceptual framework is justified by the heterogeneous way in which theorists in the debate have dealt with the issue. Tuomela speaks of *I-mode* and *we-mode* attitudes (Tuomela 2013a, pp. 72–73, 2011), Epstein talks about sets of entities (Epstein 2014b, p. 21), whereas Sawyer refers to properties of different kinds (Sawyer 2002, p. 543). In this context, List and Pettit adopt the general notion of facts (List & Pettit 2011, pp. 63–72)—further developed in List and Spiekermann 2013—which complies with the way in which Searle (Searle 1995, 2010) describes elements populating the social world: 'social facts'.

2011, p. 65).[4] The debate on 'supervenience' identifies an interconnection among levels that postulates the derivative character of the supervenient level and the objective ontological status of its basis.[5] In this sense, given a particular configuration of individual facts, a specific social arrangement supervenes. Accordingly, every time something changes at the lower level, a modification occurs at the higher level. In addition, and in contrast to the relation of emergence, the case of supervenience requires an ongoing relationship between the lower and the higher order of facts so that the latter does not acquire complete independence from the former (Kim 1999). Supervenient social facts do not cut the ties with the individual phenomena involved in their foundation. Thus, the relation between them can be viewed as a kind of co-variation (Ludwig 2003, Sawyer 2002, Zahle 2007).

The assumption that some facts or a network of facts at the lower level can produce a specific configuration at the supervenient level does not mean that the social fact in question could not have been produced by another or many other arrangements at the individual level. The only necessary determination is the one between the design in place among the individuals and the holistic phenomenon it generates. The converse, however, is not true: any particular social fact can be associated with an open-ended number of arrangements at the lower level (Currie 1984, Epstein 2014a, Kim 1992, List & Spiekermann 2013, Ludwig 2003, Risjord 2014, Sawyer 2002). Such a characteristic of the supervenience relation is called multiple realizability, for which List and Spiekermann provide a clear definition:

> Multiple realizability of high-level properties: The system's higher-level properties are determined by its lower-level properties but can be realized by numerous different configurations of them and hence cannot feasibly be re-described in terms of lower-level properties. (List & Spiekermann 2013, p. 639)

Multiple realizability establishes that a social fact, produced by a particular arrangement of individual facts, can supervene on many different, alternative configurations at the lower level. In accordance, it would be a mistake to refer that phenomenon to one single basis exclusively. In fact, different individual-level sets of facts can generate the same social fact, and, consequently, different individual-level bases, not identical to one another, can generate social facts that are instead identical. For example, the social fact 'being a family' can

---

[4] See also List & Pettit 2006.
[5] On the meanings of 'supervenience', see Kim 1984.

originate from various arrangements depending on the cultural and social environment on which we focus the attention: 'Claire and Matthew are married and have two children'; 'Sonia and Laura have been living together for ten years'; 'Thomas and Steven are married in law'. All these propositions represent individual facts, different from one another, that give rise to a supervenient fact, namely the social fact of being a family that has—or should have—the same meaning despite contextual variations in its foundations.

Moreover, multiple realizability can be broadened by introducing another property, namely wild disjunction:

> The basic idea is that for any social property, there is in principle an endless sequence of nomologically possible individual-level states such that although each of them 'realize' or 'implement' the social property, none of them is coextensive with it. (Sawyer 2002, p. 546)

To elaborate, the wild disjunction of the social level from the individual level is based on the fact that, even though the former derives from the latter, it would not be satisfactory to reduce the supervenient level to its ontological foundation, as that low-level basis—apart from being just one among many—represents only a limited sequence of factors that could vary and still produce the same outcome. In this sense, the social fact should be kept separate from the arrangement(s) from which it supervenes, and the reason for this disjunction is that none of the combinations of individual facts could ever cover all possible arrangements.

One more remark about the nature of supervenience concerns its relation to time: "[s]upervenience is a synchronic claim: the individual events and properties at a time determine everything that happens at that time" (Sawyer 2003, p. 10). Thus, supervenience represents a relation that can be grasped in a snapshot.[6]

---

[6] Further considerations on supervenience and time will be discussed in Section 7.4 and Section 10.4. As opposed to the synchronic nature of supervenience, I will underline the diachronic unfolding of agency and the indispensable role of time for enabling the capacity to have intentions for the action both in individual and in supra-individual systems. This kind of considerations might be the starting point for criticizing supervenience as the best explanation of the ontological framework in social ontology. In addition to the diachronic dimension, Chapter Nine and Chapter Ten also concern the role played by the interaction with the environment in the constitution of any system of agency, including groups.

To summarize, the main features of supervenience as a logical and ontological relation between lower- and higher-level social facts are

1. multiple levels of facts,

2. co-variation of levels,

3. multiple realizability of the social,

4. wild disjunction,

5. synchronic nature of the relation.

6.2 Ontology and methodology

Section 6.1 presented supervenience as the ontological relation adopted by holistic individualism to account for how facts about individuals connect to the social facts they determine. Now, the objective is to show how the ontological framework based on supervenience might underpin the holistic methodological perspective characterizing the GLA. The point is to explain how, according to the theorists of holistic individualism, supervenience relations could enable us to postulate (at least) two irreducible levels of the description. These foundational descriptions would ensure that speaking of phenomena concerning groups in their entirety would not represent a contrasting position if compared to the individualistic ontology on which the supervenience thesis relies. At the same time, the explanation of social facts should keep its irreducible nature without representing a redundant description of facts concerning individuals, as the individualistic ontological claim might, at first, suggest. Thus, although methodological and ontological questions have been presented as separate issues, a reconciliation between the two might yet be sketched. In particular, the outlook provided on the ontological side allows us to imagine a methodology for the social sciences, which relies on arguments and acquisitions gained from the reflection upon ontology. In this sense, the relation is:

Ontology ⟶ Methodology

It is imperative to emphasize that supervenience outlines a picture of the social world organized on the base of a hierarchical ontological scale with multiple levels; each level presents specific and increasingly complex social facts. At one level, there are individual agents and their relationships. At higher levels, there are social facts instantiated by networks of relations, norms, and organizational structures among the constituents of the lower domain (Elder-Vass 2014). Claiming that only elements located at the most basic level hold an objective ontological status does not undermine the consistency of the multi-layered structure because social facts supervene on their individual basis without being co-extensive with it. As the thesis of multiple realizability states: an open number of lower configurations could produce the same high-level arrangement (Sawyer 2002). It follows that—from an explicative point of view—the social world can be the object of various descriptions, depending on the level that each perspective purports to be focused. In this sense, the supervenient relation seems to establish a suitable ontological pattern for the formulation of holistic explanations of the social world, which need a multi-layered metaphysical conception. Moreover, supervenience provides arguments to contrast the descriptive reducibility of the higher level(s) to the lower, as the GLA would require. In fact, multiple realizability and wild disjunction postulate the failure of any equivalence that would univocally translate a social fact in terms of its individualistic foundation. According to the former statement, a certain high-level phenomenon can be instantiated by many different arrangements at the individual level, and according to the latter, none among those combinations is coextensive with the social fact it generates. In line with these considerations, explanatory holism has been considered consistent with the ontology endorsed by holistic individualism (Gilbert 1989, pp. 428– 431; List & Pettit 2011, p. 76; Tuomela 2013a, pp. 4–5).

Given the above, we could also take a step forward (or backward, depending on the perspective) and affirm that the ontological picture outlined so far has provided enough reasons to justify a certain methodological choice that established the theory. In this sense, the holistic explicative claim would be the original term from which the other (i.e., the ontological pattern) has derived. Accordingly, by starting from methodological assumptions, one could establish an ontological framework suitable to outline what there is in the social world, as in any other scientific domain: "[e]very science implies a taxonomy of the events in its universe of discourse. In particular, every science employs a descriptive vocabulary of theoretical and observation predicates such that events fall under the laws of the science by virtue of satisfying those predicates" (Fodor 1974, p. 101). Hence, the relation between ontology and methodology can be turned upside down, and what was intended to be a starting point for analysis would now become a consequent term:

Ontology   ◄————————————   Methodology

The possibility of seeing the relationship in two ways suggests that no priority should be attributed, neither to the methodological nor to the ontological domain. Instead, the connection seems to be running on a double track. If any assumption or modification belonging to one of the two perspectives is studied with these implications in mind, then such a theoretical move would register on the other field. A specific methodological approach requires an appropriate ontological framework, just as a particular ontological structure allows some methodological principles while preventing others.

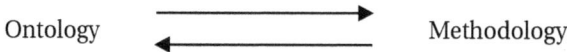

Ontology ⟷ Methodology

Therefore, it is apparent that holistic individualism might represent an extensive challenge that traditional positions in the social sciences, such as atomistic individualism and holistic collectivism, have not brought to our attention. In fact, reconciling, apparently contrasting, ontological and descriptive claims has made the investigation into the two-fold repercussions particularly urgent.

Suppose it is true that the double direction of the ontology-methodology/ methodology-ontology link should not be forgotten. In that case, the analytical reflection still requires us to proceed gradually and to bring the focus on ontology and methodology simultaneously. Given that the introduction of supervenience as an ontological relation between individual and social facts has opened a path that goes from the description of how the world is to how it should be explained, the following pages are dedicated to investigating the explicative pattern prepared by the ontological ground.[7]

6.3 The group-level account (GLA)

Now, I will turn to investigate the explicative pattern that emerges from the ontological relation of supervenience. Although the analysis could apply to any social fact, the following reflection will be developed within the limits of shared agency in regard to intentional actions realized by two or more individual agents considered as a group. In the spirit of the GLA, the group will count as the literal subject of intentional agency. Part One has already endeavored to explain shared agency as the result of shared (non-summative) intentions planning for individual contributions towards a common aim. The present reflection goes beyond the member-level account offered by that description. Now, the goal is to formulate a group-level account of shared agency consistent with the holistic individualism(s) embraced by the Big Five. Although this account shows important differences depending on the interpretation proposed, any GLA is meant to explain shared agency as a

---

[7] The target of Chapter Seven will be challenging the association of individualistic ontology and holistic methodology. If the conjunction of the patterns turns out to be a consistent account of shared agency, holistic individualism will be accepted as a valid philosophical perspective for the development of a GLA. Otherwise, some critics to current GLAs should be (and will be) advanced and some revisions suggested.

group event straightforwardly. GLAs consider the relation between shared intentions and actions from the group's perspective as if it were a single agent. In what follows, the identification of the group agent will be sketched based on some considerations provided by the investigation of the *intrinsic, extrinsic,* and *status* account as *functional* definitions of group agency.[8] The objective is to better understand how and to what extent shared agency has been viewed from a macro perspective. Concerning the mental side of the issue, the intentional event under investigation within the GLA will be the common plan in view of which everyone pursues some specific sub-plan. The common plan can thus be:

    a.   the *we-mode* attitude.[9] This happens in the case of theories that vindicate the discontinuity thesis of intentionality in combination with an intrinsic account of group agency, making the group the plural subject of intentionality;[10]

        or

    b.   the network composed by we-mode/I-mode we-attitudes or I-mode attitudes-that-we in the mind of the participants. The network plays this function when the theory endorses the extrinsic account of group agency, based either on the continuity thesis or on the discontinuity thesis of intentionality. In both cases, group intentionality is viewed as distributive, socially augmented, I/we-intentionality.[11]

Regarding the performative moment, the action to which the mental state refers is the performance realized by the group agent through the actions of

---

[8] See Section 4.2, 4.3, 4.4.

[9] The we-mode attitude meant in this passage is the prior collective intention, namely the intention planning the entire group performance. Since we-mode attitudes involve the intention of each to participate in the group effort, one is expected to associate the notion of individual contribution to the concept of intention-in-action and take the shared plan to be the prior intention. Section 6.4 will explain the issue in detail.

[10] The position matches the non-distributive view of collective intentionality, rejected by the Big Four and yet assumed in Schmid's proposal (Schmid 2009, 2017a). On the discontinuity-thesis account see Chapter Two. The intrinsic account has been introduced in Section 4.2.

[11] The continuity-thesis account was introduced in Chapter One by reference to Bratman's position (Section 1.2, 1.3). For a definition of the extrinsic account, see Section 4.3.

its members meant as primitive motors (Tuomela 2013a, p. 5) or enactors (List & Pettit 2011, p. 164).[12]

Provided that the investigation regarding the GLA touches a different level, which is still related to the level studied by the MLA, it is interesting to note that, according to what MLA one might want to follow, the GLA changes accordingly. Let us consider the MLA endorsing the continuity thesis of intentionality: in compliance with the low-level account, the GLA is bound to assume that the group attitude is the byproduct of individual attitudes and interpersonal relationships conducive to the action. Behind and beyond each individual intention, there is a common aim shared by the participants, mutual expectations among the parties, and mutual beliefs about the others' attitudes. In the case of a complex group, there might be an organizational structure regulating the effectiveness of each contribution and controlling the consistency and coherence of each sub-plan to the shared target (Bratman 2007, 2014a). This kind of system allows the network of individual agents to work as an agent in the *extrinsic* sense of the notion, namely by realizing the complex goal through the meshing sub-plans of all the participants involved (Bratman 2017). Each individual intention to join in the effort has the form: 'I-mode attitude-that-we', where the group appears in the mental state only as a representational content of the intention and as an additional background belief of each.[13]

---

[12] Four questions could be addressed: (1) What is the relevant attitude planning shared agency in GLA?; (2) what is the action relative to the attitude of (1)?; (3) who is the intentional subject in (1)?; (4) who is the actor in (2)?; (5) is the subject in (1) and (3) necessarily the same as the subject in (2) and (4)? There seem to be two different ways in which different GLAs have intended the mental and behavioral subjects of shared agency, depending on whether they have endorsed distributive or non-distributive accounts of shared intentionality. I will argue that only non-distributive accounts can rightly propose intrinsic accounts, considering groups fully-fledged subjects of intention and action.

[13] Figure 6.1 is a simple representation of a group of individuals, who—for what concerns their intentions for the action—do not form a group in an irreducible/intrinsic sense of the notion. Intentional states are, however, involved in the creation of a network, which (1) relates the members to one another and (2) provides the basis for the supervenience of a whole that is not intrinsically intentional but may counts as an agent, in functionalistic terms. Thus, the first triangle from the left represents background attitudes, relationships, and behaviors that might facilitate the formation of shared intentions for the action. With this preparatory network in the background, the second picture shows intentional attitudes in the mind of each and then the third figure illustrates the network constructed through individual intentionality (implemented or regulated by the normative apparatus associated with that system). The last triangle depicts the functional entity working as one. The dotted line represents the fictitious ontological status of the whole, whereas the

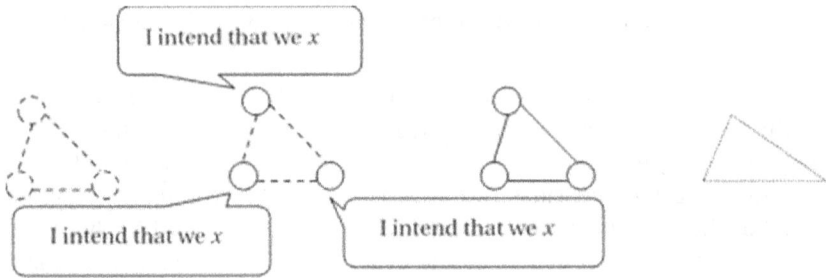

Figure 6.1. GLA and continuity-thesis accounts.

The figure shows the relation between shared intentions and actions seems to be a connection between a network of states of mind, each belonging to the members' psychology, and a performance done by the agents in concert with one another. Consequently, the embracement of the GLA has a double function. First, the GLA provides a comprehensive understanding of the intentional plan at the basis of the group's intentional action as a network of attitudes rather than the sum of individual intentions. Second, as a high-level account, the GLA must explain the fact that the network of all individual contributions counts as a system capable of action. In line with this –following the ontological supervenience relation—the concept of 'group' serves as a functional, explicative notion without any serious commitment to its ontological status. Although an event could be functionally ascribed to the group as a whole, the members in the GLA are the ultimate subjects of intentional agency in both its components (i.e., mental and behavioral). At most, group agency can be considered as an extrinsically intentional event.

Changing directions, one might want to follow the discontinuity thesis of intentionality, which maintains that group performances are planned by the members' collective/we-mode intentions to do something together. In this case, the group dimension is already part of the members' psychological perspective determining the form or mode of the attitudes for the action. Nonetheless, the fact that the participants are disposed to think of their own actions in terms of 'we'—'we intend to do such and such'; 'we have the collective intention to do x'; 'we, as a group, are ready to do x'; and so forth—does not imply that the group exists as a whole. As long as ontological individualism is accepted, the introduction of the group

---

dashed line of the first figure means the background function of the network at that level, which can be thought of in connection with mechanisms of emergent coordination enabling rational coordination and joint action (Butterfill 2017).

dimension within explanations of intentional phenomena seems to have no concrete consequence outside of the individuals' minds.[14] Hence, the discontinuity thesis does not diverge so much from the supervenient picture drawn by the theorists of the continuity thesis. Concerning the actor/action aspect, there is not a salient difference between the approaches: in group contexts, the one who realizes the intention is the group considered as a supervenient system, and the relevant performance is the action realized by the network (Tuomela 2013b). Contrariwise, on the mental attitude side, the group perspective is part of the way (i.e., the mode) in which the members formulate their thoughts. High-level concepts are already at play in the nature and explanation of the mental event. This can have two effects on the theory (List & Pettit 2011, p. 194): on one side, we-intentionality could be applied to the group straightforwardly (intrinsic account) to see the group as the term to which intentionality refers. In this sense, the group is the plural subject of collective intentions (Schmid 2009). On the other side, we-mode intentionality could be a distributive form of collective intentionality, characteristic of individual psychology and, thus, be just a mode of experience.[15] Such an important distinction in understanding the 'we'—as a subject or as a mode of intention—does not raise major problems for the perspectives considered so far. In fact, regardless of whether the 'we' refers to a plural subject or whether it is a mode of intention, the mind that thinks the attitude is the individual mind. Then, the members make the performance as those who jointly obtain the collective intention through individual contributions. Thus, proving that

---

[14] This position diverges from Schmid's idea (Schmid 2017a) that the 'we' is the actual plural subject of collective intentionality. Section 4.2.

[15] As argued in Chapter Two, I take the doctrine of collective intentionality embraced by the Big Four to be a distributive theory of collective intentionality, attributing both I-intentions and we-intentions to individual subjects. The hypothesis of non-distributive collective intentionality has been proposed by Schmid (2009, 2017a) and it will be further discussed in Chapter Ten, where I will consider the possibility to take groups as subjects of intention and action. Still, my claim and scope differ from Schmid's because I do not want to suggest a view in which the 'we' represents the plural subject of intentionality as a phenomenological trait of individual experience. My suggestion is, instead, to consider the group as a performative system that functions as an agent and question whether it could be intentionally intrinsic. My project is close to that of List and Pettit, who do not propose a distributive theory of group agency, but an attempt to consider certain groups as agents in their own right, as performative persons. It is precisely the way of understanding the notion of performative person that distances my proposal from List and Pettit's view.

there are neither collective minds nor bodies. Instead, there are networks of individuals who think and act together as if they were one. [16]

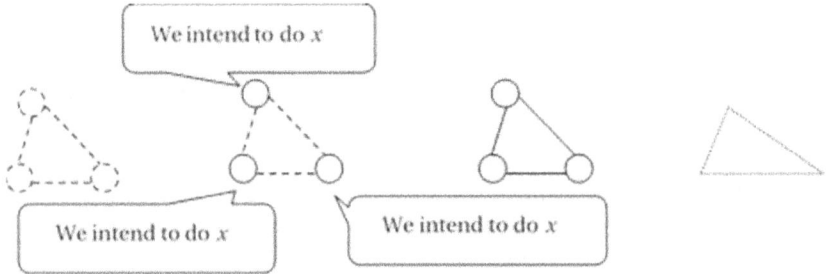

Figure 6.2. GLA and discontinuity-thesis accounts.

In what follows, I will approach the relation between shared intention and group performance by focusing on the specific features of the two models, especially those concerning intentionality. The actor/action will be instead considered through the same functional/supervenient pattern. Differences aside, and recalling the analytical framework adopted in Part One, shared intention will be associated with group action by studying constitutive, structural, normative, and causal relations between the two poles. As said, the transition from the MLA to the GLA has already been attempted in the debate by the Big Five, who have endorsed some form of holistic individualism, proposing an individualistic ontology and making it consistent with different descriptive levels of reality. The explanation of group agency, though ontologically reducible, has been presented as a non-redundant description when compared to the MLA.

6.4 The GLA and the four agency relations

What is then the relation between the intention and the action within the framework of the GLA? According to holistic individualism, how could we possibly interpret the four agency relations between intending and acting?

---

[16] The picture repeats the phases of Figure 6.1. The first dashed triangle represents background features, the second shows the mental attitude of each, and the third triangle relates those mental states to one another in order to form a network based on intentionality. The last triangle depicts the group as an executor, which is outlined by dotted lines representing the (ontological) fictitious nature of the actor. The difference between this figure and the one concerning the continuity thesis account is the form of attitudes.

6.4.1 Constitutive relation

The constitutive relation between intending and acting describes a connection in which the intentional moment is literally part of the action—where 'action' amounts to the mental state and the realizing act together. As far as the constitutive relation is concerned, shared intentions are components of the activity happening together; the physical movement (or speech act) represents its psychological counterpart. This description has been formulated based on Searle's proposal, which represents the main, explicit attempt of investigating constitutive relations (Searle 1995, 2007, 2010). In particular, regarding the MLA (Section 3.4.1, 3.4.2), it has been maintained that Searle identifies the intention that is meant to be the psychological counterpart of the action in the intention-in-action/action-intention, which corresponds to the mental state planning and happening with the gesture. Differently, the prior (or aim)[17] intention is not considered a necessary component of agency; and, when present, it works by providing the cognitive background in which each intention-in-action acquires additional meaning. While the content of the aim intention is the shared goal, the action-intention represents the goal fulfilled by every group member in pursuit of the final objective, which does not enter the content of any particular intention-in-action at all.

Now that the intentional activity has been identified with the group action, the role of the prior intention might change because—as long as the purpose is to go beyond the MLA—one cannot simultaneously regard shared agency solely in terms of individual contributions. If the group is the actor, the intention concerning all of the members as a group might, consequently, be interpreted as the intention-in-action happening with the performance. To say it with Searle's formula: "a = i.a.+ b.m." (Searle 2007, p. 18). Agency is the result of the intention-in-action in addition to the bodily movement. Similarly, shared agency should be the sum of the collective intention-in-action (that is, the prior intention of the individual contributions) and the activity performed by the group as a system. The formula could be written as:

$$a_g = i.a._g + b.m._g$$

---

[17] Tuomela refers to 'prior intentions' as 'aim intentions' (Tuomela 2007). Tuomela also introduces the concept of action intentions, which corresponds to Searle's notion of intentions-in-action. Still, the notion is not the core of his account, which is rather focused on aim intentions. Gilbert and Bratman do not dwell on this aspect and, for this reason, Section 3.4.1 discussed the notion of constitutive relation in Searle's and Tuomela's, not in Gilbert's and Bratman's accounts.

While 'a_g' represents the event of group agency, i.e., the collective action in its entirety, '$i.a._g$' stands for the intention-in-action relative to the group act and corresponding to what, in the explanation of the individual contributions, was the prior intention for the action. '$b.m._g$' is the bodily movement of the group, i.e., the group performance. Truly, this kind of non-distributive hypothesis could have been a feasible path to follow if it were not for the fact that Searle has spoken neither of group agents nor of plural intentional subjects. For this reason, there has been no need to relate prior intentions to group intentionality and behavior. As argued in Section 2.1, Searle proposes a distributive view of shared agency. Further, it was made apparent that extending the formula to other accounts among those of the Big Five would be a stretch because they do not focus on, if they even introduce, the notion of intention-in-action. Instead, group agency is explained by drawing attention to prior intentions.

6.4.2 Structural relation

The shared intention held by the members of the group—'I intend that we do x', in the case of the continuity-thesis account; 'we intend to do x', in the case of the discontinuity-thesis account—contains, as its content, the representation of the goal of the entire group activity. As remarked about the MLA, the shared plan state has a double structuring function on the action: on the one hand, it defines the horizon within which the contribution of each participant is formulated; on the other hand, it provides the motive around which all the efforts are organized (Bratman 2014a). Therefore, a shared intention can be seen both as an attitude structuring individual behavior given the group performance (MLA) and as the reason regulating the whole activity (GLA).

The structural relation between the intention and the action in group contexts seems to be less problematic than the constitutive one. The very notion of intentionality contains the idea of a project, which easily applies to various levels of complexity. Being oriented towards an object is an essential character of any intentional event, which, in the case of shared intentions for the action, coincides with the goal of the group activity. Following the suggestion of Rovane, we might refer to shared activities as coordinated activities, which "involve more than one component action; the component actions are conceived essentially as contributions to the larger joint activity; and these component actions would have no (or very little) point for the persons who perform them unless the whole activity could be completed" (Rovane 1998, p. 145). Meaning, the shared objective—the content of the prior intention—provides the setting within which every individual activity makes sense as being oriented towards a collective perspective and in conjunction with the contributions of others.[18]

Based on the continuity-thesis account of intentionality, the network of sub-plans is the aspect that fixes the shared objective and is structurally related to the whole activity of the group. Differing from the discontinuity-thesis account, the intentional attitude structuring the performance might be either the prior we-intention for the action held by each (non-distributive account) or the network of the members' we-mode we-attitudes (distributive view). The former case is ascribable to Schmid's proposal (Schmid 2009, 2017a), which assumes that the collective intention is the intentional plan referred to the group action, as such, and held by the participants as group members. The latter scenario is, instead, typical of the distributive perspective endorsed by the Big Four, and most of all by Gilbert and Tuomela, who emphasize the importance of inter-subjective relationships for the occurrence of group-oriented attitudes in the mind of each.

6.4.3 Normative relation

The normative relation between intending and acting represents a difficult step for analysis. As indicated within the member-level account (Section 3.4.3), the idea that shared agency is based upon a normative bond among the agents is explicitly accepted only in Gilbert's theory (Gilbert 1989, 1990, 2007b, 2013, 2018). Gilbert identifies two different kinds of normative relations: The first normative bond is located within the act of ascribing/accepting the role of partner, through which the participants acquire a normative status. This condition comes with expectations and duties that mediate and secure interpersonal relationships among the members, making them think and act as if they were a single body (Gilbert 1990, 1997, 2007a). Then, the capacity to act together intentionally generates the second type of normativity, which derives from the mental attitude. Sharing an intention commits the agents to the effort aimed at realizing their common goal. In this sense, Gilbert's view is

---

[18] I will further discuss Rovane's theory in Chapters Eight and Nine. At this stage, it is worth mentioning that Rovane proposes a theory of group agency (and agency, in general) for which an agent is a person committed to pursuing some rational unity. Such 'unifying project' can occur both intra- and inter-personally. In the first case the agent is committed to a long-term project, while in the second case the unity is ensured by the collaboration of several subjects, who participate in the formation of the same rational unity and therefore compose a single group-sized agent. On intra- and inter-personal relations, see Rovane 1998, pp. 136–166.

normativistic in spirit—what gives ground to the possibility of shared agency is the prior normative relation between the parties.[19]

As argued in Section 3.4.3, among the Big Four, Tuomela's approach is the only one associated with Gilbert's. Tuomela constructed a similar, multi-layered normative characterization of shared agency, articulated on two levels (Tuomela 2002, 2007, 2013a), which respectively correspond to instrumental normativity and social normativity (Tuomela 2003). The former binds the group members to the realization of the common goal represented by the intentional content, while the latter consists of a commitment that binds the individuals to each other as group members.[20]

Theoretical discrepancies aside, both approaches suggest two levels of normativity, i.e., two kinds of normative relation, that were already at play in the MLA and should now be seen through the group's perspective. The modification of our account, that is, the embracement of the GLA, has already been arranged by the MLA. Due to the MLA's most fundamental, normative bond, related to the status of being partner, the group perspective becomes a feasible alternative. As it stands, both Gilbert and Tuomela ground the possibility to have shared intentions for the action (we-mode intentions, for Tuomela, and intending as a group, in the case of Gilbert) on the acquisition of a status that, on the cognitive side, procures a new perspective. The disjointed psychological level is separate from the level to which individual intentions for the action belong, and it is straightforwardly committed to the

---

[19] In Gilbert (2018), the importance of joint commitment in social relationships is emphasized by assuming that joint commitment generates demand-rights. Such a special kind of rights can be spelled out by saying that "someone with a demand-right to some action has the standing to demand that action of the relevant agent" (Gilbert 2018, p. v). This means that joint commitment is all it takes to establish a normative bond among the agents, a bond that comes before any intention or agreement and has the power to create and legitimize mutual expectations among the participants. Gilbert asserts that "explicit agreements are not necessary for the emergence of the demand-rights of joint commitment: a given joint commitment can arise by less explicit, more gradual means, as in the case of a slowly growing collective practice" (Gilbert 2018, p. vi). This confirms that joint commitment—in Gilbert's theory—is primarily a normative connection between those who are willing to participate in the action. Joint commitment turns the individuals into partners in the action and then it enables the possibility for them to act intentionally as a body.

[20] The main difference between the two approaches is that, in Tuomela's theory, social commitment has a cognitive foundation according to which an individual assumes the status of group member insofar as there are mutual beliefs in the context. On the contrary, Gilbert regards the normative connection as a practical phenomenon that does not necessarily require any mental attitude concerning the others' intending.

intentional plans referring to individual agents as group members. In this sense, what allows the introduction of intentional phenomena planning for group performances is the kind of (horizontal) normative relation between the members, which makes them act not as a singular individual but as part of a collective. This step is important when regarding the GLA because it explains how it is possible to jump from the members' perspective to the group's perspective, without assuming the existence of any entity beyond individual minds. In fact, once the members have acquired a group perspective, they can formulate intentions for the action directly from that viewpoint. Moreover, those plan states are realizable (and rescindable) only through group performance, as the GLA requires.

To more deeply understand the explicative gap, it could be useful to recall Tuomela's way of speaking about group phenomena in contrast to facts about the members. To this extent, I want to draw attention to the acceptance of new contents as reasons for action.[21] According to the MLA, individuals collectively accept something in the *we-mode* when they engage in a process of agreement-making oriented towards an amalgam of attitudes.[22] The amalgam of attitudes represents the group attitude of acceptance, which could not be seen since the individuals are thinking and acting as members. Necessarily, members must embrace the group's viewpoint. As Tuomela explains, "a group accepts a content through its members' acceptance, but the two notions are different" (Tuomela 2013a, p. 126) because the former needs the latter as a premise, without being coextensive with it. In particular, the collective acceptance that happens at the member level allows the individuals to have something to recognize as a group. Then, from that group-level view, the members can accept the reason in question as a reason of and for the group as a whole. Precisely, the embracement of a group perspective is made possible by the collective acceptance members exert towards the group's ethos—the shared (cognitive and moral) horizon they have as parts of the same collective. Without a group dimension of contents and meanings established through collective acceptance and commitment (at the member-level), no reason could have been, in principle, accepted as suitable for the group because the consistency and coherence of that reason with the group ethos would have been managed—as happens in Bratman's approach—by the

---

[21] On acceptance, see Tuomela 2002, 2003, 2007, 2013a.

[22] Group attitudes can be the result of processes of decision making either when the individual attitudes agree with the group perspective or when there is disagreement between the positions. Concerning the latter case, see Schweikard 2017b.

individuals' rational control.[23] Accordingly, the GLA is not the same as the MLA because the latter has created the conditions for identifying a higher dimension beyond what is explicable through individual facts and laws.[24]

The normative relation embedded within the notion of shared agency can thus be seen as a relevant characteristic of the GLA. This characteristic is evident when discussing theoretical models disposed to admit that taking up a group point-of-view generates—through an act of commitment—a normative relation between the shared intention and the action. This relation is not the same as the connection in place at the individual level. In fact, the most fundamental kind of commitment turns the participants into partners and opens the possibility of accepting intentions regarding the group as a whole. The mediation of the members can be considered a premise—different from the resulting amalgam—because individuals embrace a group perspective through which they consider themselves parts of a body.

It is relevant here to recall Rovane's proposal mentioned earlier in Section 6.4.2, which holds that "any agent is always a product of effort and will" (Rovane 2014, p. 1668), meaning that whenever a project of rational unity is realized, the agent's point-of-view is constituted. Such an agent is not necessarily coincident with the contours of any human being; it can also be a group, the members of which commit themselves, as members, to act in the pursuit of group reasons. And when they do so, the members jointly commit to act as a part of a group and carry out the will of that group:

---

[23] Tuomela maintains that in group-scale contexts the association between collective acceptance and commitment has two roles: "First, it binds the members together around an ethos, serving to ground the unity and identity of the group. Second, collective commitment provides the group with the authority to decide about its members' activities in a practically efficient way" (Tuomela 2013a, p. 45).

[24] Concerning Searle's and Bratman's proposals, the normative side of shared agency seems not to play such a fundamental role. In particular, for Searle, normativity derives from intentionality (precisely, from the collective recognition of status functions with a normative characterization) without representing a constitutive dimension of collective intentionality, which is rather an original possibility of the mind (Searle 1995, 1997, 2002, 2003, 2006, 2010). Bratman (1984, 1987, 2007, 2009c, 2014a) presents the normative relation in strict connection with two principles (*consistency* and *means-end coherence*). These principles bind the individuals to act in accordance with an intention that must be goal-oriented and consistent with the network of beliefs. Such normative function, however, does not imply any shift to some collective ways of thinking that is ontologically distinct from the individual level.

when human beings achieve rational unity together at the level of a whole group, this tends to produce a certain kind of rational fragmentation in their lives, because not all of the thoughts and actions associated with their brains and bodies proceed from the same point of view—some proceed from the group agent's point of view, while others proceed from a point of view that is somewhat smaller than human size. (Rovane 2014, p. 1665)[25]

As Gilbert and Tuomela corroborate, individual psychology branches out by making the same human being capable of following her individual intentions when acting for herself and following group intentions when thinking and acting as a member. Thus, we can say that in order to move from the MLA to the GLA, the double normative relation is required "for the group to function as an agent, because without it the members could not coordinate their activities or perform together effectively to achieve group goals" (Tuomela 2013a, p. 45). Moreover, "the members are assumed to view and construct their (we-mode) group as an entity partially guiding their lives when their group membership is salient, and also requiring them to function as collectively committed ethos-obeying and ethos-furthering group members" (Tuomela 2013a, p. 45).[26]

---

[25] The last part of this quote might at first seem striking, if not implausible, in that it admits the existence of agents smaller than the human being and therefore contained within it. Indeed, in keeping with her notion of agent, Rovane believes that as long as a human being is characterized by distinct unifying projects and as long as each of these projects gives rise to a specific rational point of view to which the subject takes a commitment, there may be multiple rational units—and so many agents—within the same human being. On multiple agents within the same human being, see especially Rovane 2004 and Rovane 1998, pp. 167–208.

[26] In Chapters Eight and Nine we will find that Rovane is willing to go further than Gilbert and Tuomela in arguing that group agents and multiple personalities are individual agents just like human-sized agents. According to Rovane, human beings, as agents, should not be granted any normative priority because the definition of agent does neither derive from nor coincide with the human being as if it were an agent by nature. All normative principles that are associated with being an agent apply to every agent equally. Therefore—whenever the definition is fulfilled—there are no reasons to ascribe priority to some of its manifestations to the expense of others. Tuomela and Gilbert instead maintain the individualistic principle that individual (human) agents have a special normative status and priority over groups. The same, we will observe, applies to List and Pettit's view.

6.4.4 Causal relation

As observed in the context of MLAs (Section 3.4.4), the causal relation plays a relevant role in the explanation of shared agency as the normative relation loosens its grip. In fact, as soon as we draw attention to the mediation performed by the normative constraint, the causality that directly connects the two components of agency becomes weaker. Thus, in Chapter Three, the issue of a causal relation between intentions and actions has been primarily associated with Searle's thought, in which the normative dimension of shared agency appears mainly as a consequence of the intentional attitude, deriving from the recognition of a status function. For Searle, the causal relation can be formulated in two different ways: first, a causal bond can be found between the intention-in-action and the bodily movement realizing the mental state (i.a. causes b.m., Searle 2007).[27] Second, the causal relation occurs in conjunction with the prior intention of performing the individual gestures (taken as i.a + b.m.). This prior intention is causally responsible for the individuals' making and realizing a fitting intention-in-action regarding the common plan. Alas, the shared goal does not enter the individual intentional content, so it has no direct causal power on the action performed by the participants. Due to this structure, the collective intention influences the activity through the mediation of intentions regulating individual contributions. Based on this sort of mediation, it would be hard to maintain that the GLA could embrace a notion of causal relation that is irreducible to the causality grasped by the MLA. The reason being that the causal power exerted by the group's reason for the action only operates through the participatory intentions of each individual.

Far from Searle's notion of direct causation, the idea of causation changes meaning for theorists such as Gilbert and Tuomela, who construct a stronger normative foundation of shared agency. Challenging the MLA, it seems reasonable to affirm that the chance of considering the causal relation from a high-level perspective, as supervenient causation, is particularly grounded in the normative relation among the members. The point is that the normative bond among the agents allows a change in perspective that makes it feasible and meaningful to treat groups as causally effective structures (Tuomela 2013a). In fact, the normative relation clears the way for (1) embracing a group viewpoint from the members' side and (2) creating a network from which the group dimension supervenes. Therefore, the commitment to the status of group members and the identification with a certain group allows the members to think of themselves as a group. At the same time, the fact that

---

[27] In the case of a collective intention for the action, the intention-in-action only pertains to the contribution of each.

the members are acting by following a set of roles and functional positions sets a higher domain of social facts, which enables the holistic explanation of the group as an (intentionally extrinsic) agent. On this (normative) basis, fitting with the ontological framework of supervenience, the explanation can focus on the group dimension and consider a form of causality that directly emanates from the collective, as a supervenient social fact, without going through the mediation of member intentionality. Meaning, "although social properties are supervenient on individual properties, the causal force of social properties does not have to be mediated through a conscious awareness of them on the part of individuals". (Sawyer 2003, p. 218)

The distinction between ontological and explicative issues might be of help here. Concerning the former, groups are reducible to individuals, and individuals are the only motors of any causal chain (Tuomela 2013a, p. 5). As for the latter, due to the group perspective and to the agential system created through the double normative relation, we might notice group-related facts that cannot be described without postulating a holistic, higher-level realm of concern. Moreover, as Tuomela spells out, a group "exists causally objectively as a social system capable of causal production of outcomes in the world in virtue of its we-thinking and 'we-acting' members" (Tuomela 2013a, p. 47). To rephrase, a group can be accountable for a certain causal effect in the world when it is considered as a system comprised of intentional mechanisms at the members' level. Accordingly, the group's influence, as a system, frames the group as extrinsically intentional due to its being a structure, i.e., a system of agency, related to intentionality rather than an (intrinsically) intentional agent. To say it in Tuomela's terms, groups have causal powers because the members have collectively accepted the group and because—in virtue of collective acceptance—they are capable of realizing a structure and having effects on the world as if they were one (Tuomela 2013a). Therefore, the causal relation in the context of the GLA could be understood as a connection established between the group, considered an extrinsically intentional system, and its effects on the environment. Instead of being a link binding the intention and the action, holistic causality seems to have been better introduced as a relation between an object, i.e., the agentive system, and the effects produced on the social world in which it is located (Tuomela 2011).[28]

In the above pages, I have endeavored to profile the four agency relations as allowed by the GLA of holistic individualism. Chapter Seven will confront this account's shortcomings and explain why the Big Five have not succeeded in

---

[28] In line with methodological individualism, Bratman does not refer causality to group-level (fictitious) facts. Thus, his account has been excluded from this step of analysis.

overcoming the MLA altogether. It will be the task of Chapters Eight and Nine to unmask the roots of these limits and propose an alternative approach to the GLA and the four agency relations analyzed in Chapter Ten.

Part Three.
Shared agency as group agency

Chapter 7

Holistic individualism and flaws in the GLA

7.1 Restarting from Part Two

Part One and Part Two have been devoted to identifying various dimensions of shared agency, including:

1. descriptive dimensions:
    (1a) intentional behavior: intention (subject-mode-content) + action,
    (1b) agency relations: constitutive, structural, normative, and causal relation.

2. Conceptual dimensions:
    (2a) continuity-thesis account,
    (2b) discontinuity-thesis account.

3. Micro-macro dimensions:
    (3a) member-level account,
    (3b) group-level account.

Part One focused on the member-level account of shared agency (3a) and analyzed (1) descriptive and (2) conceptual aspects based on the micro-perspective. Part Two shifted the attention from (3a) the member-level account to (3b) the group-level account of shared agency. The objective was to investigate the possibility of considering the notion of shared agency as group agency and to study how traditional debates have dealt with the issue. To this end, I have presented holistic individualism as a way to study groups as subjects of agency by adopting specific points of view regarding two distinct issues, namely the ontological and the methodological problem. Groups might be examined for their being or not being objective features of the social world; alternatively, groups might be considered explicative terms, functional to grasp high-level phenomena that could or could not be spelled out using low-level concepts and principles. Hence, the main claim underpinning the GLA emerging from holistic individualism is the firm separation of ontology and methodology as two distinct matters of concern. This thesis has been further supported by finding it feasible to inquire into the ontological and methodological domain even by assuming two seemingly contrasting positions. Indeed, groups (as social facts) could be approached as

- objective/irreducible features with respect to both methodology and ontology,

- subjective/reducible features with respect to both methodology and ontology,

- subjective/reducible facts for what concerns ontology but objective/irreducible aspects of methods, or

- objective/irreducible ontological facts that are subjective/ reducible as far as methodology is concerned.

In brief, among the alternatives, holistic individualism corresponds to the third option. According to this approach, groups are nothing more than the (interrelated) individuals on which they depend. At the same time, group-related concepts are irreducible in terms of analysis.

Partly due to such a delicate association, investigating the notion of group agent sparked a debate about the relationship between groups as higher-level phenomena and the individuals on whom they depend. Holistic individualism interprets that form of dependence as a supervenience relation—a logical, synchronic connection between levels. I described supervenience as a form of co-variation that relates an arrangement at the lower level with a particular high-level configuration: changing something at the foundation would imply modifications of the supervenient fact and *vice versa*. Further, it has been observed that a high-level fact could be the result of many different arrangements at the lower level, and this characteristic of the relation has been qualified as multiple realizability (Currie 1984, Epstein 2014a, Kim 1992, List & Spiekermann 2013, Ludwig 2003, Risjord 2014, Sawyer 2002, Zahle 2007). Thus, groups—as supervenient phenomena dependent upon specific configurations at the members level—are ontologically the same as those networks and represent indispensable notions of the theory. In this sense, the study of shared agency as a phenomenon regarding groups has been a problematic question to investigate.[1] Considering all of this, we addressed the study of shared agency as

---

[1] In order to determine whether holistic individualism has succeeded in dealing with the matter, the second part studied the group-level account by referring to Pettit's interpretation of the puzzle (Pettit 1996, 2014). According to Pettit, the association of holism and individualism is a feasible path to follow, not just because the two positions have been assumed with respect to different concerns (methodological and ontological). In fact, the perspectives should also be considered as pertaining to specific and separate issues. Individualism—Pettit claims—regards the vertical relation between individuals and society as well as the psychological autonomy of the former from the

a proper group-level phenomenon by starting from the definition of groups as agents. In line with the conception of groups as supervenient wholes, Chapter Four outlined three different strategies:

a. *intrinsic account*: a group is defined as a group agent by its being the term to which the intentional phenomenon of agency refers (List & Pettit 2011, Schmid 2009),

b. *extrinsic account*: a group is an agent due to its being a structure realizing the plan that intentional mechanisms at the member-level have fixed (Bratman 2017, Tuomela 2013a),

c. *status account*: a group agent is an organization to which has been attributed the normative status of agent (Hindriks 2008).

In connection with each of these alternatives, providing a *functional* definition of 'agent' was endeavored. Particularly, this suggestion considered 'agent' as a concept deriving from the model of agency proposed by the theory. Once the definition of what it means to do something (together) intentionally has been provided, then the (group) agent has been functionally defined as such. Following this clarification, Chapter Six redescribed the notion of shared agency through the GLA and explored (high-level) constitutive, structural, normative, and causal relations between intentions and actions.

The present chapter begins the discussion on the group-level account of holistic individualism with the aim of unmasking eventual weak points and contradictions hidden in the explanation of shared agency as group agency. The overall objective of Part Three is to argue against the suitability of holistic individualism as a stable group-level account in social ontology (Chapter Eight) and suggest an account that might be suitable to advance a non-reductive view on group agency (Chapter Nine and Chapter Ten)—here, anti-reductionism means anti-singularism. Therefore, I will support the claim that the notion of agent does not apply exclusively to individuals: it is extended to systems made up of several individuals held together by a structure, be it intentional, institutional, or organizational (Pettit & Schweikard 2006).

---

latter. Differently, holism concerns horizontal relationships among the members and represents a thesis about the social nature of human skills. According to the holistic view, the flourishing of human faculties necessarily needs interaction. Singularism has then been presented as an even different issue concerning the debate about the agent and, specifically, whether it must be a singular individual or whether groups can be agents as well. See Section 5.3.

7.2 Problems of constitutive and structural relation

Let us now examine the problems hidden behind the description of the constitutive and structural relationships in the GLA of holistic individualism. Although Chapter Six has already presented both aspects under the ontological and explicative assumptions of that position, some critical issues are detectable.

7.2.1 Constitutive relation

Intentions-in-action are constitutive elements of agency. Assuming that "actions and intentions, in other words, are interlocking components of a system of practical activity" (Epstein 2014a, p. 218), any theory that upholds this principle should present arguments to support this relationship between the two poles—both in the case of individual-scale and group-scale forms of action. As Rovane clearly observes, in both cases, the efficaciousness of intentions for action rests on two factors: "a recognition of them and a decision that acting on them is a reasonable thing to do" (Rovane 1998, p. 159).

Concerning the MLA, Chapter Three showed that a constitutive relation, of some kind, has been formulated only in Searle's proposal; although, there is some possibility for attributing the point to Tuomela's perspective (Tuomela 2007) as well.[2] Indeed, the connection is particularly fitting for theoretical models that introduce the distinction between intention-in-action/action intention and prior/aim intention. The categorization allows the identification of intentions (i.e., intentions-in-action/action intentions) as parts of agency. The question pursued in Chapter Six inquired about the validity of the constitutive relation, even for the holistic explanation provided by the GLA, because it considers both intentional and practical components as facts related to groups as wholes. To prevent the redundancy of the GLA, the goal was to imagine the constitutive relation at the higher level of the description and avoid invoking concepts belonging to the member-level approach. To accomplish this, Searle's proposal has proved to be difficult because his compliance with the metaphysical principle that all intentionality happens in the individuals' mind has made him discard groups as proper subjects of agency by imposing strict limits to the methods, which had to ensure that ontological assumptions do not lead to contradictions. Concerning the ontological side, individuals are the only starting points of any intentional phenomenon; the explanation—although open to holistic terms and concepts—must follow that principle by accommodating the boundaries

---

[2] See Section 3.4.1.

fixed by the ontological premise. Meaning, whereas we-attitudes are defined as irreducible to I-attitudes, groups are reducible to the members.[3]

If it is true that, in Searle's perspective, collectiveness is meant to be an original trait of collective intentionality, then, in Tuomela's explanation of shared agency, the collective intention is held from a group perspective based on previous acts of acceptance and commitment through which the members have acquired a proper collective standpoint. In other words, if the collective mental state is irreducible to any individual mental state, it is because of a prior normative relation. The relation in question—denoted by Tuomela as

---

[3] Based on considerations of this kind, it becomes clear that the ontological perspective is entangled with epistemological and methodological issues. Although social facts, as mind-dependent items, are ontologically reducible to individuals, they are still described as epistemically objective. It is a matter of knowledge among the members that statements, representing social facts, are true within the network of beliefs shared in that particular social context. Thus, recognizing the existence of a social fact represents an objective belief as long as, among the members, it is an accepted assumption that such a social fact has some function in society. Consequently, the epistemic objectivity regards the epistemological status of claims about social facts and not the ontological status of social facts as such. However, the epistemic viewpoint, in Searle's account, is not the same as the methodological concern. In particular, the objectivity that Searle ascribes to social facts is limited to the epistemic context in which the social fact is accepted. At the same time, within that domain, social facts are treated as reducible features, in a manner that makes the description of the social world be consistent with the ontological account. As long as one does not distinguish between the epistemological status of social facts and the explanatory power of high-level notions, the reducibility of groups to the level of the members would threaten the objectivity fixed by epistemology. Let us consider the following statements, each of which applies to Searle's view. (1) Social facts are "ontologically subjective", "observer-relative", "intentionality-relative", (Searle 2010, p. 17); (2) social facts are "epistemically objective", (Searle 2010, pp. 17–18); (3) high-level explanations of social facts are reducible to the explanation based on what happens at the individual level; (4) it follows that social facts are not objective. The objectivity mentioned in 4 may (a) contrast with the objectivity claimed by 2 or (b) represent another kind of objectivity. My suggestion is that 4 concerns methodology and argues against the irreducibility of the GLA to the MLA, while 2 upholds the epistemological objectivity of knowledge in a social context. In relation to the classification of 'dimension' endorsed so far, it could also be said that the rejection of a macro-perspective in Searle's account comes with ontological individualism and with the endorsement of the discontinuity thesis of intentionality, which refers to individual psychology. Then, individual psychology is considered capable of having objective beliefs about the social domain, meant as a mind-dependent realm. Thus, the interpretation of Searle's position could not be associated with arguments in favor of the methodological non-redundancy of the GLA.

'social commitment' (Tuomela 2002, 2003)—derives from the mutual recognition through which individuals ascribe to one another the status of being partners and parts of the same collective. In this sense, the constitutive relation theorized by the GLA can be found irreducible to the MLA only by assuming that the normative relation on which it is established, and which enables the possibility of fully-fledged collective intentions for the action, is irreducible in the first place. Thus, the commitment initiated by the individuals to be part of a group should be ascribable to the group straightforwardly or to the individuals as members, and not to the individuals as autonomous agents just enacting the capacity to act with others (Rovane 2014). The fracture in individual psychology resulting from individuals assuming the group viewpoint, in addition to the individual viewpoint, should therefore be deep enough to allow us to say that the individual—as an individual subject—and the individual—as a group member—belong to the unity of two, different intentional subjects, not reducible to one another. On the level of intentions, this implies that group intentions would not be reducible to individual intentions.

As the psychological fragmentation is an implication of the normative agency relation, it will be discussed further in Section 7.3.

7.2.2 Structural relation

The assumption for which intentional mental states and, more precisely, shared mental states have the structural power to generate a certain kind of performance, oriented towards an end, does not necessarily imply that the framing role exerted upon the group activity is irreducible to that played upon the members' contribution. In fact, what the GLA has a stake in is the non-redundancy of the holistic explanation that seems to be threatened by the double structuring relation already grasped by the MLA (Section 3.4.2). More specifically, the difficult question is that the two influences of intention on the action—the former upon the individual participatory act and the latter upon the group performance—were already part of the picture when the group perspective had not yet been endorsed. In fact, the intention to obtain a common goal might regulate the actions of the group of agents as the result of the mediation operated by the individuals. This mediation consists of securing each individual's consistency with their actual behavior when envisioning the goal.

For example, Bratman's *means-end coherence principle* (Bratman 1990, 2014a) applies to actions that happen over time, as well as among subjects, providing rational guidance along and among the various stages/components of the performance (Bratman 2017). Still, the principle only refers to individual-level descriptions, which, according to Bratman, are well suited to explain both time-spanning and shared actions. Comparing to Rovane's view, Bratman's theory shows many points of commonality—the building blocks that serve to construct the explanation of individual actions are the same ones that allow us to account for group agency. Nevertheless, there is a substantial difference between the two approaches worth noting: as far as Bratman's account is concerned, what we can say about shared actions is derived from the explanation of individual agency and, for this reason, the GLA figures as methodologically reducible to the MLA. The GLA is just a development of member-level descriptions (Section 1.2 and 1.3).

In contrast, Rovane argues that the components of temporal individual action and group action are the same because, in both cases, there is a single rational point of view at the center of the project that unifies the efforts into the same agent. Thus, if in the case of individual action over time, one can speak of an individual agent who is likely to be a particular human being; in the case of a group action, the agent is the group, and the individuals are counted as members, not as individual agents. This viewpoint fractures being an individual subject and being a member in such a way that it prevents the reduction of group agents to individual agents and the reduction of the GLA to the MLA. So, for Rovane, the role of the intention that structures any group action is not graspable by merely defining the participants as individual agents because the individuals are now pursuing a different point of view from their personal one. In contrast, Bratman's account maintains that the structural role of intentions that program both individual contributions and the entire shared performance can already be explained with an individualistic lexicon because there is no fracture, neither methodological nor metaphysical, that hinders reduction.

The question concerning the double structural influence could also be addressed through the proponents of the discontinuity-thesis account of intentionality, whose accounts consider individual intentions as we-mode attitudes for action. One might argue that, especially regarding Gilbert's and Tuomela's theory, the structural role of collective intentions could be adequately and non-redundantly grasped through the GLA if and only if the normative relation enabling the we-mode perspective requires unavailable explanations so long as one holds fast to the psychology and agency of individual agents. Again, it must be ensured that the normative relationship that grounds the group point of view is not a vector for reduction.

Another obstacle to the irreducibility of the structural connection's high-level descriptions can be found, on entirely different premises, in List and Pettit's account of shared agency as group agency (List & Pettit 2011). By assuming the *intrinsic* intentional nature of group agents (Section 4.2), the authors consider the intentions held by the group as rational attitudes, autonomous from the attitudes of the individuals (cf., List & Pettit 2011, p.76).[4] Hence, List and Pettit (2011) seem to suggest that the structuring role of the attitude is to be attributed to the group's plan-states directly. However, what is it, then, that allows such an attribution and makes it likely that the group's action is regulated directly by the intentionality of the system instead of that of the members? The answer can be found in the notion of 'agent' adopted by List and Pettit: any system granted agency status has "representational states, motivational states, and a capacity to process them and act on that basis in the manner of an agent" (List & Pettit 2011, p. 32). As long as the group consists of members, it can have representations that coincide with the inputs provided by the individuals.

Moreover, as long as the group is organized in such a way as to have deliberative procedures aimed at processing the inputs, the group can form reasons for the action and, thus, have intentions that are the outcome of complex rational procedures. These procedures are complex enough to be supervenient and not reducible to the members' intentions. The mechanism through which the intentions of individuals are aggregated and made into a single supervenient output is the element that assures the autonomy of the group's intention; accordingly, it is precisely such a rational plan that guides the actions of the entire group. On these grounds, List and Pettit vindicate the epistemic autonomy of group agents and the non-redundancy of talk about group agency.

Yet, the non-redundant realism they propose sticks to the individualistic principle that individuals are the ultimate ontological components of the

---

[4] I would like to make a clarification regarding the sense in which List and Pettit can be said to defend an intrinsic account. As defined in Chapter Four of this book, the intrinsic account is one that treats groups as subjects of intention. And this is the meaning I want to give to the term and refer to their view. It should be noted, however, that List and Pettit propose a characterization of the *intrinsicist* account that is based on the idea that an agent—more specifically, a person—is as such "by what it is in itself" (List & Pettit 2011, p. 171). List and Pettit say they do not adhere to this interpretation and see themselves closer to the *extrinsicist* position, whereby agents or persons are distinguished by what they do extrinsically, i.e., by the roles they play. This is different from denying that the group can be the subject of intention, as my definition of the extrinsic account instead suggests (Section 4.3). What List and Pettit mean is that they do not acknowledge any essence associated with being an agent but rather argue for a performative notion of agent/person according to which an agent is the subject of intention and action. Thus, I do not see how the extrinsicist view they endorse could prevent their proposal from being considered an example of intrinsic account as understood in Section 4.2.

social world and are also the primary sources of any normative judgment and preference. Individualism holds because the status of agent granted to groups is not quite equivalent to that granted to individuals. In Chapter Eight of List and Pettit (2011), they clearly state that while groups are artificial agents or persons, the individual possesses the status of agent by nature. The reason is that individual agents coincide with human beings who are taken to be natural agents as well as the bearers of rights and values that do not apply to groups. Although it is unquestionable that human beings have particular dignity, especially when compared to artificial subjects, this pre-eminence should not be related to the agency status but to that of being human. Insofar as the notion of agent is considered in a functionalist and performative sense—an aspect that List and Pettit endeavor to defend—then appealing to substantive arguments to address normative issues would seem misplaced.[5]

It might be observed that the normative argument does not weaken the definition of the structural relation as non-reducible. Indeed, epistemic reducibility is no threat to List and Pettit's account. Instead, what can undermine the structural autonomy of group intentions is the way in which such attitudes are affected by normative considerations regarding the members, to whom normative priority is ascribed in virtue of the fact that they are human beings and, therefore, natural agents. Because groups are not human beings, but entities made of human beings, they are not credited as natural agents. Thus, although both groups and humans are agents, the former must comply with normative principles calibrated to the latter. Such an imbalance between two kinds of agent casts doubts on the autonomy of the intentions and actions of group agents from the intentions and the actions of individual agents.[6] There is a sense in which the group comes first. Although risking repetition, I agree with this insight but not with the reasons advanced by List and Pettit to support it.[7]

7.3 The normative issue

To adjudicate the case of GLA's (non)reducibility regarding constitutive and structural relations, it is important to investigate the normative issue and determine whether it provides enough stability for shared agency as some

---

[5] I am inclined to agree with Rovane's criticism as presented in Rovane 2014. Section 7.3 further elaborates on this.

[6] In defense of groups' intentional and moral autonomy, see also Copp 2006, 2007, Haji 2006, Hindriks 2014, Rovane 2014.

[7] Compelling criticism to List and Pettit (2011) has been provided by Kusch (2014).

proponents of holistic individualism seem to suggest (Gilbert 2013, List & Pettit 2011, Tuomela 2013a).

As Chapter Three and Chapter Six highlighted, the normative relation between the intentional and the behavioral moment of agency in group contexts leads to different discussions, depending on which source of normativity one considers (Zeibert & Smith 2007). In particular, the normative force connected to shared agency has a double meaning: (1) a form of basic normativity committing the participants to group member status and (2) a normative bond generated by each individual sharing a plan for the action. The first kind of normativity, characterized through Gilbert's and Tuomela's theories, is called social normativity, and it depends on individuals having the status of being partners. Until the entire group agrees to the entrance or departure of the individual(s) claiming involvement (Gilbert1990), the condition of being partners can neither be acquired nor eschewed by anyone personally. The only requirement needed for a joint/social commitment of this sort is the common awareness among the participants about the readiness of the others to take part in doing something as a body. Gilbert writes:

> Just as the readiness of each is required to bring the joint commitment into being so the concurrence of each is required in order to rescind the commitment. No one party can rescind it unilaterally. Nor can any one party rescind any part of it unilaterally, since it does not have parts. Each of the parties to a joint commitment is indeed committed in the sense that each one is subject to a commitment. It is tempting then to refer to the parties' 'individual commitments' when there is a joint commitment. If one does this, one must bear in mind that these individual commitments have important special features: they depend for their existence on the joint commitment; and the person who has a given individual commitment of this sort is not in a position unilaterally to rescind it. (Gilbert 2013, p. 32)

Therefore, the normative relation established by the joint commitment of the members is not an aggregative attitude that one could describe as the sum of all personal commitments brought together. Instead, the only way to grasp and explain joint commitment is by looking at the group as a whole and considering that such a collective represents an ontological fictitious ontological fact that has just acquired a normative salience. In fact, individuals, by way of a commitment act, have become partners or group members, and have consequently lost their personal autonomy to decide and act as a group. Thus, the moment an agent engages in full-blown we-attitudes, namely in states of mind held from the group-perspective, her thinking (as a we-thinking) could only happen as part of a wider group-thinking. As a group member, the individual has intentions for the action formulated from the group's point of view, which is an independent epistemological perspective, detached from the typical mindset of individual agency (Gilbert 2009, Rovane 1998). According to the disjunction criterion, we could imagine two different psychological levels in the mind of each individual: one concerned with individual attitudes and the other directed toward collective mental states.

By incorporating normativity in place at the group level directly (that is the second kind of normativity examined here), the GLA can, thus, provide a holistic perspective focused on the group-level explanation and not reducible to the description given by the MLA. In this sense, facts related to individuals as group members could be accounted for in the GLA as they occur within each member's mind from the group's rational point of view. Accordingly, being committed to a group dimension would be the condition through which an individual can act as a partner and hold intentions in the group's name. One might even say that, concerning the psychological dimension, the GLA appears to be more fundamental than the MLA because the former provides the horizon within which any individual ceases acting as a single agent and starts thinking and acting in the we-mode as a group member.

However, such non-redundancy (and priority) of collectivistic explanations seems to be challenged by two aspects that can be found, primarily, in Tuomela's and Gilbert's accounts. In order to forge the group viewpoint, an agreement-making process or some episode of collective acceptance at the members' level should occur. Then, the group perspective can be established on its foundation (Tuomela 2002, 2003, 2007, 2013a, Gilbert 1989, 2009, 2013).[8] Although we could say that a basic understanding of the group perspective is possible only by looking at the collective, how the normative source exerts its power on the individuals requires the use of concepts that belong to the dimension of member-level explanations. In fact, the we-mode perspective enables the group members to act as a single body if and only if the process of acquiring the shared viewpoint intervenes at the members' level by opening and grounding the theoretical possibility. Problematically, such a possibility does not introduce any real high-level subject of intentionality but instead offers a perspective into the mind of each. Despite the group perspective being epistemologically stable, the group is still a metaphysically fictitious entity, which makes sense to talk about while not constituting an actual individual

---

[8] The only author—among those considered here—assuming the original character of we-attitudes is Searle (2010). However, as argued in Section 7.2.1, it would be misleading to consider Searle a proponent of holistic individualism.

agent.[9] Therefore, to be understood (both by an external observer and by the agents' perspective), any discontinuous account needs the mediation operated by the MLA because it is only at that level that one can find irreducible attitudes. As mentioned above (Section 3.1), the 'we' of collective intentions is distributive in a way that makes it impossible to acknowledge the group as an intrinsic intentional subject. In other words, while the normative bond between the individuals generates a group viewpoint, it stops short of seeing the group as a genuine intentional agent.

Let us now consider the second kind of normativity Tuomela and Gilbert characterize: the normativity emanating from the shared intention for the action. Once the joint/social commitment to the group dimension has been established, the members act in accordance with the reasons they endorse as part of a group. Their intentional state of mind is something established and required by the group and, as such, is not an attitude representing an individual objective, pursued with individual/personal commitment. Tuomela writes:

> The members are, so to speak, assumed to have at least temporarily given up or delegated to the group a relevant part of their authority and autonomy to act, and this entails that they are normatively bound to comply with the group's directives. The most central group reasons are those relating to the group's ethos, which the group members have collectively accepted for the group and are publicly available to the group members. On the basis of their membership in a we-mode group the members in general ought to act as proper group members and to put aside their countervailing private desire and interests. (Tuomela 2013a, p. 115)

Thus, as group members, individuals are supposed to have intentions for action that represent the contents established through the group's ethos—the set of values, reasons, and motives for the action. Accepting the elements collectively composing the ethos enables the group to assume a reason selected from that shared horizon in the name of all the participants, without violating their rational autonomy. In fact, by becoming part of a group, individuals go through a leveling process through which they accept setting their personal inclinations aside—since they act as group members—and embrace a collective goal grounded in the common ethos as a suitable reason

---

[9] Rovane admits the possibility of group-sized intentional subjects, for she argues that groups can qualify as individual agents in their own rights (Rovane 2014, p. 1665).

for action.[10] In addition to forming the group perspective, the group might make its decisions by following at least two different strategies: if it is a hierarchical group, i.e., a group in which the members cover positions with different degrees of responsibility, decision making happens from the top down through be "operative members (leaders) authorized to make decisions for the rest of the group" (Tuomela 2013a, p. 126). Contrariwise, "in egalitarian groups all the members are operatives with an equal say about the views that the group will adopt" (Tuomela 2013a, p. 126). In brief, a group can endeavor to pursue a rational plan for action by (1) a decision made by the operatives or (2) through some sort of agreement among the members. Indeed, this assumption seems to build the GLA upon the MLA because the intention for action, fixed for the entire group, requires the membership structure to be evaluated—or so some might argue.

Tuomela could reply to this criticism by maintaining that the members act in the we-mode, not as individuals but as a group. Meaning that the operatives (be they a few or all of the members) are allowed to speak in the name of the group, to decide what targets should be pursued or rejected, what reasons might benefit the group, and what others diverge from the common good. Presenting the group as one unit becomes possible through a more basic form of commitment—where individuals commit themselves to the status of group members—and by the collective acceptance of the common ethos: "the main point of collective acceptance is to amalgamate member attitudes into a group attitude collectively binding the group members" (Tuomela 2013a, p. 125). The assumption of the we-mode requires individuals to become part of a whole by losing some of their autonomy. Indeed, in Tuomela's and Gilbert's proposals, the separation of psychological domains (concerning the members' perspective and the group's point of view, respectively) is functional to protect individual personality from the intrusion of the collective and, consequently, preserve some individualism in the theory (Pettit 1996). Nonetheless, the assumption that the group can influence individuals' psychology, creating a homogeneous intentional viewpoint, could be challenging to conciliate with the kind of individualism endorsed in the approach. In fact, the ultimate reason motivating members to act would be the one determined by the normative commitment assumed with respect to the ethos, which—when working properly—may overstep individuals' inclinations and preferences. This determination would undermine the

---

[10] An agent need not accept all of the group's motivating ethos in order to be a group member.

distinction between two psychological levels established in the discontinuity thesis of intentionality.[11]

It would seem, then, that in Tuomela's (and Gilbert's) theory, the issue of psychological determination is a delicate one in that the intentional amalgam required for any well-functioning group psychology is at risk of equating individual reasoning to collective reasoning.

The case is different in List and Pettit's account (List & Pettit 2011), who consider group agency as intentionally intrinsic and based upon a network of individual attitudes. Here, problems arise when List and Pettit claim to be realistic and treat groups as proper intentional agents.[12] As argued already about the structural relation, their realism about group agency is a form of epistemological realism with neither ontological nor normative counterparts in the theory. First, there is no ontological counterpart because groups are described as ontologically non-autonomous (List & Pettit 2011, p. 76), meaning that the existence of group agents depends upon the existence of individual members who constitute them. Further, this applies both in the context of material constitution, whereby "group agents are not flesh-and-body persons" (Ibid., pp. 176–177) and must have members to serve as

---

[11] To better understand the members' normative priority, it could be helpful to mention another issue investigated by Tuomela: group responsibility. The point is difficult because it shows a methodological ambiguity that the distinction between the MLA and the GLA might help to clarify. Tuomela affirms that the group is straightforwardly responsible for the dissident actions of its members, because a disobedient (individual) act means a lack of control or a weak influence of the group on the individuals' mind. Still, the group is only indirectly responsible for the action that it brings about through the members' contribution. In this sense, if it is possible to ascribe a performance to the entire collective, this can only be done retrospectively: the group can be identified as the agent only if the event is seen afterword. From a third-person perspective, the action is seen firstly as realized by individual agents; then, those agents can be recognized as group members. It is just after those steps that the action can be ascribed to the group as such (Tuomela 2007, pp. 233–253). Hence, Tuomela seems to be disposed to assume that the group has direct responsibility concerning the homologation of individuals' psychology to the group intentional horizon, whilst rejecting a direct/prospective responsibility of the group with respect to the members' action. Yet, the group is indirectly responsible for what the members do. This way of introducing indirect responsibility is consistent with not accepting the intrinsic account of groups as intentional agents (Section 4.2). At the same time, the kind of individualism Tuomela embraces would require members' psychological autonomy, which is rather undermined by the leveling process that the group is expected to operate.

[12] The requirements that a group agent needs to satisfy in order to be held responsible can be found in List and Pettit 2011, p. 158.

physical support, and in the context of the constitution of groups as agents. By context of constitution, I mean that while some groups can be agents, the status they have as agents is not distinct from the fact that members are agents themselves. In fact, even though both individuals and groups can qualify as agents, the former are agents by nature while the latter are agents only in a derivative way.

And yet, according to List and Pettit, every agent is a performative person: "what makes an agent a person is not what the agent is but what the agent does" (Ibid., p. 171). Here, they suggest that the difference between natural agent and derivative agent does not fit the characterization of individuals and groups as agents in the sense of performative persons. Indeed, performative persons are considered as such regardless of what they are and only by virtue of what they do. Opposing the functionalist view, we can consider the following framework instead: both groups and individuals are agents (performative persons), and while individuals are agents originally, by nature, groups are agents depending on the fact that there are individual agents, some of whom are members. Therefore, it would seem that ontologically speaking, groups are supervening entities, not eliminable, and yet derived from what constitutes them. At the same time, the complexity that characterizes them legitimizes explanatory non-redundancy. It seems reasonable to observe, with Rovane, that while consistent with the kind of individualism defended in List and Pettit's account, the distinction of natural and derivative persons clashes with the performative notion of person and with the realistic aspiration of the theory (Rovane 2014). If only individuals are genuine agents, then group agents would seem to be denied the full agency status.

Advocating for realism about group agency shows weaknesses even on the normative level: provided that groups are derivative agents, the rational plan they endorse must first be calibrated to the protection of members as natural persons. The reason is explicit: "something is good only if it is good for individual human or, more generally, sentient beings" (List & Pettit 2011, p. 182). Therefore, the normative aspect in List and Pettit's proposal seems reducible, or at least relatable, to the normativity captured by the MLA because it is precisely that normativity generating and guiding any legitimate, group-level rational commitment.

Although it is undeniable that individuals have greater normative (moral) salience by virtue of being humans or moral persons, it is not entirely convincing to assert this priority by relying on the notion of a performative person or agent as this is a functional notion that should be applied indistinctly to any suitable case.

7.4 Troubles with causality

Questioning what happens to the psychological autonomy of the members in group-scale contexts of agency becomes extremely important when we consider causal relations. In fact, as far as the GLA is concerned, the causal relation is supposed to regard the influence that the group plan for the action has on the agential system composed of joint members. From this perspective, one of the main problems is determining whether and in what terms the shared intention (be it a collective intention or a network of interrelated I/we-attitudes) could have a causal impact on the activity performed by the group agent and preserve, at the same time, the psychological autonomy of the members. Indeed, if the plan state of the group is the cause of the activity, the issue concerning individual psychology might be subject to dual interpretations: on the one hand, member intentionality could be determined by some fact belonging to the group level (downwards causation)[13]—the participants act in compliance with the group's claim because a higher-level attitude necessitated their individual contribution. On the other hand, the members' intentional stance could be overridden, and the group might act and have effects on the world, independently from what happens among its members (Pettit 1996).[14] According to the former possibility, the individualistic claim regarding the members' psychological autonomy would collapse, and the collectivistic assertion that groups are causally influential on individual agency would be confirmed. Under these circumstances, the group's impact would alter individual thinking and acting. Instead, regarding the latter, the individuation of a causal force located at the group level could be effective, as it would neither violate nor alter the intentional process operating at the level of the members. In this case, the hurdle would be the possibility to hold the group as the bearer of any causal power even though, as a social fact, it is ontologically reducible to the individual basis. Thus, what must be determined is whether a collective "exists causally objectively as a social system capable of causal production of outcomes in the world in virtue of its we-thinking and 'we-acting' members" (Tuomela 2013a, p. 47). More to the point, the difficult question is adjudicating whether the causal effectiveness of the group (if any) could concern group-level intentionality and allow us to say that group intentions are causally effective on group activities.

When dealing with causation, the GLA should fix whether the supervenient, ontologically reducible group dimension can have any kind of causal impact

---

[13] On downwards causation in social ontology, see Elder-Vass 2012.
[14] See Section 5.3 and 5.4.

on the world and/or members. Ultimately, the causal relation is a two-folded issue: first, there is the problem concerning the possibility of attributing causal power to social facts that, in compliance with the individualistic principle, would be ontologically reducible. Second, in the case of granting causal power to social facts, the point is to establish the domain upon which social facts exert their influence. It is important to notice that the social facts considered in what follows are group intentions, namely, group-level rational plans that might eventually exert some direct/indirect causal influence on the activity of the collective. Then, it may be that:

    a.   high-level social fact C is the cause of another high-level social fact E that is the effect,

    b.   high-level social fact C is the cause of social fact E, at the individual level, that is the effect.[15]

If high-level social facts are considered as causally and directly effective on other high-level social facts, individual psychology will not be compromised but bypassed; if they are, instead, considered to exert top-down causation, individual psychology will be compromised, and high-level social facts will be indirectly affected. Moreover, it should be acknowledged that in the case of top-down causation (b):

    c.   social fact C, at the higher level, may have a causal impact on any fact E, at the individual level,

    d.   high-level social fact C may have a causal impact on its own individual basis.

Concerning the first issue (c), the problem arises when considering a group, like any other social fact,[16] as the starting point of a causal chain. Here, the puzzle begins with the ontological status of the elements populating the social sphere defined as ontologically dependent upon the individual. Indeed,

---

[15] In view of the analysis of the agency relations developed so far, C is a group intentional property. Assuming groups have intentional properties only if approached by the intrinsic account (Section 4.2), one might also interpret group intentional properties to be networks or outcomes of individual attitudes as proposed by the extrinsic account (Section 4.3). Then, E could represent either an action or an attitude. While in the case of downwards causation E represents individual-level facts, high-level (S-S) causation needs E to be a group-level fact.

[16] The set of social facts includes high-level properties of intentionality and agency.

holistic individualism holds that social facts are supervenient features. Accordingly, one could adopt two strategies: (1) rejecting the possibility of any causal power of social facts; (2) acknowledging the causal power exerted by some supervenient facts on other supervenient facts. Although the former option seems easier to uphold, theorists engaged in holistic individualism have more often followed the latter. As a matter of fact, the idea that high-level facts have explanatory significance in the social sciences has contributed to the attribution of causal power to social facts (List & Pettit 2011, Pettit 1996, 2003, Sawyer 2003, Tuomela 2011, 2013a).[17] The outcome has been defined as supervenient causation (SC),[18] which validates the causal power of groups as supervenient facts. For its connection to the principles governing the ontological supervenience relation, supervenient causation requires considering the causal power of social facts dependent on the individual basis from which the social fact arises. Accordingly, group intentions for the action are member-dependent[19] properties, having a causal influence on group activity only through the supervenience relation:

> SC. Social properties do not have autonomous causal force, because their causal consequences obtain in virtue of their realizing individual supervenience base. (Sawyer 2003, p. 207)

Thus, the causal force in the GLA would still be dependent on what happens within lower-level reality.

Sawyer proposes to improve the holistic account (keeping the ontological individualism associated with it) by introducing an interesting variation. This improvement incorporates time and its relation to supervenience. Insofar as supervenience is the only relation of dependence on focus, groups might be accounted for by virtue of being supervenient facts, namely social facts occurring if and only if a corresponding lower-level arrangement occurs (Sawyer 2003, pp. 207–208). The same correspondence applies to high-level properties, such as group agentive properties, which can be instantiated only once individual agentive properties have occurred. However, Sawyer observes,

---

[17] To be precise, Tuomela considers the causal power of groups as intentionally extrinsic social structures. Meaning, the influence groups might exert depends on their being structural and institutional components of the social world. In other words, groups might have causal powers as social objects. Groups as intentionally intrinsic agents are not meant to have any causal power (Tuomela 2013a).

[18] Kim (1979) provided a first definition of 'supervenient causation'. For further developments of the concept, see Sawyer 2003.

[19] Member-dependent means mind-dependent.

causation is a relation that happens as time passes; for this reason, it is quite challenging to study that relationship based on the synchronic temporal dimension that supervenience has set. An alternative way to approach the causal relation is through the diachronic perspective. According to this, some particular social fact is investigated not for its being a supervenient fact but for the consequences it generates over time. Given the explicative non-redundancy of group-level facts (fixed by the criteria of multiple realizability and wild disjunction), considering group phenomena as causally effective over time is meaningful—methodologically—especially because understanding group phenomena could influence what happens next, both at the individual and the social level:

> a social property S, with supervenience base I at time t_1, can lawfully be identified as the cause of social property S^* and individual property I^* at time t_2, even though I cannot be lawfully identified as the cause of I^*. (Sawyer 2003, p. 207)

Despite its explanatory power, the supervenient causal efficacy of group-level facts raises, once again, a difficult problem: that is, determining the dimension upon which social facts could show their influence. *Prima facie*, social facts could have the causal power to produce outcomes on the social world by having an impact on other social facts (S-S causation). In addition, one might associate social facts with a top-down, causal power directed towards individual facts. More precisely, top-down causation could lean towards (1) lower facts in general or (2) facts belonging to the individual basis of the group. In Sawyer's framework, the latter form of top-down causation should be rejected because the basis from which the group supervenes is unaffected by any causal impact coming from the higher level. This reason being the synchronicity of the two levels, which does not legitimate the individuation of any effect happening over time. The other top-down option, albeit feasible, would threaten the individualistic claim; according to which, group events could not interfere and causally determine individual intentional agency. In fact, being capable of intervening on intentional agency would imply the power to modify individual psychology. Therefore, it seems that assuming some form of downwards causation means affirming a psychological collectivistic principle that has been, instead, excluded from the pattern of holistic individualism (Pettit 1996, 2014).[20]

---

[20] See Chapter Five. In particular, Sections 5.3 and 5.4.

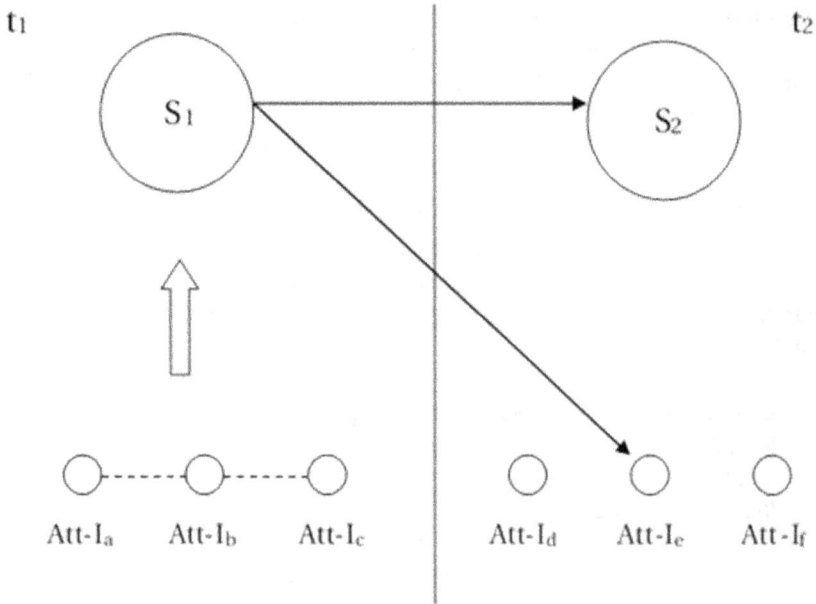

Figure 7.1. Supervenience causation.

Thus, regarding S-S causation (S1-S2 in Fig. 7.1) [21], the puzzling issue concerns the ontological thesis maintained by holistic individualism. Defining social facts as effects (and sources) of causality challenges the fundamental idea that only facts about individuals are real: setting a causal relation between fictitious items seems oxymoronic. Insofar as ontological individualism denies the existence of any social fact, the troublesome

---

[21] Figure 7.1 represents supervenience and causal relation over time. On the left side, a high-level social fact S_1 supervenes on a network of individual attitudes. The upwards arrow draws the supervenience connection happening at a moment in time (t_1). The right side of the figure represents a high-level social fact S_2 and other facts about individuals, all happening at a later stage (t_2). The thin arrows going from S_1 to S_2 (S-S causation) and from S_1 to Att-$I_{d,e,f}$ (downwards causation) represent eventual causal relations. What is excluded from the context is the top-down causation connecting S_1 with Att-$I_{a,b,c}$. Causation would have been between elements occurring at the same time (t_1), whereas causation needs the unfolding of time. An alternative version of the picture can be found in Sawyer 2003, p. 208, and in List & Spiekermann 2013, p. 637.

identification of the effect in S-S causation immediately affects the identification of the source.[22]

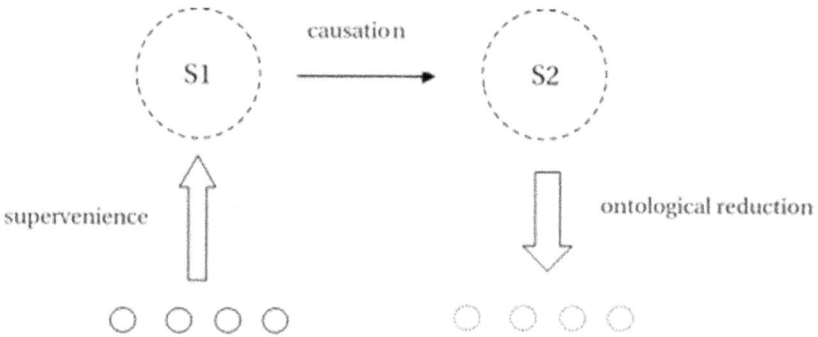

Figure 7.2. S-S causation.

Therefore, the riddle of supervenient causation might be approached in two ways. First, one could dissolve the GLA and build the explanation of causality in the social world through the MLA. In this sense, refusing the ontological consistency of groups and high-level facts in general would lead the theory to describe both S-I and S-S causality in reductive terms, and the GLA would finally collapse downwards on the description provided by the MLA.[23] Second, the solution to the dilemma might be to support the holistic ambition of the explanation, which aims at contrasting methodological individualism and reduction. Then, the challenge would be integrating the diachronic dimension into the GLA of shared agency to make the theoretical framework better suited to fulfill the explanatory desideratum. Otherwise, social causation would continue to represent an unstable aspect of high-level descriptions and an argument in favor of methodological individualism. It is indeed difficult to

---

[22] The problem of the source is relative to S-S causation and S-I causation, as well. As it is, a causal bond might start either from a high-level social fact and produce a low-level fact as its outcome (S-I), or it could be a relation that has a social fact as its source and another social fact as its effect (S-S).

[23] Figure 7.2 concerns S-S causation. Dashed contour lines of S1 and S2 represent the non-objective ontological nature of social facts in holistic individualism. Then, I used dotted lines to draw the basis of ontological reduction, which—according to multiple realizability—cannot be uniquely derived from the supervenient phenomenon. The small, dotted circles just stand for any possible configurations of individual-level facts forming S2.

believe that social facts with a fictitious ontological status might be causally effective or be the subject of autonomous intentions for the action.

Giving more thought to the temporal dimension might help to articulate the problem of causality better. However, we must first consider whether this modification would also solve other problems in the GLA and help explain what exactly the reasons for these problems are and if an alternative framework may be more adequate than holistic individualism. Chapter Eight will clarify the source of the instabilities identified so far in the GLA. Then, Chapters Nine and Ten will offer an anti-reductionist and anti-singularist argument based on a minimal and performative notion of agent and the dismissal of the individualistic mindset embraced by the Big Five. We will see to what extent individualism's reception has been shaped by ontological, normative, intentional, and metaphysical claims.

Chapter 8

A disturbing premise

8.1 A shared trait among shared action theories

Holistic individualism and current group-level accounts have been extensively discussed throughout this text. Now, the objective is to investigate specific contradictions prompted by the GLA and make broader (meta-theoretical) observations concerning its (theoretical) foundations. The inconsistencies encountered in the re-construction of the GLA might signal deeper theoretical problems connected by a shared premise underlying different versions of the account. Accordingly, this chapter unmasks that premise as a form of normative and metaphysical individualism that comes with the endorsement of intentionalism as a theoretical approach to action theory.[1] This interpretation is connected to the kind of intentional individualism considered in Chapter Three: all MLAs are distributive given the basic assumption that all intentionality is attributed to individual psychology. If we say that all intentionality is individual, then it means that group intentional behavior must somehow be individualistic. A few flaws in the GLA corroborate the argument. This chapter primarily focuses on the problems identified regarding normativity and the kind of normative individualism the four agency relations revealed.

It is imperative to underline how crucial normative relations are when compared to constitutive, structural, and causal relations (Chapter Seven). To account for such an endorsement, I will argue that although the Big Five (except for Gilbert) have not explicitly accepted a normativistic action theory, the intentionalism they uphold seems to require a normative grounding

---

[1] The double connotation of the premise serves to enrich Hindriks' (2008, 2014) and Rovane's (2014) definitions of normative individualism, according to which individualism in the social sciences has been framed on the basis of the idea that individual human beings have special rational and moral status. I want to follow the insight and connect the model of intentional agency to moral individualism. In addition, it will be argued that ethical and moral assumptions are also bound to a metaphysical position establishing conditions that inevitably lead to individualistic views about morality, ontology, and methods. Taking individual human beings as the seeds of any possible action and rational thought represents a transcendental, meta-theoretical condition characteristic of the entire intentionalistic approach (Section 3.1).

principle. Far from being just one of the ways to relate intending and acting in group-scale contexts, the normative relation seems to be considered a necessary condition for the happening and the description of group agency— the normative relation is the foundation for the other connections characterizing the event.

Normativity as an agency relation consists of two levels; the unique role of that dimension must be viewed through both. As mentioned in Tuomela's (2002, 2003, 2007, 2013a) and Gilbert's (1989, 1990, 2007b, 2013, 2018) accounts, the two interpretations of normativity in the description of group intentional behavior can be spelled out in two ways: the first way maintains that the normative bond arises from mutual recognition and joint/social commitment of the members to the status of being partners/parts of the collective and acting in its name, as one. The second way asserts that the normative force can be associated with sharing an intention for the action. In this case, the joint/collective commitment is relative to the members' pursuit of the intended goal. The aspect that the analysis of the GLA has emphasized the most is that the kind of normativity concerning the goal of we-attitudes is second-level normativity because it arises from the normative bond set up by the prior form of commitment. Thus, the basic attitude is the commitment that the agents mutually assume to the status of being group members—a condition that enables the participants to have collective intentions for the action and realize those plans jointly, as the second kind of normativity binds them to do. From this perspective, and in compliance with the *disjointed criterion*,[2] individual agents are enabled to think and act in a way that cannot be adopted (when they do what they intend to do) as singular individuals. Clearly, one could find this kind of separation within the domain of the normative relation just by referring to accounts, such as Tuomela's and Gilbert's, that assume both individual and collective intentionality. Indeed, postulating two disjointed theoretical levels is meaningful because the fracture implicitly acknowledges a psychological gap between the individual and the collective intentional domain.[3]

---

[2] For a definition, see Section 2.4 and Gilbert 2009, pp. 171–173.

[3] Even though Searle defends the discontinuity thesis account of intentionality, his proposal is not a proper form of holistic individualism, since the notion of group agent is not really part of the account (Section 7.2.1). Indeed, among the theorists of the discontinuity thesis, Searle's view might be an exception, because it maintains that "collective intentionality is a fundamental and irreducible fact of human and some animal psychology" (Searle 2007, p. 13). According to this, we-intentions for the action are attitudes that occur in the mind of each the same way—but with a difference in

The idea that the normative relation, especially in its basic form, might be a fundamental requirement of shared agency in the group-level account can also be maintained by referring to approaches framed on the continuity thesis of intentionality. In fact, the assumption that shared agency is the result of attitudes and networks of attitudes occurring at the individual level in the I-mode might be associated with normative bonds securing the aggregation of individual intentions for action. Regarding Bratman's account, the building blocks of shared agency are the bricks taken from the explanation of individual agency and re-arranged to explain group events as phenomena of the same kind. The foundational role of normativity might be identified, as Bratman suggests, in the application of two normative principles—the *means-end-coherence* and *consistency* principles—responsible for the suitability of each single, individual sub-plan in view of the realization of the common goal (Bratman 1987, 2014a). More precisely, the appropriateness of individual efforts to that of the others and with respect to what should be done for obtaining the goal secures the rationality of agency by providing a rational control over the entire activity. Even though the control, in Bratman's individualistic view, is a duty of individual rationality and not a goal pursued by the group as such, the function it

---

form—as I-intentions for the action. Assuming the original and irreducible character of both intentional forms, collective intentionality does not require any 'prior attitude' paving the way for the happening of we-intentions. Instead, the possibility to have shared attitudes oriented towards cooperative actions is presented by Searle as something that happens in the individual's mind without being necessarily referred to the participation (or willingness to participate) of others. The only element mentioned by Searle (and that might recall the content of the basic form of commitment introduced by Tuomela and Gilbert) is the "background sense of the others" (Searle 1990, p. 415). Such a feature, in Searle's theory, represents a belief about the presence of other participants and, as a belief, it is part of the cognitive background of the individual agent, who might also be wrong in assuming the cooperative character of the performance. On the matter, Searle holds that the presence of the other as an agent, willing to cooperate in the action, is just an assumption. Any individual might assume it even if she were a brain in a vat. Therefore, the actual cooperation of the others seems to be not an essential character, necessary for the logical possibility of we-intentionality. Instead, the background sense of others might be a wrong belief, claiming the collective nature of the attitude even when no actual relationship with others is set. For these reasons, Searle's proposal is an account of collective intentionality and yet not a theory of group agency.

fulfills still represents a necessary condition for the occurrence of shared agency as a proper event of intentional agency.[4]

An additional consideration about the normativism entangled in social ontology emerges within List and Pettit's proposal. As we have observed already, their account embraces a kind of individualism that does not prevent the theory from assuming the epistemological salience of group agents as proper, rational systems capable of planning, controlling, and realizing intentional actions. Group agents are agents in the *intrinsic* sense, having autonomous intentions for action the same as individual agents. To rephrase this: group attitudes might be described as intentions of the system, and they can be grasped through the same concepts and principles employed in the explanation of individual agency. Both individuals and groups—if compliant to the conditions that being an agent requires—are systems of agency, accountable for by the same methodology (List & Pettit 2011). Considering this position, the normative foundation of shared agency might be grounded in the fact that the decision-making procedure, through which the group deliberates, is based on the individuals' commitment to and the acceptance of (and participation in) the procedure as well as to the organizational structure it may generate. In this sense, group attitudes are only possible insofar as individuals are mutually committed to acting in view of the group's interest.

8.2 Normativity as constitutive dimension

Normative agency-relations seem to play a prominent role in the makeup of shared agency extensively enough that normative agency-relations might work differently than constitutive, structural, and causal relations between intention and action and count as a precondition for those dimensions.[5]

First, it is important to consider the constitutive relation. In this respect, one can observe that, instead of being a premise for the instantiation of the

---

[4] Moreover, the network of common beliefs held by the participants, and regarding the intentions of the other fellows, might be considered as creating (even if not necessarily) a kind of normative ground, close to that proposed by Gilbert (1989, 1990, 2007b, 2013, 2018) and Tuomela (2002, 2007, 2013a), upon which constructing shared agency (Bratman 2014a, pp. 110–120). The mutual awareness of the others' willingness to participate creates expectations among the agents, who act for the benefit of the collective partly for the pressure of others. In some sense, Bratman suggests that being considered as an agent gives to the individual a (normative) status, which relates to the "obligations of each to each" (Bratman 2014a, p. 119). Doing things together thus generates obligations among the parties. See Section 1.2, 1.3, and 1.4.

[5] I am considering only the account of shared agency based on holistic individualism.

constitutive relation, the normative connection operates as a kind of constitutive relation itself. Particularly, this fundamental role of the normative aspect does not concern the intentional phenomenon and commitment towards its pursuit; instead, it concerns the obligations that assuming/ascribing the role of partner/group member has evoked. Meaning that the aspect that plays a constitutive role in the explanation of shared agency is a basic form of commitment—the attitude oriented towards the assumption/ascription of a status—which generates a new theoretical (collective or group-oriented) perspective in the individuals' minds or a decision-making mechanism binding individual attitudes together. The basic normativity associated with the mutual recognition of partner/group member status at the member-level reality might be a constitutive feature of shared agency in the GLA as it provides the conditions for which the group's viewpoint can be established. Then, the supervenience of the group perspective might be seen, depending on the theory, either as an autonomous rational point of view (*intrinsic* accounts of group agent) or as a mode (i.e., we-mode) of individuals' intentionality (*extrinsic* accounts). [6]

A second consideration involves the structural relation. According to the critical investigation proposed in Chapter Seven on the unstable conditions of the GLA, it appears that the capacity for shared intentions to structure group activities can be grasped only by considering the normative relation among the individuals as partners. Let us take Bratman's perspective as an example (Bratman 1999, 2007, 2014a). First, Bratman regards the common goal for the regulative function it has on the individual contributions (Section 1.2); then, he takes the shared plan to be the goal of shared agency (Section 1.3). An intention shapes the action thanks to the normative principles securing the means-end-coherence and consistency of the attitude, pertaining to individual intentional agency and affecting the suitability of the contribution of each individual toward the broader group plan.

Different, but with some commonality, is the case of structural relation presented by Tuomela (2003, 2005, 2007, 2008, 2013a, 2013b) and Gilbert (1989, 2003, 2011, 2013), who introduce group attitudes which establish a group perspective in individual psychology. Without the social/joint commitment to the mutual recognition of that status, a collective way of thinking and acting could not emerge.

---

[6] Intrinsic and extrinsic accounts of shared agency have been proposed in Section 4.2 and 4.3.

As for the causal relation, we found that this dimension also conceals a normativistic core, similar to the structural agency relation. In fact, the causal power of high-level social facts can be grasped in the GLA if and only if member-level descriptions have correctly set up the high-level domains. Necessarily, shared agency has supervened upon a particular set of attitudes among the members, allowing the introduction of such a social dimension. In this sense, mutual obligations between members, binding them to one another as part of the same collective, are the condition *sine qua non* a set of individuals could function as a group, have group-level intentions for the action and, eventually, exert some high-level, causal power. Moreover, the capacity to exert such a causal influence, be it downwards or S-S causation (Section 7.4), might occur only once the group agent has been formed and recognized as a system. No matter if the collective represents an *intrinsic* or an *extrinsic* intentional system of agency (Section 4.2 and 4.3), what the causal relation requires is a social fact to treat in the GLA as the source of the power it aims to describe. Thus, like in the structural relation, even the account of group-level causality seems to depend upon the modification of perspective generated by the individuals once they have acquired group status and the rational viewpoint of group members/partners. Without the network of mutual obligations accompanied by that status and perspective, it would be hard to conceive a group plan for the action (and a group act as well) having a causal power that is not reducible to the causal power of individual attitudes. In order to grant causal power to some system, it is necessary to ascertain whether that system is real.

The normative relation, hidden within all connections, coincides with just one of the two sides of normativity in shared agency (namely, the basic form of normativity generated by social/joint commitment). In this way, the same range of considerations regarding structural and causal relations could also apply to second-order normativity. First, basic normativity might be the premise upon which the group members can form a group perspective. From this basic normativity, group members can hold and commit themselves to collective intentions for the action (as in the case of Tuomela and Gilbert)[7] and common plan states (as in Bratman).[8] Basic normativity can help in the generation of autonomous group attitudes as well (List & Pettit 2011). It follows then that the explanation of second-order normativity resembles the account relative to structural and causal relations, about which basic normativity has appeared to be fundamental.

---

[7] References can be found in Section 2.3 and 2.4.
[8] See Section 1.3.

From what we have observed so far, it is reasonable to infer that there is, or seems to be, a normative relation embedded within the concept of shared agency advanced by holistic individualism. This normative relation, in particular, considers mutual relationships occurring at the level of the members and entitling individuals to the status of group members. In what follows, I will be questioning to what extent the GLA reflects the normative relation's unstable condition and appears reducible to the MLA. I will mainly refer to basic normativity and the foundational role of the inter-subjective (member-to-member) attribution of status in the construction of high-level explanations regarding group agency. More clearly, it is not implied that any normative account of shared agency is unstable or reductive. The target of the criticism is specifically at the interpretation provided by the Big Five, which remains consistent with a normativistic action theory, yet bound to some form of individualism which hinders that project. An example of action theory that claims to be both normative and non-reductive, i.e., in support of the possibility that some groups are to be regarded as individual agents, is the one proposed by Rovane (Rovane 1998), who grounds the notion of agency on the commitment of the subject to some specific rational point of view. The normative relationship between the subject and the rational point of view is what makes the subject an agent, regardless of whether it is a human-sized or a group-sized individual.[9] The agent is the result of a commitment undertaken toward a project of rational unification, and it is in this sense, being an agent is inherently normative and non-reductive.[10]

8.3 Normative and metaphysical individualism(s)

Normative relations between members alone are insufficient to determine the instability of any GLA because, as mentioned already, such a normative foundation could be the guiding principle of a normative, and yet non-reductive, theory of agency such as the one proposed by Rovane. Instead, I claim that what makes such member-to-member normative bonds problematic is a deeper kind of normativism regarding the priority attributed to individual agents over group agents. This section clarifies to what extent this kind of normativity is a form of normative individualism—it will then be referred to as NI_2, meaning second-level normative individualism.

---

[9] Rovane also concedes that within the same human being there might be multiple rational viewpoints disconnected from one another and thus multiple persons (Rovane 1998, 2004).

[10] More will be said about Rovane's account in Chapter Nine.

To understand the sort of priority here under investigation, incorporating some insights from Chapter Three might be helpful. Let us consider the point made by Stoutland (1997), who offers an explanation of individual priority as an anti-social bias, assuming that intentional attitudes are ascribed "not to social groups per se but to their members" (Stoutland 1997, p. 46).[11] Here, Stoutland suggests that individuals are the only intentional subjects that have been really introduced by (the greatest part of) the debate on group agency. This assumption is in line with the endorsement of intentional individualism, which states that "[A]ny interpretation of an individual's behavior has to be given in terms of individual intentional states" (Schmid 2009, p. 23).[12] Thus, the GLA has to be through MLAs focused on individual attitudes. In other words, the theory hints at the idea that intentional subjects must be individual subjects in the same way that agents must be individual agents. Individuals here are human beings. Therefore, the GLA of shared agency is constructed upon a standard concept of agency. Since that standard refers to individual agency, specifically, the GLA is necessarily oriented towards individual agents. This makes second-level normativity emerge clearly as a form of individualism, for the reference point of any agency theory is identified in individual agents of human proportions. This observation denotes theory normativism designed for adhering to a normative principle and a kind of intrinsicism concerning the notion of agent. Indeed, no matter how thoroughly it has been said that an agent is generally described functionally, we are now confronted with a metaphysical characterization that seems to move away from that functionalist idea.

Let us take a step back. When considering the view of the Big Five, I highlighted that the action theory they endorse comes with a functional notion of agent—according to which a system is an agent insofar as it fulfills the conditions of agency (Section 4.4). Such a claim has been developed specially by List and Pettit (List & Pettit 2011). They have argued that both terms, namely 'individual agent' and 'group agent', refer to subjects ('individual' and 'group') fulfilling the status of agent for their conformance to

---

[11] Full quotation can be found in Section 3.1.

[12] Further observations on intentional individualism and its implications on the MLA can be found in Chapter Three.

the definition of what it means to be an agent for the theory.[13] Thus, both individuals and groups have been considered centers of intentional action because they function exactly how the theory expects an agent to function.

There are reasons to believe that this framework can be promising to set up the group-level account of shared agency, especially because it undertakes to apply the notion of agent to systems of various kinds regardless of their nature.[14] Introducing the functional notion of agent is consistent with holistic individualism because the demands of high-level explanations do not necessarily require any ontological commitment to its material components. In fact, to say that systems of different kinds, such as individual and group agents, function in a way that can be described similarly does not mean that the two objects are of the same ontological kind. On the matter, List and Pettit made an interesting remark when they defined any system functioning as an agent a performative person.[15] This characterization is opposed to the substantive conception of personhood according to which a person is such by virtue of what it is. List and Pettit have called this latter account the 'intrinsicist perspective' and observed that, [16]

> There are two conceptions of personhood. According to the one, there is something about the 'stuff' that persons are made of that distinguishes them from non-persons: something that makes persons stand out. This is the 'intrinsicist' conception of personhood. According to the other, what makes an agent a person is not what the agent is but what the agent does; the mark of the personhood is the ability to play certain role, to perform in a certain way. We call this view the 'performative' conception of personhood and later adopt it in our argument. (List & Pettit 2011, p.171)

This notion of personhood relates to the adequacy of systems for establishing meaningful relationships with others through the mediation of normative

---

[13] As said, the agent can be identified through *intrinsic, extrinsic,* and *status* accounts. The first one considers shared attitudes as the features that allow us to recognize and treat the collective as a group agent (Section 4.2); the second individuates group agents based on extra-psychological elements—such as norms and functional roles—that make the shared attitude performed through the realization of a structure (Section 4.3). Finally, according to the *status* account, a group is an agent insofar as it is attributed that status (Section 4.4).
[14] Chapter Nine and Ten will elaborate on the model.
[15] On personhood, see List & Pettit 2011, pp. 170–174.
[16] Interesting in this regard is Kusch 2014, where it is noted how List and Pettit' notion of personhood could also be approached as a form of intrinsicism.

expectations and obligations that correspond to the social normativity underlined in the previous section.

> The performative conception of personhood maps the distinction between persons and non-persons onto the divide between agents who can be incorporated in a conventional system of mutual obligation and agents, such as non-human animals on the standard pictures, that do not have this capacity. (Ibid., p. 173)

Thus, a person, either singular or plural, is what counts as such in ordinary social practices as "persons, natural and corporate, are distinguished by the fact that they can enter a system of obligations recognized in common with others [...]". (Ibid., p.178)

Although this form of functionalism might seem attractive, I find it problematic that the account, having attempted the holistic (and realistic) characterization of high-level facts by ascribing a priority to individual-sized agents over group agents, has non-neutrally characterized the metaphysical level. In support, after defining the performative meaning of personhood, adopting it into the theory, and applying it to both individuals and groups, List and Pettit (2011) find the following:

> While we agree that group agents count as persons, and that they are inevitably given certain rights, we deny that the rights they enjoy are on a par with the rights of natural persons. (Ibid., p.180)

Here, 'natural persons' seem to denote individuals' original status that is not ascribable to groups. In fact, to be a natural person means to have the capacity to bear a rational point of view and have moral preferences and inclinations by nature. The main offering, in this case, is that individual agents as human beings have a special intentional standing due to their natural endowment of rationality and "sensitivity" (Ibid., p. 182).[17] In contrast, group agents are not thought to have a rational standpoint originally because they are not 'natural'. Group agents, as social facts, acquire their status through the interaction among the members and through the agreement-making

---

[17] This is agreeable but misplaced especially insofar as the argument is grounded on a performative notion of personhood and not on an intrinsicist one, which would consider individual agents for being human creatures. Because of this, I see the notion of person as weakening when applied to groups.

procedure leading to the formation of the group perspective over time.[18] List and Pettit have offered this distinction, which I believe takes a step back from the functionalism characterizing their notion of agency, by introducing a metaphysical requirement that can be seen as the source of intentional, metaphysical, and normative individualism (NI_2).

The priority of individual agents over groups brings into the discussion another form of normative individualism concerning morality.[19] Provided that moral standards are fixed by what is good or blameworthy for individuals, they say: "something is good only if it is good for individual human or, more generally, sentient beings" (Ibid., p. 182). There is undoubtedly an intuitive sense for which individual agents, as humans, have rights that groups do not have. Nevertheless, being the bearer of certain rights does not depend on an individual's agency status—it depends on being human. Since the notion of agent is functionalist, it would be consistent to ascribe deontic powers to the applicable systems that are equally based on the property of agency and not on other carrier-specific properties. For example, if one believes that it is fair to ascribe speech rights to human beings as agents, then the same should be said for groups. Conversely, if one believes that the right to speak is the prerogative of human beings, then it would be consistent to think that this right does not belong to groups because they are not human beings (and not because they are non-natural agents). I am not saying that List and Pettit would disagree with this position. Rather, I am highlighting ambiguous phrasing within their descriptions. To exemplify:

> Whether or not a group person should exist, and whether it should function within this or that regime of obligation, ought to be settled by reference to the rights or benefits of the individuals affected, members and non-members alike. And it is extremely unlikely that giving group persons equal status with individuals could be in the interest of individuals. (List & Pettit 2011, p. 182)

What is unconvincing about List and Pettit's account is that they define the notion of agent in such a way that it becomes hybridized. An agent is both a

---

[18] On groups as persons, see List & Pettit 2011, pp. 174–178.

[19] According to Rovane, normative individualism comes as a corollary of ontological individualism. It is important to say that by 'normative individualism' Rovane refers to 'moral individualism': normative individualism "recommends that group agents be expressly organized so that they do not dominate their human members, and moreover, so that they safeguard the individual rights and interests of their human members" (Rovane 2014, p. 1664).

performative person and a natural or corporate person. This ambiguity is what makes their discussion of morality not entirely convincing—or this is what I have been contending.

To conclude, it is worth mentioning that metaphysical and second-level normativity are premises that can be found in List and Pettit's view, which is shared by the Big Four. Although, they do not always make it explicit. Indeed, ontological individualism is the only kind of individualism openly defended by all of the Big Four. Ontological individualism generally upholds the ontological priority of individual mental properties, facts, and events over social properties, facts, and events in compliance with the special standing ascribed to individuals as naturally rational beings. This position obscures claims of normative and metaphysical individualism that will be discussed in the next section.

8.4 Second-order assumptions

So far, I have suggested viewing the instability of high-level approaches to group agency in social ontology through a deep-rooted, individualistic mindset, including:

i.   ontological individualism: "the thesis that facts about individuals exhaustively determine social facts" (Epstein 2009, p. 187),

ii.   normative (moral) individualism: "the principle according to which the design of our socio-political institutions should ultimately be sensitive only to the concerns of human beings" (Hindriks 2014, p. 1566), since "something is good only if it is good for individual human or, more generally, sentient beings" (List & Pettit 2011, p. 182),

iii. intentional individualism: the conception that "[A]ny interpretation of an individual's behavior has to be given in terms of individual intentional states" (Schmid 2009, p. 23),

iv.   metaphysical individualism: the claim that rational human beings are *natural persons* or agents (List & Pettit 2011, pp. 170-74),

v.   second-level normative individualism (NI_2): the meta-theoretical characterization of intentional action theory for which agency is first and foremost human agency.[20]

---

[20] The same classification can be found in the Introduction, Section 5.

Such an individualistic mindset at the meta-theoretical level represents a difficult problem to face for those who want to defend a GLA based on holistic individualism. While individual agents are viewed as special components of the (social) world, naturally endowed with the capacity to have preferences and to act intentionally on that basis (Hindriks 2014), groups (and group attitudes) are considered derivative features, supervening on the rational network and normative relations among individuals (Bratman 2014a, 2017, Gilbert 1989, 2013, 2018, Tuomela 2013a). In this sense, the contradictions of the GLA that seemed, at first, to be generated from the individualistic reading of ontological issues emerge as the outcome of the metaphysical notion of agent. This concept influences the doctrine of intentionality and even how to approach agency-related moral questions. Accordingly, the GLA would seem to be just a fictitious perspective, ultimately deriving from the MLA, focused on individual psychology and behavior. In this context, ontological individualism would become an obstacle that the explicative effort of being realistic about groups and group agency has not managed to face successfully because the delicate balance between ontological and methodological issues rests on deeper metaphysical foundations. In fact, the element that has seriously endangered the holistic account, even more so than ontological individualism, has been the metaphysical notion of agent and the normative standard establishing a priority of individual agents, as natural agents, over the corporate units of group agents.[21] Ontological individualism has followed accordingly.

If it remains reasonable to assume that the normative dimension of the theory represents a corollary of ontological individualism, as Rovane suggests,

---

[21] On this basis, we could say that current accounts of group agency have been able to describe such social constructions as the outcomes of processes of recognition, acceptance, commitment, and decision-making procedures that relegate the group agent to the realm of supervenient phenomena, and its explanation to one of useful and yet reducible descriptions. The priority of individual agents, together with the intentional individualism connected to it, makes the intentionality of the group dependent on the intentionality of the individuals and the functional notion of agent subordinated to that of natural agent. In short, the supervenient level has been framed in a way that cannot avoid reduction. This is not a direct reduction of high-level facts to the member-level explanation, which is hindered by multiple realizability and wild disjunction. The reducibility at stake here rather concerns meta-theoretical assumptions of the GLA as a theory: what is reducible is, basically, the group-level account as a description built on the same individualistic premises that are at the root of the MLA. I do not mean to change the premise for the GLA, but base both accounts on anti-individualistic assumptions.

it is primarily because different accounts often concern different definitions of normativity. While Rovane's claim is based on the premise that normative individualism concerns morality, the notion of normative individualism meant here implies considering normativity as second-level normativity. According to this variation, NI_2 becomes a premise of ontological individualism, located on a deeper level compared to the ontological question about what it is that populates the social world. As noted previously, the metaphysical standard represented by individual human beings—combined with the normativism of the approach—is the aspect that has bound the theory to a certain (objective) ontological status granted to human beings as natural agents at the expense of other systems of agency. The ontological position can be viewed as the outcome of a kind of metaphysical anthropocentrism regarding agency: it constructs the social world to be consistent with the normative/metaphysical foundation (cf., Archer 1995, p. 16). Therefore, changing some features in the ontological survey without having prepared the modification within that foundation would be of little use. In fact, if one opts for keeping a substantial correlation between agency and human beings, one will also be bound to a (individualistic) thesis about the ontological issue and to the MLA as its most suitable explanation. The attempt of proposing a GLA in social ontology has failed, partially, because of this underlying implicit perspective about the priority of humans as agents, which is not a consequence of the ontological choice but a grounding condition of the entire research plan.

Such considerations supplement what Chapter Six presented as a double relation between ontological and methodological issues in the social sciences. In that context, I have suggested that the ontological framework, rather than representing a starting point for the description, could be seen as just one side of a bidirectional connection. As claimed, both terms of the relation might be subject to changes whenever the conciliation between the perspectives requires revisions. In this sense, no priority has been ascribed to neither the ontological nor the methodological side.

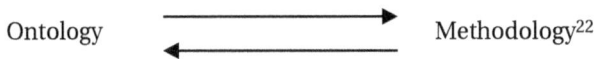

Ontology $\longrightarrow\atop\longleftarrow$ Methodology[22]

Here, it is suggested to assume the priority of metaphysics over both the ontology and methodology endorsed in the explanation.

---

[22] The picture replicates the one proposed in Section 6.2.

Ontology ⟶ Methodology
⟵

⇑

Metaphysics

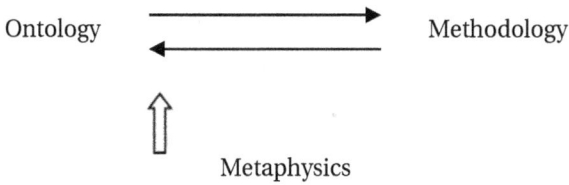

The arrow from metaphysics to the correlation of ontology and methodology is what I have referred to as 'second-level normative individualism'. Given the acknowledgment of the human being as the original agent affects ontological, moral, and methodological assumptions of holistic individualism, it can be argued that such a metaphysical claim fixes the standard and underlies the entire group-level account.

All things considered, one might ask what would happen with the GLA in the context of the proposed critique. If the attempt to defend the high-level approach's irreducibility has been found unconvincing due to reasons that are not attributed to the double connection between methodology and ontology but that are located at the foundation of that association, then a hypothesis for revision could not be addressed because that premise is left undisturbed. In fact, adjusting the balance and providing a stable GLA by working on the ontological picture in view of the problems highlighted by the explanation would not be enough because the entire theory would still rely upon the same (individualistic) metaphysical premise. Instead, one could consider a revision of the ground level—a meta-theoretical range of assumptions that lay the foundations for constructing the theory of shared agency in all its dimensions. The dashed arrow stands for the revision process necessary to overcome the metaphysical bias that, by virtue of second-level normative individualism, determines the instability of the GLA.

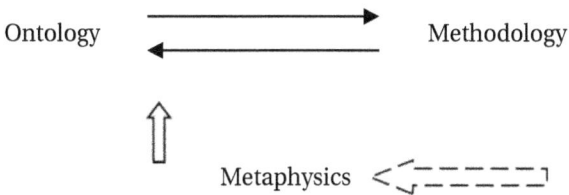

Ontology ⟶ Methodology
⟵

⇑

Metaphysics <⸺ ⸺ ⸺ ⸻

Chapter Nine will focus on the dashed arrow by proposing a possible metaphysical revision related to the definition of an agent.

Chapter 9

Hypothesis for a revision

9.1 Alternative solutions

Pursuing explanatory holism and treating groups as if they were agents has made it necessary to ascribe to groups an objective ontological status that could function as a source of stability for the theory. By adopting the holistic individualism proposed by the Big Five and denying ontological realism about group agents, some inconsistencies in the explanation become unavoidable, as the inquiry developed so far has demonstrated. An obstacle to the revision of the ontological thesis presents itself in the recognition that the ontological dimension is not the deepest foundation of the received account—adjusting the ontological level would require a preliminary modification of its grounds. I suggest that the metaphysical claim that considers the human being to be the paradigmatic agent represents the anti-holistic bias endorsed in the debate (Stoutland 1997). According to this widely accepted anthropocentric view, human-sized agents hold, by nature, a rational and moral stance, according to which individuals are meant to be the ultimate subjects of any form of intentional agency and moral judgment (Hindriks 2014, List & Pettit 2011).

Thus, intentional agency is likely to hold that any kind of intentional behavior is understood in terms of individual intentional behavior. I have been arguing that metaphysical individualism accompanies second-level normative individualism (NI_2): the meta-theoretical characterization of intentional action theory for which agency is, first and foremost, human agency insofar that the explanation of agency, in general, must be related to the explanation of human agency.[1] Therefore, recognizing groups as agents depends on one's willingness to modify the kind of embedded anthropocentrism that exists within agential metaphysics and one's willingness to consider groups as centers of agency, on par with individuals.

As the *desideratum* is to search for the conditions of a stable GLA in social ontology, we could follow one of the alternative strategies: (1) leaving the metaphysical thesis unchanged and advancing a functionalist notion of agency or (2) abandoning metaphysical individualism altogether. Both options represent viable paths to follow, but preference will be given to the

---

[1] See Section 8.3 and 8.4.

latter in this context. To understand this selection, the reasons for discarding the former option are noteworthy. According to the first strategy, individual agents maintain priority, but this should not prevent the development of a group agency theory. Actually, holistic individualism has already attempted a research plan of this kind.[2] Promoting a holistic explanation alongside an individualistic viewpoint about the ontological issue has indeed represented a way to reconcile ontological individualism with divergent explicative objectives. In fact, holistic individualism has proposed a functionalistic notion of agent, according to which an agent is what functions as an agent in society. This notion has somehow allowed a kind of *epoché* about primary individualistic principles framing the definition of agent and left the holistic explicative purpose undisturbed (List & Pettit 2011). As argued in Chapters Seven and Eight, this solution was unsuccessful because the theory was subject to the reduction required not just by ontological individualism but also by intentional and metaphysical individualism(s). In fact, working on confining the implications of metaphysical choices to the meta-theoretical level does not change that, even though inclined to accept group-level facts in the description of the social world, one would still be doomed to ascribe some special status to the individual agent as required by metaphysical individualism. Suppose the functionalistic notion of agent, aimed at taking individual and group agents on par, has failed. In that case, the failure resulted primarily because the (first-order) comparison was conceptualized through a (second-order) priority of individual agents over group agents. Here, the key weak point has been omitting the grounding function of metaphysical concepts, especially when applied to conceptualizing what it means to be an agent. I argued that a point of agreement among those who defend an interpretation of shared agency based on the notion of intentionality is, indeed, the ratification of intentional individualism—proof of metaphysical individualism. In other words, intentional individualism confirms the trend to consider individual human beings as special (if not even the only) agents. This position makes it difficult to acknowledge that holistic individualism could even defend the functional notion of agent it intended to propose.

If we now consider the second solution, abandoning the metaphysical premise, the main, radical implication of this solution would be the denial, in line with the individualistic characterization of being an agent, of the rationality model related to it. Indeed, the intentionalistic action theory is a perspective that complies with a concept of rationality and rational being that vindicates the characteristic nature of the human being as the original bearer

---

[2] A critical investigation of the position has been developed in Chapter Seven.

of that faculty. This view implies that rationality and its connected capacities are typical traits of humans, which are endowed with such 'special gifts' by nature. Therefore, for systems, such as groups, the possibility of belonging to the same kind of beings as humans, i.e., the kind including all 'fully-fledged' agents, is precluded.

In an effort to overcome the limits imposed by metaphysical individualism, I will endorse a form of holism concerning the concept of rationality and rational attitudes that can be ascribed both to human-sized and group-sized agents equally.[3] Pettit's account (1996, 2014) inspires the characterization of agency as a holistic concept: being an agent has been primarily associated with the image of individual agents, endowed by nature with basic skills that can be magnified and improved progressively. The ability to reason, Pettit affirms, "presupposes interaction with others; it is not something that we could enjoy out of society" (Pettit 2014, p. 89). As opposed to what the advocates of the atomistic perspective maintain, the kind of (ontological) individualism associated with (explanatory) holism in holistic individualism appears to be compliant to the holistic assumption regarding the development of individual skills, which are indeed expected to happen gradually, through interaction with other individuals, and by learning how to deal with empirical circumstances as time goes by. Meaning, human beings mature their rationality and capacity to act intentionally and meaningfully in the social world because of constructive relationships entertained with others over time. Therefore, the special rational and moral standing that metaphysical individualism assigns to an individuals' mental properties, as the ultimate 'metaphysical reason' of the social world, does not seem to be the only thing that matters regarding the range of the theory's premises. On the contrary, holistic individualism has the potential to associate the distinctive value of individual mental faculties with the idea that the full flourishing of those faculties requires some horizontal interaction with others of their own kind within a social context of rules and practices (Section 5.3).[4] Although this

---

[3] In this case 'normative' means 'moral'.

[4] Improving the account of shared agency by focusing on horizontal, intra-, and interpersonal relationships is a task that could benefit from recent insights and theoretical perspectives proposed in cognitive sciences and phenomenology. Both research fields encompass huge and multifaceted debates, embracing various, fast evolving viewpoints about the notion of human agency. This book has been giving preference to top-down approaches in social ontology and in the social sciences, considering group-scale events of agency, by focusing especially on intentional behaviors. However, the investigation on shared agency would certainly profit from a dialogue with bottom-up approaches, such as those developed by cognitive scientists

conception is consistent with holistic individualism, it has often been overlooked or not considered in its full meaning and consequences. Thus, the idea has spread that intentionalism is assuming rationality is a natural human capacity. Instead, a major thesis of holism asserts that rationality and agency are better described as processes that shape the rational viewpoint from which the agent operates.

In what follows, I will be addressing the social and diachronic process of rational development as a metaphysically essential aspect of being an agent. Considerations of this kind might be the key to a hypothesis of revision aiming at transforming the individualist notion of agent into a functionalist notion that can be applied to a wider variety of systems indistinctly. Starting from Pettit's consideration that the formation of individual rationality requires (as a necessary condition) an inter-subjective, diachronic process, I will argue that there should be no reason for assigning priority to human-sized agents over groups. This argument dismisses the metaphysical standard responsible for making the received GLA an unstable approach. The focus then changes to finding suitable (second-order) foundations for a (first-level) comparison between agents of different proportions as they all become centers of rational agency over time and through rational efforts.[5]

To briefly foreshadow, it is worth quoting Epstein's point that comes extremely close to the one defended here:

> Our strategy for understanding group intention is no different than the strategy for understanding individual intention. We take both individual and group action to be functionally anchored kinds and take them to play the same functions in their respective systems of practical activity. (Epstein 2014b, p. 248)

Not only should the metaphysical revision support a functionalist explanation of agency, but it is also expected to provide reasons to doubt ontological

---

and phenomenologists (Bianchin 2015, Butterfill, Vesper, Knoblich, & Sebanz 2010, Butterfill 2011, Butterfill & Sebanz 2011, Huebner 2013, Pacherie 2014, Theiner & Wilson 2013, Tollefsen 2002b, Tollefsen & Gallagher 2017, Tollefsen, Kreuz & Dale 2014).

[5] The comparison of individual agents and group agents as systems, equally formed over time and through interaction, can be set especially if we consider such processes as involving not just individuals as human beings but also material components of the environments, rules, costumes and, of course, individual, group, and artificial agents. In this sense, any type of system that becomes an agent would be the result of complex and extensive interactions with the environment as well as with the other agents that populate it.

individualism. If found convincing that any agency system is formed through social and temporal processes, then it should be rather inconvenient to ascribe different ontological statuses to different instances of being an agent.

9.2 On different premises

Given the inclusion of diachronic and social dimensions among the premises of intentional agency, greater attention should be paid to the role of time and interaction. The challenge is to see what the effects of such processes on the GLA might be. Decoupling the functionalist notion of agent from the prioritization of the individual over other kinds of rational systems is the strategy I will pursue. The objective is to argue that if the *functional* notion of agent has not produced a stable account with respect to complex systems, it was primarily because of metaphysical individualism—assuming that individuals are entitled to an indispensable rational priority—which required establishing a group rational autonomy that relies on individuals' rationality. This is the reason why the GLA has been conceived as ultimately reducible to the MLA. However, once the notion of agent is adequately conceptualized and applied both to individuals and groups, the two occurrences of the concept should be treated, if not in the same way, at least similarly. Individuals constitute groups, which does not allow a perfect analogy. However, the focus here is not on what constitutes the systems realizing the notion of agent; but rather on agency status, which should be applied without relying upon different degrees of complexity in material constitution. In this respect, I find it useful to dwell upon the notion of performative person proposed by List and Pettit and generally shared by those who acknowledge the salience of talks on group agency. According to the performative person account, any system can function as an intentional agent insofar as it fulfills the conditions that the notion implies, such as: (1) being receptive to the stimuli of the environment, (2) processing/accommodating those stimuli, (3) intervening in the environment based on (1) and (2).[6] Let us take social groups as an example. The list of requirements says that as long as a group intervenes in the social context based on any reason, the group can be defined as an agent

---

[6] The list of requirements is inspired by List and Pettit's definition of agents (List & Pettit 2011, p. 20).

(French 1979, List & Pettit 2011).[7] This characterization of group agents especially applies to organized groups, in which a certain network of relations among the members secures the unity of the group around some decision-making procedure. If a group follows the procedure, then the complexity of reasons adopted through it constitutes the group's rational point of view. As a part of the organization, each member is committed to playing her role in performing the group's goal, even when this performance conflicts with her personal inclinations (Hess 2020).

This account of group agency embraces a minimal concept of being an agent, according to which an agent is a system that fulfills some basic requirements. If each condition is met, the social group interacts with the environment and intentionally intervenes in it. Therefore, groups come into agency with all of the tasks and duties connected with the concept in the same way individuals do. In fact, as Pettit suggests, the rational point of view of individual agents defines itself over time and through a constitutive interaction with the social context. Following this suggestion, one could argue against metaphysical individualism about 'agent' by assuming that there is no reason why we should defend the derivative character of group intentional agency as opposed to the primitive nature of individual agency, as both capacities are the outcome of diachronic, social processes.

List and Pettit's proposal sticks to the functionalist thesis until they introduce the notion of natural person, which serves to ensure a fair moral framework that preserves human dignity in the face of group interests: "While we agree that group agents count as persons, and that they are inevitably given certain rights, we deny that the rights they enjoy are on a par with the rights of natural persons" (List & Pettit 2011, p. 180). Generally shared by the Big Four, this point is fundamentally important in a theory that does not intend to limit itself only to speculative aspects but, on the contrary, wants to confront practical and ethical questions. And I certainly do not mean to deny the specificity of human rights. Rather, what I have in mind is reframing the imbalance between individuals and groups by distinguishing the moral issue from the performative one. We might, for instance, rephrase the quotation

---

[7] This definition of being agent is mainly concerned with functional organizations centered on decision-making mechanisms. I am not going to argue in favor of the fact that also other kinds of organization deriving, for example, by the division of labor among the parties can guarantee the instantiation of agentive properties (Bird 2015, Hess 2014, Theiner 2018). However, I find the functionalist model could also be applied to organized social groups in which the ability to act is based on different ways of achieving cohesion.

and say the following: *While we agree that group agents count as performative persons, and that they are inevitably given certain rights, we deny that the rights they enjoy as performative persons are on a par with the rights of human beings.* Qualifying 'persons' as 'performative persons' is, I believe, a legitimate move because the notion of person assumed by List and Pettit is performative and opposed to that of the person in the substantial or intrinsic sense (List & Pettit, pp. 170–171). While the former defines a person by what it does, the latter defines a person by considering what it is. Characterizing a person as natural can, therefore, have two meanings. In the first case, the appeal would be to the substantive conception that ascribes meaning to natural persons based on their metaphysical nature. In the second case, the person would be called natural based on how it has come to have the properties that qualify it as such. Therefore, a person would be 'natural' whenever the properties of being a person were derived from factors possessed by nature and not acquired through practice. Since the former hypothesis is explicitly discarded by List and Pettit, the only option left is the latter, which, however plausible it may sound, is not strong enough to support the introduction of the normative discrepancy between individual-sized and human-sized agents. In fact, if an agent is a performative person, and if a performative person is defined by what the person does, it remains unexplained how a system that performs the function of agent could affect its status to the point of implying different ways of being an agent.[8] Besides being unconvincing, this seems at odds with how List and Pettit have characterized their notion of agency and personhood in functionalist and performative terms.

Even assuming that how a system is or has become an agent might be decisive to the identification of its own nature—the differences between individuals and groups do not seem to warrant that the two types of systems necessarily correspond to different types of agent or performative person. To demonstrate, I would like to draw on Rovane's theory. Suppose the argument proves

---

[8] In an insightful piece on corporate legal personality, Dewey discusses the misunderstanding arising from speaking of personal rights as natural rights and from attempting to refer such personal/natural rights to all persons including legal persons, which are persons though not by nature. Dewey contends that one should not consider natural personality when dealing with legal matters: "for the purposes of law the conception of 'person' is a legal conception; put roughly, 'person' signifies what law makes it signify" that is "a right-and-duty-bearing unit" (Dewey 1926, p. 655, p. 658). The person in this field is simply the legal person. I would like to argue for something similar regarding agency: 'person' signifies what action theory makes it signify, i.e., performative person. To invoke the notion of natural person rather leads to considerations that derive from the nature of the agent and not from its status as performative person.

convincing and shows that the process that constitutes agency can be treated analogously in the case of the individual and as well as of group agents. In that case, the distinction between the rights of individual-sized agents and group-sized agents should be based on whether, in addition to agency status, they are human beings. In this sense, if it is right to grant certain rights to individual-sized agents this does not depend on their being agents but on their being human creatures. Then, human beings will also have rights related to agency, but these rights will have to be shared by any system, including groups, that qualifies for agency status under the same circumstances.

Perhaps the most problematic aspect of List and Pettit's account is what Rovane broadly defines as a certain type of rhetoric, which discriminates against group-sized persons as persons that are denied full personhood. Based on such rhetoric, "they might have some of the distinguishing capacities of persons, but in such diminished degree that they cannot really be engaged with as persons" (Rovane 1998, p. 120). In Rovane's view, this conception is guilty of hypocrisy that can be unmasked and avoided by concentrating on the fundamental principles of being an agent, which apply—Rovane suggests—to both individuals and groups.[9] These fundamental principles are the following: "(1) a person is something with a first-person point of view; (2) the identity of a person consists in the unity and continuity of such a first-person point of view; (3) the first person point of view of an individual person need not coincide with an individual soul or an individual animal" (Ibid., p. 14). To put it in the terminology adopted so far, the first tenet holds that an agent is a system with a first-person point of view—that is, the point of view from which a person deliberates and decides what would be best to do (Rovane 1998, p. 21; p. 80). The rational point of view is a perspective that the agent commits to in an effort to ensure her full rationality and to guarantee her own personal identity. In light of this, Rovane characterizes the notion of a rational point of view as essentially normative: "a rational point of view is something in which contradictions and conflicts ought to be resolved, implications out to be accepted, preferences ought to be ranked, means and consequences ought to be taken into account [...]" (Ibid., p. 21). Essential to being an agent is the commitment to achieve overall rational unity (Ibid., p. 23). For the unifying project to be carried out successfully, the agent will have to exercise intentional control over the reasons that move her action and select only those compatible with the overall rational unity. Therefore, deliberation is an ongoing, goal-oriented,

---

[9] Rovane also admits the case of multiple personalities, that is, the presence of multiple agents within a single human being (Rovane 1998, 2004).

universal effort that is inherent in all agents: its goal "is to bring the events that fall within the agent's domain of intentional control into line with the dictates of its rational point of view, so that what it does is what it has most reason to do" (Ibid., p. 86).

Thus, the first two principles tell us that for any system to be an agent, it must be capable of deliberation, commitment, and intentional control. The development of these three characteristics leads the system to define a rational unifying project that is the distinctive viewpoint of any agent. No system could ever possess that viewpoint by nature, not even a human being. On this point, Rovane clarifies that,

> [...] what human beings are born with is a capacity to deliberate, which cannot be exercised at all until fairly late in its cognitive development; and insofar as human beings are born with a capacity to deliberate, they are also born with a potential to form a deliberative point of view by coming to recognize different deliberative considerations as things to be taken into account together. (Rovane 2014, p. 1680)

All that human beings naturally possess is potential, not a current condition of being rational agents. Hence, "[...] once the process of deliberation begins, there arises within the human being a temporally extended deliberative point of view that encompasses more than 'current' thoughts" (Rovane 2014, p. 1681). This explains why with the third principle Rovane assumes that an agent's rational point of view does not have to coincide with a system of human proportions. The project of rational unification could be based on an effort involving several subjects, as in the case of group agency, or only part of the rational activity of a single subject, as found in cases of multiple personalities. Therefore, the personal viewpoint will neither be bound by necessity to a single soul nor a single body as each agent identifies with some specific rational purpose and not with the consciousness or body of the system that achieves it. Most recently, Rovane has clarified that,

> as human beings come to exercise their deliberative capacities, in order to coordinate thoughts and actions for the sake of realizing various goals, there is no metaphysical or natural necessary that dictates that they must forge rational unity within the biological boundaries set by their existence as separate organisms; and so there is no metaphysical or natural necessity that they must forge deliberative points of view that fall one-to-one with human bodies and human centers of consciousness. (Rovane 2014, p. 1682)

Having tied the notion of agent to a rational unifying process and a commitment to its fulfillment thus allows for no discrimination among systems that qualify as agents. Rovane notes that some might still believe that "human beings would already have to be persons in order to generate persons" (Rovane 1998, p. 185) and replies that the issue is not a paradox but a puzzle that should be framed in the right way, which means by setting aside the individualistic bias. The point is not to determine whether the human-sized person generally forms before higher or lower-sized persons. Something important to understand is that no individual could ever participate in the formation of the group's rational point of view as a single person who contributes to the collective undertaking. Individuals together forge the group's point of view by assuming that point of view themselves. Members are not autonomous persons participating in the group but are contributors who together create a viewpoint that is specific to the group. Participants do not need to become persons before taking part in the formation of a person. The possibility of group agency, as well as that of multiple personalities, is opened up by the fact that the contributions subsumed under the same point of view can belong (1) to the activity of a single human being in its rational integrity and temporal continuity, (2) to a group of human beings who communicate with one another and make commitments to one another, (3) to just one part of the rational life happening inside a single human being that is distinguished from other parts of the rational life happening inside that human being committed to some other rational plan.[10]

It appears that the Big Five want to account for at least the first two cases without, however, refraining from assigning a metaphysical, and therefore normative, priority to human-sized agents.

9.3 The subject of group agency

To defend the idea that the group-level account is an indispensable theory focused on a domain other than the one considered by the member-level account, it has been argued that the attribution of intentionality and agency to social groups might become feasible by questioning the principle that individuals are agents of a fundamental kind. I have referred to this principle as metaphysical individualism and explained to what extent ontological, intentional, and moral individualism derives from it. Then, the suggestion has

---

[10] The third scenario can happen both in cases of psychic disorder and when the subject compartmentalizes in a very rigid way her reasoning according to the various activities. For example, one may be a different person depending on whether she is playing or working.

been that, to legitimize realistic claims about group agency, we should first revise the characterization of what being an agent means by starting from the individualistic, metaphysical foundation of the notion. On this point, Section 9.2 observed how Rovane has provided a fruitful approach for addressing the scope: shift the focus from the human being to the process that constitutes the very notion of agent. This reorientation has allowed for a minimal notion of agent, applicable to different circumstances, each of which would be neither reducible to nor derived from the other. The crucial aspect is to recognize that agency can be embodied in systems of variable size and complexity. Such variability has not only been important for studying the metaphysics of personhood but has also been developed in the cognitive sciences, especially among those who work on socially distributed cognition (SDC). In general, SDC assumes that "what constitutes the relevant unit of cognitive analysis is not fixed but can change dynamically within the context or development of a cognitive activity" (Theiner 2018, p. 234). Regarding groups as socially extended systems, SDC's main claim is that designing the group rational activity based on the party contribution does not mean that all actions are based on cognitive processes, reducible to individual mental attitudes. Indeed, the notion of mind, traditionally characterized as a self-conscious mind (Block 2008), does not overlap with the concept of cognition, which refers to the capacity of receiving, processing, and giving information. This definition is reminiscent of List and Pettit's description of the agential system, excluding its development into the notion of natural/corporate performative person (List & Pettit 2011, p. 20). As long as a system meets the requirements of cognition, it can be described as a cognitive system, regardless of how it is materially composed. Cognitive systems are not necessarily instantiated by individual human beings; on the contrary, they may extend to artificial as well as social systems. Within these systems, human beings count as members (Wilson 2004). SDC suggests interpreting group mentality as a kind of rational unity shown by cognitive systems of variable matters and sizes that change over time and through interaction (Theiner 2018). Whenever there is unity in the high-level (group-level) process that enacts cognitive activity, SDC takes the process to be the actual bearer and realizer of such cognitive activity. No member-level contribution or mere aggregation of contributions, aside from the entire system, could ever recreate the process or lead to the same result. In this sense, groups are considered to have emergent cognitive properties that go beyond the properties of the individuals; as such, properties are not present at the members' level.

Although it sounds like a bit of a stretch, there are reasons to say that this perspective has clear points of contact with Rovane's theory (despite being grounded on different assumptions). Both accounts view the agent's point of view as a ceaseless process of rational unification, which can be embodied in systems of different kinds and dimensions. Moreover, in both cases, rationality (Rovane) and cognition (SDC) are dissociated from the concept of soul and self-conscious mind, respectively.

An example of SDC in the cognitive sciences is provided by the so-called transactive memory system (TMS). In TMS, a group of individuals pursues a goal by divvying up the labor (both practical and cognitive) and relying upon the knowledge, memories, and skills (once again, both practical and cognitive) of the participants.[11] Considering the case study of a group assembling a radio (Liang, Moreland & Argote 1995), TMS is a mechanism that emerges from the organization, training, and habitual practices of the participants, who solve the problem of assembling the radio through the individual expertise and mutual trust. In particular, TMS occurs if and only if the group is trained to develop the following conditions:

- memory differentiation: the tendency of group members to specialize in recalling distinct aspects of the assembly process,

- task credibility: how much members trust one another's expertise,

- task coordination: the ability of group members to work together smoothly.[12]

Because 'group cognition' refers to group-scale mechanisms performing rational activities that cannot be deduced by aggregating all the attributes of its constituents and because TMS is a group-scale mechanism of that kind, TMS can be (and has been) viewed as a form of group cognition.[13] Group members are still parts of the process—they are the nodes of the network on which cognition distributes. However, when taken singularly, they do not bear the group's perspective. Rather, that perspective is embedded within the whole system. The group members share the cognitive activity by contributing to a cognitive process that cannot be reduced to any I-mode/we-

---

[11] TMS has been first studied by Daniel Wegner (Wegner, 1986, 1995) and proposed by Theiner et al. as a good example of emergent cognitive mechanisms (Theiner & O'Connor 2010; Theiner, Allen & Goldstone 2010).

[12] Cf., Theiner & O'Connor 2010, p. 93.

[13] The argument is discussed and objected in Ludwig 2015, pp. 189–224.

mode member-level attitudes and forms of interaction.[14] Thus, similar to what Rovane suggests, it is noticeable within the framework of SDC that the bearer of the overall rational point of view is the system taken as a whole. The system is not necessarily a mind. However, the mind—in the sense of brain and head—instantiates the example par excellence of cognitive system, which has, after all, questioned its metaphysical priority over other kinds of cognitive systems.

Broadening the applicability of 'cognitive system' is not the same as saying that all systems function equally or that all systems could bear similar cognitive properties. It merely means that there can be heterogeneous cognitive systems, all able to do some cognitive labor in their interaction with the environment. As noted in Rovane's view, when it comes to rationality (and agency), the nature of the realizer does not matter because the issue for SDC, as well as for Rovane, is not determining what a mind is but what scale of analysis fits with the cognitive process under investigation (Hutchins 1995).[15]

While metaphysical individualism limits the boundaries of intentionality to human beings, SDC finds that those boundaries are flexible, dynamic, and sensitive to contextual, temporal, and social forms of influence. This shift of perspective emphasizes to what extent "choosing the brain as our unit of cognitive analysis" has led to a misframed image of group rationality and intentional action (Theiner 2018, p. 244). Rovane's metaphysics of personhood and SDC accounts in the cognitive sciences prove that overcoming the impasse generated by the image of human beings as prime cognizers is an urgent issue shared by distinct disciplines. It is worth specifying that the projects and scopes pursued by the two approaches are different, and analogies are particularly related to explanations of group-scale phenomena that have uncovered some

---

[14] Group-scale cognitive processes are not reducible to individual-level mechanisms, since they show aspects that exceed the contribution of the individual agents (heterogeneity), depend on the organizational structure of the group (organization-dependence), can be neither intended nor foreseen by the members (novelty), and can be equally realized by many different low-level arrangements (multiple-realizability). On the irreducibility of group-scale cognition, see Theiner 2018, Theiner, Allen & Goldstone 2010.

[15] This view implies a paradigm shift in action theory and philosophy of mind, with relevant connections to the notion of extended mind (Chalmers & Clark 1998) and to the interplay of methodological assumptions concerning the philosophy of group agency (Hindriks 2014, List & Pettit 2011, Tollefsen 2006, 2015), social metaphysics (Epstein 2015, List 2018, Rovane 2014, 2004), philosophical functionalism (Fodor 1974) and recent works on social distributive cognition (Hutchins 1995, Theiner & O'Connor 2010, Rupert 2005).

critical aspects of the intentionalistic view and demonstrated the necessity of modifying the anthropocentric paradigm of the subject to extend the notion beyond humankind to other suitable systems.

9.4 How does the GLA relate to the MLA?

Once the notion of agent is disassociated from the individualistic metaphysical premise, it should become possible to compare individual and group agency based on the equal status they gain. Each case consists of an action ascribable to an agent and intentionally directed towards the fulfillment of a goal represented in the content of the intentional attitude. This comparison does not imply that individual and group agency are the same; in fact, differences reside in the subject, the complexity of the goal, and the variety and number of efforts needed to realize it. For what concerns the subject, the MLA and the GLA diverge due to the system that bears the intention and performs the action. On the one hand, any interpretation of shared agency that intends to study the phenomenon regarding individual behavior and psychology is expected to offer a member-level account. On the other hand, when the entire group counts as the subject of intentional behavior, the theory proposes a group-level account. Thus, the two accounts assume different perspectives of shared agency when it happens in group-scale contexts. Considering the classification based on the dimensions of shared agency considered so far (Section 1.1 and 4.1), the MLA and the GLA represent alternative perspectives as micro/macro views on the phenomenon. Then, each account focuses on specific traits by slicing the descriptive dimension based on its perspective and adopting adequate theoretical tools to provide appropriate explanations of those descriptive components. When the perspective is a micro-level investigation focused on member-level details, the account will certainly show high degrees of complexity, focused on the content, the mode, and the interconnection of individual attitudes. Then, in the case of a macro-perspective, details will give way to broader theoretical horizons, looking at the group of agents as a single group agent with unified group-level attitudes enacted through the performance of the system as a whole. As a result, the account is granular when it is least comprehensive and most comprehensive when least granular. In other words, we can say that if compared to the dense network of attitudes, commitments, and phenomenological perspectives investigated by the MLA, the GLA is a panoramic view, centered on a portion of reality, composed of social events that are studied in the framework of a macro-level account.[16]

Different levels of analysis are conceded by the fact that various kinds of beings can be agents—including systems consisting of more than one singular individual. This is the reason why I find the proposal developed in this book to be in line with the anti-singularist perspective (Pettit 2014).

Moreover, the multiple realizability of agency allows for analogous group-level performances that can differ in member-level contents, modes, and objects of intentions. The same group action can be associated with different forms of individual experience without necessarily affecting the nature of the action.[17]

To conclude, it is important to point out that not all intentional actions carried out by two or more individuals together can be the target of a group-level account. In fact, if the action does not depend on the organization of the parties and if it does not enact any group-level attitude, then the group is not a system that functions as an agent. So, it would be misleading to introduce some high-level subject in the theory. An exemplary case is that of crowds, formed by scattered individuals, who follow common tendencies but do not show any group rationality (Le Bon 1985). However, such cases can be well explained by the MLA and classified as individual or even joint actions, which do not show any decision-making process or division of labor stable enough to ensure a rational unity of the members. While people might follow a common goal and perhaps even some shared rules during a mass demonstration, the overall activity is not a single action. Instead, it seems to be an aggregate of individual actions directed towards some specific shared goal. What is missing is a group decision-making process, mutual expectations, and a plan to guide everyone's contribution as part of the same initiative. Therefore, the group cannot be considered as an agent, and thereby,

---

[16] Claiming that the GLA does not offer a fine-grained analysis of individual-level facts does not necessarily exclude that the range of questions asked by member-level accounts might concern group-level facts as well. Assuming groups are agents, it makes sense to ask what kinds of thoughts, rational processes, and phenomenological experience (if any) affect supra-individual rational systems specifically (List 2016).

[17] A further implication of multiple realizability is that group agents and individual agents represent different instantiations of the same concept, because they both satisfy requirements, including being receptive to the stimuli of the environment, processing those stimuli, and intervening suitably in the world. Therefore, individuals and groups can be agents, not because they coincide with one (or a set of) natural person(s), but because they have become performative persons themselves.

the GLA does not apply. Nevertheless, such socially oriented behavior can be studied through the MLA.[18]

In light of these considerations, Chapter Ten aims to re-read the four agency relations through an account that disengages from metaphysical individualism and, therefore, from the imbalance between individual-sized and group-sized agents.

---

[18] Some authors have focused on the ability that a group of agents might have to organize into a group agent and thus solve a collective problem like reducing pollution. The main idea behind this project is that the ability to act as a group is mediated by the group-formation process, which charges the individuals with the responsibility of forming a group agent (Collins 2019, List & Koenig-Archibugi 2010, Pinkert 2014, Wringe 2019). Although this intuition advances an interesting perspective on group agency, here I consider cases of this sort as pertaining to the member-level account and still not suitable to be considered as proper phenomena of group agency.

Chapter 10

Agency relations in the GLA

This chapter dwells upon the implications that abandoning metaphysical individualism might have on the four agency relations of shared agency. The goal is to outline a non-reductive account of agency suitable for explaining intentional actions performed by systems of different proportions, specifically focusing on groups.

10.1 Constitutive relation

The first way to explain the constitutive relation says that intentional attitudes and actions are constitutive parts of agency.[1] In particular, among the Big Four, Searle has considered the combination of intending and acting as the nucleus of agency both in cases of individual and collective activities (Searle 2010). Taking the latter into consideration, the intention and the action correspond to occurrences performed by the individuals from a collective perspective. This point of view is characterized by the plural grammatical form of the attitudes (we-attitudes) and the belief that other individual agents cooperate towards the goal. Nonetheless, the 'we' just counts as an epistemological standpoint in the individuals' minds, namely "a psychological primitive in the individual heads of individual agents" (Searle 1997, p. 449). More directly, "the fact that I have a we-intention does not by itself imply that other people share my we-intention, or even that there is a 'we' that my we-intentions refer to" (Searle 1997, pp. 449–450). Thus, the structure of collective intentional behavior is compatible with a kind of methodological individualism[2] because it treats individuals as subjects of we-intentionality while keeping collective attitudes in mind. Consequently, in Searle's account there is no need to introduce a genuine group perspective or a GLA distinct from the MLA (Section 7.2.1).

---

[1] This definition is not a challenging aspect in the context of holistic individualism, because the approach has generally focused on others meaning of the relation (Section 6.4.1 and 7.2.1).

[2] I mean methodological individualism to be different from the epistemological one. See Section 7.2.1.

In addition to Searle's interpretation of the constitutive relation, holistic individualism has associated that dimension to another facet of constitution that regards the chance of taking the normative relation to be constitutive of shared agency. I have presented this hypothesis in Section 8.2 as an assumption that complies with acknowledging shared agency as a social practice aimed at pursuing a common goal, jointly obtainable through individual agents intending and acting as a group. Hence, I argued the normative bond connecting individuals to one another as partners constitutes shared agency—without that normative constraint, no group agency could have ever occurred. In line with this position on the constitutive relation, the GLA of holistic individualism procured a model of shared agency as group agency that was different from individual agency; the latter did not need the normative bond that brings the members together in a group. In fact, this process of constitution requires normative attitudes that individual agency does not necessitate thanks to the special status attributed, as a premise, to individual agents. As human-sized subjects are meant to be capable of acting intentionally by nature, shared agency cannot be a phenomenon of the same kind. However, if one is disposed to abandon such individualistic assumptions, the constitution of agency becomes a necessary process within both group and individual agency. Given that the rational point of view is considered the result of an ongoing process, it can be assumed that the intentional perspective develops over time through normative commitment, deliberation, and interaction with the social environment both in individual and group contexts. Therefore, if different rational steps brought together by an act of commitment constitute group intentions, the same should apply to individual attitudes. It follows that the GLA of the constitutive relation is not reducible to the MLA because neither of the two perspectives comes before the other. The GLA focuses on the system, whereas the MLA concerns the psychology of the parts.

Based on the functionalist view, group and individual agency can be two instantiations of the same notion—i.e., agency—and can be considered comparably indispensable and complex.[3] On one side, each element is necessary because they concern a rational system of agency as the subject of

---

[3] This comparison has brought theorists of the continuity thesis to say that the GLA is compatible with methodological individualism. Here I would like to affirm the contrary: if both groups and individuals function as agents, it is not because groups function as individuals. Rather, the comparison aims at understanding any rational system as a complex and diachronically anchored whole, bearing attitudes from a point of view that is not a given.

intentional behaviors. On the other side, each component is complex because any kind of intentional agency can occur only within a social and diachronic process of constitution of the rational perspective from which intentional attitudes and actions can derive.

10.2 Structural relation

The action theory based on intentionality "sees the intentions of individuals as plan states" (Bratman 2014a, p. 18) which give a structure to individual behavior by fixing its target. In addition to representing the goal of every single action, the intentional character of agency also secures the consistency of each individual action to the activities performed either by the same individual over time or with the contribution of other agents. Then, intentionality ensures the coherence of each individual's actions with the scope it aims to realize. Thus, the role of intentional attitudes regards the structure of individual agency and the structure of shared agency as a derivative. In fact, the approach "takes the intentions of individuals seriously as basic and distinctive elements of individual human agency" (Bratman 2014a, p. 11). To summarize, individuals' intentionality might generate (1) individual intentions for the action directed to individual performances (individual agency), (2) individual intentions of contributing to shared performances (*continuity thesis* of intentionality), or (3) we-intentions located in the mind of each and oriented towards some common goal (*discontinuity thesis*). Regardless of what interpretation one adopts, intentional attitudes establish the target of the individual contribution as a participant/group member. Accordingly, they would also represent the first step towards the organization of shared agency as a group intentional performance. Thus, in the case of both original collective attitudes and meshing individual sub-plans, to speak of group planning attitudes requires the mediation of the MLA, which operates at the level of the members by grasping the structure of individual (group-oriented) agency as a fundamental component of the whole.

What if individuals' intentions are no longer considered basic and distinctive elements? Would the GLA still need the mediation of the MLA? In some sense, it would. If the structural relation is a relation that, by definition, happens over time and in conjunction with further intentions aimed at the realization of a broader goal, referring to those steps still represents an unavoidable theoretical move. Indeed, the structural dimension itself implies such mediation (Section 3.4.2, 6.4.2, and 7.2.1). However, being the outcome of a process composed of several stages is not equivalent to being reducible to those components, especially if (at the meta-theoretical level of reasoning) there is no priority attributed to them. The GLA refers to member-level facts the same way in which the MLA refers to each attitude involved in the diachronic, inter-subjective process that prepares the individual intention for the action. None of the two cases necessitates reduction, or so I have argued. In fact, if the low-level process is not granted metaphysical priority over the higher-level one, individual and group agency may just represent two different forms of agency—where the former is about the parts and the latter concerns the entire agential process. Accordingly, the structural relation can intervene both at the higher and the lower level of reality and description.

In line with such considerations, the structural relation between intending and acting can maintain relevance without the GLA being reducible to the MLA. More precisely, the relation can exert a double influence at both levels. As showcased in Chapter Three and Chapter Six of this book, the first dimension of the structural relation pertains to the role exerted by each intention in guiding and securing the consistency/coherence of every single action, whereas the second dimension refers to the organization of all contributions towards the same goal. Concerning the MLA, I noted that the structural relation works in the same way in both cases that the efforts are sub-plans of the same, individual agent occurring at different temporal moments and in the case that they are intentions belonging to different subjects. Such continuity is supported particularly by Bratman's view based on the fact that diachronic and shared agency can be treated equally (Bratman 2014a). Now, regarding the GLA, I want to suggest that the comparison between micro- and macro-level structural relations finds its roots in the equal status one can ascribe to individual-sized and group-sized agents. This way of interpreting the issue also has repercussions on the MLA framework. The difference, if compared to Bratman's perspective, consists in questioning the special position allocated to individuals as primitive subjects of rational attributes from which the construction of any diachronic and social agency starts. In contrast, my proposal considers that the notion of individual agent (and agency) also needs the diachronic and social dimension as transcendental conditions necessary for turning individual human beings into individual agents capable of intentional action.[4] In this sense, the vectors of time and social interaction are not external dimensions of a (given) rational point of view. Instead, they are brought into the notion of agent as

---

[4] By reference to Epstein's vocabulary, we could also say that diachronic and social vectors represent anchoring conditions of agency, in the sense that the temporal and social development of agency are what ground the grounding principles of agency, such as collective intentions and commitments. As anchoring aspects (grounds of grounds), the two vectors may ground a model of agency released of intentional individualism and suitable for providing a foundational framework based on which one could account for intentional attitudes and behaviors (Epstein 2014b, 2015).

constitutive and structural features of the individual and the collective meaning of the concept.

10.3 Normative relation

Apart from the second-order normative premise (NI$_2$) of holistic individualism, two additional first-order dimensions of normativity can be found in group agency. On the one hand, the relation regards the constraint that individuals establish as members of the group. On the other hand, normativity concerns the obligation of each member to the pursuit of the collective goal.[5] On this matter, I have been arguing that the GLA collapses downwards on the MLA because the collective commitment to realize the common goal jointly can occur only insofar as the individuals mutually recognize themselves as part of the same whole. The predominant aspect that threatens the GLA is not the theoretical achievement, according to which the group perspective represents the outcome of aggregation and commitment happening inter-subjectively and diachronically. Instead, the particular challenge is the meta-theoretical principle—assuming the naturally given, rational standing of the individual members. I suggest that once the metaphysical premise is abandoned, the issue addressed by the comparison of 'group agent' and 'individual agent' can be seen as a question about whether both kinds of normativity found in group agency contribute to generating individual agency as well. If group and individual agency are particular instantiations of the same concept, it should be possible to describe each case through the same explicative pattern used for the other by setting concrete discrepancies aside.

Let us begin with the most basic normative relation and introduce the second kind of normativity afterwards. First, basic normativity encompasses mutual expectations and obligations that individuals acquire once they have committed themselves to the status of group member/partner (Schweikard 2017a). Such a social/joint commitment shifts the individuals' perspective from an individual to a collective in a way that all that they intend from the new point of view is related to the group context and is intended, not personally, but on behalf of the whole, i.e., in the we/role-mode.[6] This perspective shift works particularly when referring to those theories that defend the discontinuity-

---

[5] Those forms of normativity might be considered as grounding conditions of agency, while NI$_2$ is the anchoring (Section 8.4).

[6] On the relation between role-mode and we-mode intentionality, see Section 5.2. The analysis is based on Schmitz 2017.

thesis account of intentionality.[7] Differently, the continuity-thesis account does not identify any discrepancy between individual and collective intentionality (Alonso 2018). So, the basic normative bond helps to tie the members in stable relationships and establish networks of attitudes and decision-making mechanisms capable of producing original (in List and Pettit's approach) or joint (regarding Bratman's view) group intentions.

I want to suggest that basic normativity easily applies to the analysis of individual agency—thanks to the endorsement of the diachronic and social constitution of the agent.[8] In particular, one way to extend the commitment concerning partner status to the case of individual agency is considering the endorsement of the rational point of view held by the individual as an agent.[9] In fact, the rational perspective characterizing the agent does not coincide with the individual's position as a human being because human beings do not have a rational point of view by nature. Agency is, instead, a capacity that requires the subject (be it individual or plural) to construct a perspective through rational effort directed to the establishment of rational control over future decisions and intentional actions (Rovane 2004, 2014). This attitude in shared agency was denoted as social or joint commitment (Tuomela 2003, Gilbert 1989), and thus can be defined in individual contexts as a commitment to the rational project one pursues as an agent.[10]

Once the rational stance becomes a stable viewpoint, the agent can commit herself to a particular goal as described by the second normative relation. This goal is represented in the intentional attitude's content and is pursued by the rational system, established on the foundation of basic normativity. In this sense, if one accepts the role of basic normativity, for both individual and group agency, the commitment regarding the action's goal can be consequently understood as the subject's obligation to the goal's realization, regardless of the kind of agent involved.

10.4 Causal relation

Chapter Seven argued that the causal dimension—defined as a direct agency relationship between a cause (the mental state) and an effect (the action)—is

---

[7] See Chapter Two.

[8] Since this assumption is missing, "it is argued that joint actions are inherently normative phenomenon and that individualists deny this" (Miller 2007, p. 74).

[9] On rational commitment in individual agency, see Rovane 1998, 2004.

[10] As a normative attitude, this form of commitment exerts a role that we could also define in terms of self-governance, where the self is the subject of agency (Bratman 2018, Schmid 2017a).

excluded from the GLA, as it is accountable for in terms of member-level descriptions (Section 7.2.2).[11] Then, in addition to direct causation, I considered another level of causality that is called 'indirect' or 'supervenience causation'. Theorists of holistic individualism have been questioning the issue of indirect causation, especially in connection to supervenience. Hence, it has been observed that this kind of causal power can be exerted by high-level facts on (1) other high-level facts or (2) individual facts that can be either (2a) facts belonging to the foundation of the social event or (2b) individual facts in general (Section 6.4.4). No matter how one interprets the issue, the causal chain grasped through the GLA faces problems related to the assumption that high-level facts have no objective ontological counterpart in the theory (Section 7.2.2).[12] As long as ontological individualism is preserved, holistic explanations can be incorporated as convenient considerations, and the realistic claim of the group-level account cannot contrast redundancy. In this sense, a group agent "*exists causally objectively as a social system capable of causal production of outcomes in the world in virtue of its we-thinking and 'we-acting' members*" (Tuomela 2013a, p. 47).[13] Therefore, the comparison between group agency and individual agency is compromised, on the ontological side, because individual agents, as group members, have been assumed to be human beings, holding an objective, ontological status and a primitive rational perspective by nature. Consequently, group members have been considered in possession of an original causal power that groups do not have. As Sawyer (2003) remarks, social facts are high-level supervenient facts and can be motors of causal chains insofar as their causal power derives from the power of the members. Following the same line of thought, Tuomela observed that "individuals are ultimately the only causal 'motors' in the social realm" (Tuomela 2013a, p. 50):

> Individual agents are 'in the last analysis' the sole causal initiators or ultimate sources of causation in the social world. There is derivative

---

[11] Direct causation has been included only in Searle's explanation, as a relation between the intention in-action and the bodily movement fulfilling it. This meaning of causation applies to the member-level notion of agency, although it is not suitable for designing high-level explanations of the event. Section 2.3.4 argued that Searle has avoided constructing a GLA.

[12] Case 2a presents also the problem that groups as supervenient phenomena cannot have any causal influence upon their basis, because: (1) supervenience is synchronic; (2) ontological individualism implies the psychological autonomy of the individuals from any social influence, causally speaking (Sawyer 2003).

[13] Italic font in the original.

causation, e.g., the fact of people spending 'too' much money on goods can be the cause of increase in inflation, etc. (Tuomela 2011, p. 309)

According to this account, group agents and high-level facts, in general, have derivative causal powers. The point leaves no room for a non-redundant GLA regarding causation. Nonetheless, by questioning metaphysical individualism and doubting the original status of individual agents, one might seek to contest those premises and underline the similarity of individuals and groups as systems of agency. In fact, if one takes the notion of individual agent to overlap neither with the body nor with the mind of any human being, causal power will become a problem concerning individual agency, too. Indeed, recognizing the first causal motor in the human body or mind would not mean recognizing the first causal motor in the individual agent. As said, individual agents do not coincide with biological beings. Thus, if causal powers do not apply to group agency due to the ephemeral ontological status of group agents, the same causal power should also be discarded in the case of individual-sized agents because—for the sake of argument—no causality could properly refer to the functionalist and fictitious concept of agent. Still, abandoning normative individualism can help question the original status of individual agents with the intent to consider them as systems built over time and through interaction.

By this, I do not mean to argue in favor of no agent having causal powers. Observing that an agent is a system that builds its deliberative point of view over time and through interaction is not the same as describing it as an ontologically fictitious system. Instead of being dissolved, the ontological objectivity of agents could be grounded precisely on a process of construction that, by unifying different components around a single rational plot, guarantees the formation of stable structures that can influence the surrounding environment even causally.

I take the social and diachronic dimensions of agency to develop Sawyer's intuition (Sawyer 2003)—considering agentive properties at different moments in time. Sawyer maintains that although high-level facts cannot exert any causal influence on the individual basis from which they supervene, they could, however, have power on other high/low-level facts happening ahead in time (Section 6.4.4). [14]

---

[14] Figure 10.1 replicates Figure 7.1. On the left, S_1 is a high-level fact that supervenes on a network of individual attitudes. The upwards arrow represents supervenience at time t_1. High-level social fact S_2 and individual-level facts on the right side all happen at time t_2. The thin arrows going from S_1 to S_2 (S-S causation) and from S_1 to Att-$I_{d,e,f}$ (downwards causation) represent eventual causal relations.

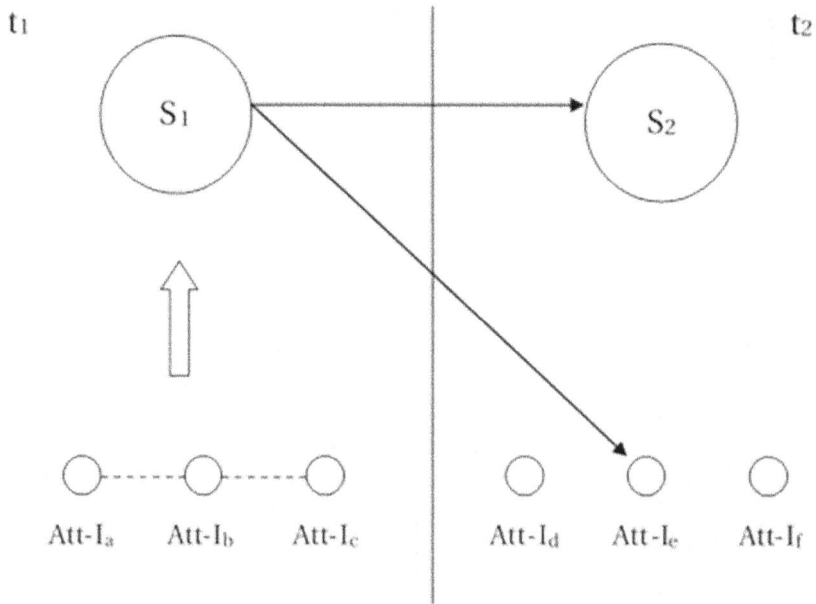

Figure 10.1. Supervenience causation revisited.

Introducing the unfolding of time allows a causal dependence that is not in conflict with the supervenience of social facts on individual facts. Further, the unfolding of time does not lead individual psychology to be subjugated under the direct influence of high-level phenomena.

Even so, the perspective still faces difficulties: as S_1 supervenes on individual attitudes, S_2 will represent an ontologically reducible element. This reduction cannot be contested because it is embedded within holistic individualism as one of its fundamental premises. Therefore, it seems that the causal power of group-level facts can only be understood by assuming their objective status in our ontology.[15] The problem is challenging, and the first step towards solving it focuses on the diachronic dimension of agency. Here, the idea is to interpret time as an inherent dimension of intentional agency rather than a line along which the faculty is exercised as a given. Thus, thinking about agency as a rational capacity constituted over time, through rational effort and commitment, might help conceive the subject of intentional agency as a

---

[15] Theorists of critical realism have endorsed the ontological objectivity of high-level social facts (Archer 1995, 1998a, 1998b, Baskhar 1998, Baskhar and Lawson 1998, Elder-Vass 2010, 2012, 2014).

system made up of multiple steps, all involved in the agent's design and performance of the action. In this sense, groups as high-level facts would not just derive from the snapshot of the individual-level foundation, but they would be formed by all attitudes, rules, reasons, and obligations that have been contributing to the constitutive process of the rational system as well as of its stable rational perspective. Thus, the attitudes of each individual agent would be just part of a process of rational identity formation, establishing, throughout time, a particular perspective that does not need to be traced back to individual intentionality. Although the process, as an open system, involves the members' contribution, the inputs should not be ascribed priority over the entire system. Similarly, one could think of individual agents as rational systems with a perspective that is the (open) outcome of decision-making processes, commitment, and interaction with the world. Given the group system's status of performative person (List & Pettit 2011, Rovane 2014), agency is constructed rather than "naturalistically grounded" (Tuomela 2013a, p. 49)—individual agents are comparable to groups.[16] Both individual and group rational perspectives come to be centers of agency due to a giving-

---

[16] For what concerns the material constitution of agentive systems, this means that any group can be more than the sum of its members just as any individual agent can be more than her physical body. Systems include in their constitution facts incorporated over time and gathered from the environment, such as artificial parts of the body, mechanical tools, computers, physical and social objects (Elder-Vass 2017). This remark crosscuts the increasing sociological interest in socio-materiality studies (Leonardi 2012), focused on forms of intentional agency equally including human (socio) and artificial (material) components, and philosophical concerns about identifying the only foundation of group agency in facts about individuals. In this thought line, Epstein has questioned the supervenience relation endorsed by holistic individualism as a position focused exclusively on facts about individuals. The Starbucks example makes the point clearly: "On a typical day at Starbucks, pots of coffee are being brewed, baristas are preparing frappuccinos, cash registers are ringing, customers are lining up, credit cards are being processed, banks are being debited and credited, accountants are tallying up expenses, ownership stakes are changing in value, and so on. At least on the face of it, some of these facts about Starbucks fail to supervene on facts about the people and their interrelations. To be sure, the employees are critical to the operation of Starbucks. But facts about Starbucks seem also to depend on facts about the coffee, the espresso machines, the business license, and the accounting ledgers. Groups can also be made of rules and material parts even when individual members are lacking" (Epstein 2015, p. 46). If one is disposed to endorse the social and diachronic constitution of agents, the standard account of supervenience (Chapter Six) will be difficult to defend, because it presents the relation as a synchronic relation producing high-level facts ontologically derived from individual-level facts, which are meant to be facts about individuals and, especially, about individual intentional attitudes.

identity process, fixing the consistency and autonomy of the viewpoint based on the continuity created by the rational effort and the commitment to the plan (Rovane 1998, 2004). Thus, if it is reasonable to attribute mental causation to non-fictitious systems of intentional agency, capable of having effects on the environment, group agents should represent first causal motors in the same way that individuals do. By conceding that both systems acquire rational stability diachronically, both systems should be viewed as capable of intervening in the social world due to their equal incorporation of rational stability. Differences would concern the level of complexity associated with each case, but formally, if intentions can have some causal influence on actions, this must be true no matter what instantiation of the concept is in focus. Otherwise, mental causation should be discarded in its entirety.

Conclusion

The world, it seems, runs in parallel, at many levels of description.
You may find that perplexing; you certainly aren't obliged to like it.
But I do think we had all better learn to live with it.
(Fodor 1998, p. 23)

This book has addressed the GLA problem in social ontology—questioning whether the debate has proposed a stable group-level account of shared agency, capable of regarding groups as (proper) subjects of agency. I outlined the main positions and distinguished between two ways of approaching shared agency: shared agency as an exploration of members' mental attitudes, relationships, and behaviors (MLA); and the group-level account (GLA) as an attempt to recognize groups as centers of agency. The latter approach has been found reducible to the former due to the widespread tendency to study shared agency (when conceived as a group-level phenomenon) based on holistic individualism. When studied in this way, holistic individualism maintains that high-level explanations are objective as long as ontological issues are left aside. Therefore, I proposed a framework for devising a non-reductive GLA based on agency's functional and performative properties.

Here, the main thesis defended claims that for how holistic individualism is construed, the GLA is reducible to the MLA. The reason is that holistic individualism upholds ontological individualism based on a second-order, individualistic, metaphysical, and normative premise, fixing the special status of individual agents as human beings, naturally endowed with rationality and intentionality. The premise generates first-order contradictions between reductive ontology and high-level explanations that cannot be solved by working on the two issues directly. Consequently, holistic individualism can propose an MLA where the group is the outcome of members' intentions and actions, but it cannot offer a stable GLA that accommodates group agency accordingly. I conclude that we should revise the approach and abandon individual-sized agents' metaphysical priority and holistic individualism, in turn. This abandonment allows for the construction of a functionalist and performative notion of agent—suitable for grasping any rational system that fulfills the conditions required by intentional agency. The resulting perspective is an account that accepts high-level explanations of agency alongside low-level explanations. The difference from holistic individualism is that, in my view, no form of agency is granted metaphysical priority. Given the capacity to act intentionally is regarded as the result of rational unification, processes of different scales have equal ontological statuses. Therefore, explaining what an agent does should not be affected by what an agent is. The nature of the agent lies precisely in its being a performing system that is committed to the realization of rational plans. This functionalist and performative interpretation of agency is made possible by abandoning the metaphysical bias, resulting in the received functionalist account of agency being combined with the intrisicist idea that agents of human proportions are agents of a special kind. To reject this premise is not to deny that different systems have specific properties. Instead, it denies that the specificity of those properties resides in the nature of the agent as if there were a clear ontological gap between agents of different scales.

The hypothesis for revision started by considering and criticizing the same assumptions that framed holistic individualism. In particular, it questioned the metaphysical priority of the individual's mind, securing its immunity from the influence of high-level social tendencies. This assumption has been called into question considering a further premise of holistic individualism that takes the individual's mind as constituted through interaction with other agents over time. Thus, the rational faculty of individuals can be seen as a skill one develops through interacting with others and learning how to live in a shared social environment:

> Individuality—identification as an individual person—emerges out of a certain kind of social order. Such an order is defined by multiple, distinct spheres of social life, none of which comprehensively defines anyone's agency, individual freedom of mobility among those spheres, and individual membership in multiple spheres. Only when these social conditions are in place can people become individuals, understood as agents authorized to set their own priorities, on their own, according to an autonomously defined self-conception. (Anderson 2001, p. 36)

In this sense, the individual rational perspective loses its priority over group intentionality due to the identity-giving process through which both rational perspectives emerge.

Conceiving individual rationality as the outcome of a process of constitution has allowed us to compare individual and group agents as rational systems developing their rational point of view over time. This conclusion defends a kind of performative and functionalist notion of agent, but it does not imply a homogeneous interpretation of different instantiations of the concept. The homogeneity the proposal claims concerns the explanatory model. If the theoretical *desideratum* is to describe intentional agency and if intentional agency is a phenomenon ascribed functionally to a subject fulfilling its definition, then any system satisfying these conditions should count as an agent—no matter its degree of complexity and how it comes to realize it. Agency is functional: explaining its functioning should work in the same manner across cases. Understanding high-level events should be possible based on the same framework needed to understand the individual-level tokens. Hence, we can define the GLA as a high-level account, analogous to the individual agency account, where agency is attributed to a group rather than ascribed to individuals becoming agents over time and through social interaction. Both agents are rational systems constituted through rational efforts, commitments, and decision-making procedures developed diachronically. Neither of them has a special status, nor are they naturally endowed with an original rational viewpoint that the other does not hold. Therefore, the GLA should not be defined by analogy to the explanation of individual agency because the direction of the comparison going from individuals to groups would keep alluding to the derivative nature of the latter as supervenient phenomena. Rather, I would contend that the processual nature of agency requires us to treat both individual agency and group agency using a non-reductive account based on a performative and functionalist definition of 'agent'. More clearly, treating different instantiations of the same concept equivalently without proposing conceptually or principally redundant accounts. Simplicity is the target.

Yet, simplicity does not necessarily mean homogeneity, and the MLA is proof of that. Illustrating different approaches to the study of shared agency from the individuals' perspective, the member-level account has shown to what extent the case of two or more individuals acting together represents a complex topic of research. This area has been explored by selecting one of the alternative positions between the continuity thesis and the discontinuity thesis of intentionality. The former considers group agency, analogous to individual agency in the sense of being a phenomenon that we can explain with the same theoretical tools required to account for individual agency. Both cases involve individual intentionality in the individuals' minds plus interaction among the parties, either over time or across agents. This account might seem similar to the one proposed in this book. Indeed, the idea of comparing individual and group agency, and employing the same explicative framework for both has been one of the goals of this investigation.

While the goal is similar, methodology and conclusions differ. The continuity-thesis account explains shared agency by endorsing methodological individualism and avoiding the introduction of concepts and principles characteristic of individual psychology. In contrast, my point is to regard shared agency as a particular event in the individual's mind that needs specific concepts and principles. While the continuity-thesis account relates the continuity to the explanation of individual psychology, the approach defended in this study concerns the analogy between tokens of 'agent'. Individual and group agents are equal in that they are both rational systems capable of intentional agency. At the same time, to understand how individual components are committed to the rational individual/collective plan of the individual/group agent, we need concepts suitable for grasping the specificity of attitudes. In fact, attitudes can occur with singular or plural mode based on the context (whether individual or collective). They can refer to other attitudes in the individual's mind, others' attitudes, or attitudes that happened in the past. All of these degrees of complexity belong to psychology and phenomenological experience.

The approach proposed here aligns with the part of the debate embracing the discontinuity thesis of intentionality, which describes shared agency through concepts such as collective intentionality and commitment that are not part of the explanation of individual agency. The version of shared agency sustained by the proponents of the discontinuity thesis studies group agency based on what happens at the members' level. My proposal diverges when I argue that individuals' efforts do not define—at least, not completely—the group as an agent. The group is an agent because it fulfills the criteria of a rational system of agency. The members' intentions and actions are important to grasp the complexity of the event in the same way in which a study of individual psychology can be relevant to understand the constitution of individual agency in depth.

The GLA of holistic individualism has been considered reducible to the MLA because it aims at explaining group agency based on the description of intentionality and agency of group members. As showcased by the way we generally refer to the actions of social groups like committees, orchestras, and universities, group agency does not constitute a distributive form of shared agency. When we say that the contest committee has decided on a winner, we are not talking about what each judge individually thinks. To say that the orchestra gave a marvelous performance refers to the accomplishment of the entire group. Similarly, to state that the university issued us a graduation certificate involves recognizing the university as the subject of that action. The metaphysical, individualistic premise, assuming individuals as primitive subjects, has compromised the functionalist notion of agent—preventing us from considering the group an agent in its own right. The mediation of the member level and the ontological thesis that only individuals exist has made it necessary to frame the GLA based on the MLA without allowing the former to go beyond the latter (Ludwig 2017b). I argued that the strength of ontological individualism has deep roots. In fact, the holistic account has been impeded by the metaphysical notion that establishes the priority of individual agents, as natural agents, over the corporate units of group agents. Such a metaphysical principle works as a normative standard upon which any account of intentional agency has to be given in terms of human agency because the (individual) human being has represented the most original example of agent. I called this position second-order normative individualism (NI$_2$). Then, ontological individualism has followed accordingly.

The present research suggests the abandonment of metaphysical individualism and the treatment of the GLA as a high-level account of agency, structured like the account of individual agency. The MLA can help study how individuals engage themselves in individual and collective contexts of agency, and these can be approached from either the continuity thesis or the discontinuity thesis of intentionality. The member-level account concerns the experience of the parties. The group-level account regards the group as a rational system of agency, considered in its entirety and in analogy to other performative persons—just like individual agents.

List of references

Alonso, F. M. (2018). Reductive views of shared intention. In M. Jankovic & K. Ludwig (Eds.), *The Routledge Handbook of Collective Intentionality* (pp. 34–44). New York: Routledge.

Anderson, E. (2001). Unstrapping the straightjacket of 'preference': A comment on Amartya Sen's contributions to philosophy and economics. *Economics and Philosophy*, 17, pp. 21–38.

Andina, T. (2016). *An Ontology for Social Reality*. London-New York: Palgrave MacMillan.

Anscombe, G. E. M. (1957). *Intention*. Cambridge (MA)-London: Harvard University Press.

Archer, M. S. (1995). *Realist Social Theory: The Morphogenetic Approach*. Cambridge: Cambridge University Press.

Archer, M. S. (1998a). Introduction: Realism in the social sciences. In M. Archer, R. Bhaskar, A. Collier, T. Lawson, A. Norrie (Eds.), *Critical Realism: Essential Readings* (pp. 189–205). London-New York: Routledge.

Archer, M. S. (1998b). Realism and morphogenesis. In M. Archer, R. Bhaskar, A. Collier, T. Lawson, A. Norrie (Eds.), *Critical Realism: Essential Readings* (pp. 356–382). London-New York: Routledge.

Archer, M. S. (2010). Morphogenesis versus structuration: on combining structure and action. *The British Journal of Sociology*, 61, pp. 225–252.

Austin, J. L. (1962). *How to do Things with Words (William James Lectures)*. Oxford: Clarendon Press.

Bach, T. (2016). Social categories are natural kinds, not objective types (and why it matters politically). *Journal of Social Ontology*, 2(2), pp. 177–201.

Bhaskar, R. (1998). Philosophy and scientific realism. In M. Archer, R. Bhaskar, A. Collier, T. Lawson, A. Norrie (Eds.), *Critical Realism: Essential Readings* (pp. 16–47) London-New York: Routledge.

Bhaskar, R. & Lawson T. (1998). Introduction: Basic texts and developments. In M. Archer, R. Bhaskar, A. Collier, T. Lawson, A. Norrie (Eds.), *Critical Realism: Essential Readings* (pp. 3–15). London-New York: Routledge.

Bianchin, M. (2015). Simulation and the we-mode. A cognitive account of plural first persons. *Philosophy of the Social Sciences*, 54(5), pp. 442–461.

Bird, A. (2015). When is there a group that knows? Distributed cognition, scientific knowledge, and the social epistemic subject. *Oxford Scholarship Online*, DOI:10.1093/acprof:oso/9780199665792.003.0003.

Block, N. (2008) Phenomenal and access consciousness. *Proceedings of the Aristotelian Society*, 108, pp. 289–317.

Bratman, M. (1984). Two faces of intention. *The Philosophical Review*, 93(3), pp. 375–405.

Bratman, M. (1987). *Intention, Plans, and Practical Reason*. Cambridge (MA): Harvard University Press. Re-issued by center for the study of language and information, (1999).

Bratman, M. (1990). What is intention?. In P. R. Cohen, J. Morgan, & M. Pollack (Eds.), *Intention in Communication* (pp. 15–32) Cambridge (MA): MIT Press.

Bratman, M. (1992). Shared cooperative activity. *The Philosophical Review*, 101(2), pp. 327–341.

Bratman, M. (1999). *Faces of Intention: Selected Essays on Intention and Agency*. New York: Cambridge University Press.

Bratman, M. (2004). Three theories of self-governance. *Philosophical Topics*, 32(1-2), pp. 21–46.

Bratman, M. (2007). S*tructures of Agency: Essays*. Oxford: Oxford University Press.

Bratman, M. (2009a). Intention, belief and instrumental rationality. In D. Sobel & S. Wall (Eds.), *Reasons for Action* (pp. 13–36). Cambridge: Cambridge University Press.

Bratman, M. (2009b). Intention, belief, practical, theoretical. In S. Robertson (Ed.), *Spheres of Reason: New Essays on the Philosophy of Normativity* (pp. 29–61). Oxford: Oxford University Press.

Bratman, M. (2009c). Intention, practical rationality, and self-governance. *Ethics*, 119, pp. 411–443.

Bratman, M. (2009d). Modest sociality and the distinctiveness of intention. *Philosophical Studies*, 144(1), pp. 149–165.

Bratman, M. (2010). Agency, time, and sociality. *Proceedings and Addresses of the American Philosophical Association*, 84(3), pp. 7–26.

Bratman, M. (2012). Time, rationality, and self-governance. *Philosophical Issues*, 22, pp. 73–88.

Bratman, M. (2013). The interplay of intention and reason. *Ethics*, 123(4), pp. 657–672.

Bratman, M. (2014a). *Shared Agency: A Planning Theory of Acting Together*. New York: Oxford University Press.

Bratman, M. (2014b). Rational and social agency: Reflections and replies. In M. Vargas & G. Yaffe (Eds.), *Rational and Social Agency: The Philosophy of Michael Bratman* (pp. 294–343). New York: Oxford University Press.

Bratman, M. (2015). Shared agency: Replies to Ludwig, Pacherie, Petersson, Roth, and Smith», *Journal of Social Ontology*, 1(1), pp. 59–76.

Bratman, M. (2017). The intentions of a group. In E. W. Orts & N. C. Smith (Eds.), *The Moral Responsibility of the Firm Revisited*. Oxford: Oxford University Press.

Bratman, M. (2018). *Planning, Time, and Self-Governance: Essays in Practical Rationality*. New York: Oxford University Press.

Brentano, F. (1874). *Psychologie vom empirischen Standpunkt*, 3 vols., Hamburg: Felix Meiner Verlag.

Burge, T. (1986). Individualism and psychology. *The Philosophical Review*, 95(1), pp. 3–45.

Butterfill, S. A. (2011). Joint action and development. *Philosophical Quarterly*, 62(246), pp. 23–47.

Butterfill, S. A. (2017). Collective action and agency. In M. Jankovic & K. Ludwig, (Eds.), *The Routledge Handbook of Collective Intentionality* (pp. 68–82), New York: Routledge.

Butterfill, S. A. & Sebanz N. (2011). Joint action: What is shared? Introduction to the special issue. *Review of Philosophy and Psychology*, 2(2), pp. 137–146.

Butterfill, S. A., Vesper C., Knoblich G., & Sebanz N. (2010). A minimal architecture for joint action. *Neural Networks*, 23(8-9), pp. 998–1003.

Castelfranchi, C. (2015). Healing social sciences' psycho-phobia: Founding social action and structure on mental representations. In A. Herzig & E. Lorini (Eds.), *The Cognitive Foundations of Group Attitudes and Social Interaction* (pp. 25–57). Cham-Heidelberg New York-Dordrecht-London: Springer.

Chalmers, D. (2004). How can we construct a science of consciousness?. In M. S. Gazzaniga (Ed.), *The Cognitive Neurosciences III*, third edition (pp. 1111–1120). Cambridge (MA): MIT Press.

Chalmers, D. & Clark, A. (1998). The extended mind. *Analysis*, 58, (pp. 10—23).

Chant, S. R., Hindriks, F. & Preyer G. (2014). Beyond the big four and the big five. In S. R. Chant, F. Hindriks & G. Preyer, (Eds.), *From Individual to Collective Intentionality. New Essays* (pp. 1–9). New York: Oxford University Press.

Clarke, R. (2015). Abilities to act. *Philosophy Compass*, 10(12), pp. 893–904.

Collins, S. (2019). *Group Duties: Their Existence and Their Implications for Individuals*. Oxford: Oxford University Press.

Copp, D. (2006). On the agency of certain collective entities: An argument from normative autonomy. *Midwest Studies in Philosophy*, XXX, pp. 194–221.

Copp, D. (2007). The collective moral autonomy thesis. *Journal of Social Philosophy*, 38(3), pp. 369–88.

Crane, T. (2014). *Aspects of Psychologism*. Cambridge (MA): Harvard University Press.

Currie, G. (1984). Individualism and global supervenience. *The British Journal for the Philosophy of Science*, 35(4), pp. 345–358.

Davidson, D. (1963). Actions, reasons and causes. *Journal of Philosophy*, LX(23), pp. 685–700.

Davidson, D. (1970). Mental events. In L. Foster & J. W. Swanson (Eds.), *Experience and Theory* (pp. 207–225). Amherst (MA): University of Massachusetts Press.

De Caro, M. (2008). *Azione*, Bologna: Il Mulino.

Descombes, V. (2011). The problem of collective identity: The instituting we and the instituted we. In H. Ikäheimo & A. Laitinen (Eds.), *Recognition and Social Ontology* (pp. 373–390). Leiden: Brill.

Dewey, J. (1926). The historic background of corporate legal personality. *The Yale Law Journal*, 35(6), pp. 655–673.

Düber, D., Mooren, N. & Rojek T. (2016). What is the foundation of Pettit's non-redundant realism about group agents?. In S. Derpmann & D. Schweikard (Eds.), *Philip Pettit: Five Themes from his Work. Münster Lectures in Philosophy 1* (pp. 91–100). Cham: Springer.

Durkheim, E. (1895). *Les Regles de la Methode Sociologique*. Paris: Félix Alcan éditeur. Translated by S. Lukes, *The Rules of Sociological Method*. New York: The Macmillan Press (1982).

Durkheim, E. (1897). *Le Suicide: Étude de Sociologie*. Paris: Félix Alcan éditeur. Translated by J. A. Spaulding, G. Simpson, *Suicide. A Study in Sociology*. Glencoe: The Free Press (1951).

Effingham, N. (2010). The metaphysics of groups. *Philosophical Studies*, 149, pp. 21–67.

Elder-Vass, D. (2007). A method for social ontology. *Journal of Critical Realism*, 6(2), pp. 226–49.

Elder-Vass, D. (2010). *The Causal Power of Social Structures: Emergence, Structure and Agency*. Cambridge: Cambridge University Press.

Elder-Vass, D. (2012). Top-down causation and social structures. *Interface Focus*, 2, 82–90.

Elder-Vass, D. (2014). Social entities and the basis of their powers. In J. Zahle & F. Colin (Eds.), *Rethinking the Individualism-Holism Debate. Essays in the Philosophy of Social Science* (pp. 39–54). Cham: Springer.

Elder-Vass, D. (2017). Material parts in social structures. *Journal of Social Ontology*, 3(1), pp. 89–106. DOI: 10.1515/jso-2015-0058.

Epstein, B. (2009). Ontological individualism reconsidered. *Synthese*, 166(1), pp. 187–213.

Epstein, B. (2014a). How many kinds of glue hold the social world together?. In M. Gallotti & J. Michael (Eds.), *Social Ontology and Social Cognition* (pp. 41–55). Dordrecht: Springer.

Epstein, B. (2014b). What is individualism in social ontology? Ontological individualism vs. anchor individualism. In J. Zahle & F. Collin (Eds.), *Rethinking the Individualism-Holism Debate. Essays in the Philosophy of Social Science* (pp. 17–38). Cham: Springer.

Epstein, B. (2015). *The Ant Trap. Rebuilding the Foundations of the Social Sciences*. New York: Oxford University Press.

Epstein, B. (2017). What are social groups? Their metaphysics and how to classify them, *Synthese*, pp. 1–34 (2017). DOI: 10.1007/s11229-017-1387-y.

Epstein, B. (2018). Social Ontology, in *The Stanford Encyclopedia of Philosophy*, E. N. Zalta (ed.), https://plato.stanford.edu/archives/sum2018/entries/social-ontology/.

Fodor, J. A. (1974). Special sciences (Or: The disunity of science as a working hypothesis. *Synthese*, 28(2), pp. 97–115.

Fodor, J. A. (1998). *In Critical Condition: Polemical Essays on Cognitive Science and the Philosophy of Mind*. Cambridge (MA): MIT Press.

French, P. (1979). The corporation as a moral person. *American Philosophical Quarterly*, 16(3), pp. 207–215.

French, P. (1984). *Collective and Corporate Responsibility*. New York: Columbia University Press.

Gallotti, M. (2014). Objects in mind. In M. Gallotti & J. Michael (Eds.), *Perspectives on Social Ontology and Social Cognition* (pp. 1–13). Dordrecht: Springer.

Gallotti, M., Fairhurst, M. T. & Frith C. D. (2017). *Alignment in Social Interactions. Consciousness and Cognition*, 48, pp. 253–261.

Gallotti, M. & Michael, J. (Eds.) (2014). *Perspectives on Social Ontology and Social Cognition. Dordrecht: Springer.*

Garrod, S. & Pickering, M. J. (2009). Joint action, interactive alignment, and dialog. *Topics in Cognitive Science*, 1, pp. 292–304.

Gilbert, M. (1989). *On Social Facts*. Princeton: Princeton University Press.

Gilbert, M. (1990). Walking together: a paradigmatic social phenomenon. *Midwest Studies in Philosophy*, 15, pp. 1–14.

Gilbert, M. (1997). What is for Us to intend?. In G. Holmström-Hintikka & R. Tuomela (Eds.), *Contemporary Action Theory 2*. Dordrecht: Reidel.

Gilbert, M. (2003). The structure of the social atom: Joint commitment as the foundation of human social behavior. In F. F. Schmitt (Ed.), *Socializing Metaphysics. The Nature of Social Reality* (pp. 39–64). Larzham-Boulder-New York-Oxford: Rowman & Littlefield.

Gilbert, M. (2006). *A Theory of Political Obligation*. New York: Oxford University Press.

Gilbert, M. (2007a). Mutual recognition, common knowledge and joint acceptance. In T. Rønnow-Rasmussen, B. Petersson, J. Josefsson & D. Egonsson (Eds.), *Hommage à Wlodek: Philosophical Papers Dedicated to Wlodek Rabinowicz*. http://www.fil.lu.se/hommageawlodek.

Gilbert, M. (2007b). Searle and collective intentions. In S. L. Tsohatzidis (Ed.), *Intentional Acts and Institutional Facts* (pp. 31–48). Dordrecht: Springer.

Gilbert, M. (2009). Shared intention and personal intentions. *Philos Stud*, 144, pp. 167–187.

Gilbert, M. (2010). Collective action. In T. O'Connor & C. Sandis (Eds.), *A Companion to the Philosophy of Action* (pp. 67–73). Chichester: Wiley-Blackwell Publishing.

Gilbert, M. (2011). Mutual recognition and some related phenomena. In H. Ikäheimo & A. Laitinen (Eds.), *Recognition and Social Ontology* (pp. 271–286). Leiden: Brill.

Gilbert, M. (2013). *Joint Commitment: How we Make the Social World*. New York: Oxford University Press.

Gilbert, M. (2018). *Rights and Demands. A Foundational Inquiry*. New York: Oxford University Press.

Greenwood, J. D. (2003). Social facts, social groups and social explanation. *Noûs*, 37(1), pp. 93–112.

Guala, F. (2014). On the nature of social kinds. In M. Gallotti & J. Michael (Eds.), *Perspectives on Social Ontology and Social Cognition* (pp. 57–68). Dordrecht: Springer.

Habermas, J. (1981a). *Theorie des kommunikativen Handelns, Bd. I. Handlungsrationalität und gesellschaftliche Rationalisierung*. Frankfurt am Main: Suhrkamp.

Habermas, J. (1981b). *Theorie des kommunikativen Handelns, Bd. II. Zur Kritik der funktionalistischen Vernunft*. Frankfurt am Main: Suhrkamp.

Haji, I. (2006). On the ultimate responsibility of collectives. *Midwest Studies in Philosophy*, XXX, pp. 292–308.

Harman, G. (1976). Practical reasoning. *Review of Metaphysics*, 29, pp. 431–463.

Harman, G. (1983). Rational action and the extent of intentions. *Social Theory and Practice*, 9, pp. 123–141.

Hauswald, R. (2016). The ontology of interactive kinds. *Journal of Social Ontology.* DOI: 10.1515/jso-2015-0049.

Hayek, F. A. (1942). Scientism and the study of society. *Economica,* 9(35), pp. 267–291.

Hess, K. M. (2013). "If you tickle us…": How corporations can be moral agents without being persons. *Journal of Value Inquiry,* 47(3), pp. 319–335.

Hess, K. M. (2014). Free will of corporations (and other collectives). *Philos Stud,* 168(1), pp. 241-260.

Hess, K. M. (2020). Assembling the elephant. Attending to the metaphysics of corporate agents. In D. Tollefsen & S. Bazargan (Eds.), *Routledge Handbook of Collective Responsibility.*

Hindriks, F. (2008). The status account of corporate agents. In H. B. Schmid, K. Schulte-Ostermann & N. Psarros (Eds.), *Concepts of Sharedness—Essays on Collective Intentionality* (pp. 118–144) Frankfurt: Ontos Verlag.

Hindriks, F. (2012). But where is the university?. *Dialectica,* 66(1), pp 93–113.

Hindriks, F. (2013). The location problem in social ontology. *Synthese,* 190, pp. 413–437.

Hindriks, F. (2014). How autonomous are collective agents? corporate rights and normative individualism. *Erkenntnis,* 79(9), pp. 1565–1585.

Hindriks, F. (2017). Group agents and social institutions: Beyond Tuomela's social ontology. In G. Preyer & G. Peter (Eds.), *Social Ontology and Collective Intentionality. Critical Essays on the Philosophy of Raimo Tuomela with His Responses* (pp. 197–210). Cham: Springer.

Hirvonen, O. (2017). Groups as persons? A suggestion for a Hegelian turn. *Journal of Social Ontology,* 3(2), pp. 143–166. DOI: 10.1515/jso-2016-0019.

Hobbes, T. (1651). *Leviathan.* Edited by R. Tuck. Cambridge: Cambridge University Press (1996).

Hodgson, G. M. (2007a). Meanings of methodological individualism. *Journal of Economic Methodology,* 14(2), pp. 211–226.

Hodgson, G. M. (2007b). Institutions and individuals: Interaction and evolution. *Organization Studies,* 28(1), pp. 95–116.

Huebner, B. (2013). *Macrocognition. A Theory of Distributed Minds and Collective Intentionality.* New York: Oxford University Press.

Husserl, E. (1973). *Die Gegebenheit konkreter sozialer Gegenständlichkeiten und die Klärung auf sie bezüglicher Begriffe. Soziale Ontologie und descriptive Soziologie* (1910), In I. Kern (Ed.), *Husserliana XIII. Zur Phänomenologie der Intersubjektivität. Texte aus dem Nachlaß. Erster Teil: 1905–1920* (pp. 98–104). Den Haag: Martinus Nijhoff.

Husserl, E. (1975). *Logische Untersuchungen. Erster Band. Prolegomena zur reinen Logik.* Text der 1. und der 2. Auflage. In E. Holenstein (Ed.), Hua XVIII. Den Haag: Martinus Nijhoff. Engl. trans. by J. N. Findlay (2001). In D. Moran (ed.), *Prolegomena to pure logic. In logical investigations, vol. I* (pp. 9–162). London-New York: Routledge.

Husserl, E. (1984). *Logische Untersuchungen. Zweiter Band. Untersuchungen zur Phänomenologie und Theorie der Erkenntnis,* in 2 Bänden. Text der 1. und der 2. Auflage ergänzt durch Annotationen und Beiblätter aus dem

Handexemplar, in U. Panzer (Ed.), Hua XIX/1, 2. Den Haag: Martinus Nijhoff.

Hutchins, E. (1995). *Cognition in the Wild.* Cambridge (MA): MIT Press.

Ikäheimo, H. & Laitinen, A. (2011). Recognition and social ontology: An introduction. In H. Ikäheimo & A. Laitinen (Eds.), *Recognition and Social Ontology* (pp. 1–21). Leiden: Brill.

Jackson, F. & Pettit, P. (1992). In defense of explanatory ecumenicalism. *Economics and Philosophy*, 8(1), pp. 1–21.

Jankovic M. & Ludwig K. (Eds.) (2018). *The Routledge Handbook of Collective Intentionality.* New York: Routledge.

Kim, J. (1979). Causality, identity, and supervenience in the mind-body problem. In P. A. French, J. Theodore, E. Uehling & H. K. Wettstein (Eds.), *Midwest Studies in Philosophy*, 4(1), pp. 31–49.

Kim, J. (1984). Concepts of supervenience. *Philosophy and Phenomenological Research*, 45(2), pp. 153–176.

Kim, J. (1992). Multiple realizability and the metaphysics of reduction. *Philosophy and Phenomenological Research*, 52(1), pp. 1–26.

Kim, J. (1999). Making sense of emergence. *Philosophical Studies*, 95(1-2), pp. 3–36.

Kincaid, H. (1996). *Philosophical Foundations of the Social Sciences. Analyzing Controversies in Social Research.* New York: Cambridge University Press.

Knoblich, G. & Sebenz N. (2008). Evolving intentions for social interaction: From entrainment to joint action. *Philosophical Transactions of the Royal Society. Biological Sciences*, 363(1499), pp. 2021–2031.

Kusch, M. (2014). The metaphysics and politics of corporate personhood. *Erkenntnis*, 79, pp. 1587–1600.

Kutz, C. (2000). Acting together. *Philosophy and Phenomenological Research*, 61(1), pp. 1–31.

Laitinen, A. (2011). Recognition, acknowledgment, and acceptance. In H. Ikäheimo & A. Laitinen (Eds.), *Recognition and Social Ontology* (pp. 309–347). Leiden: Brill.

Laitinen, A. (2014). Collective intentionality and recognition from others. In A. Kontzelmann Ziv & H. Schmid (Eds.), *Institutions, Emotions, and Group Agents. Studies in the Philosophy of Sociality 2* (pp. 213–227). Dordrecht: Springer.

Laitinen, A. (2017). We-mode collective intentionality and its place in social reality. In G. Preyer & G. Peter (Eds.), *Social Ontology and Collective Intentionality. Critical Essays on the Philosophy of Raimo Tuomela with His Responses* (pp. 147–167). Cham: Springer.

Lasagni, G. (forthcoming). Two interpretations of Gilbert's plural-subject account. *Rivista di Estetica.*

Le Bon, G. (1895). *Psychologie des Foules,* Paris: Alcan.

Leonardi, P. (2012). Materiality, sociomateriality, and socio-technical systems: What do these terms mean? How are they related? Do we need them?. In P. Leonardi, B. Nardi & J. Kallinikos (Eds.), *Materiality and Organizing: Social Interaction in a Technological World* (pp. 25–48). Oxford: Oxford University Press.

Liang, D. W., Moreland, R. L., & Argote, L. (1995). Group versus individual training and group performance: The mediating role of transactive memory. *Personality and Social Psychology Bulletin*, 21, pp. 384–393.

List, C. (2016). What is it like to be a group agent? *Noûs*, 52(2), pp. 295–319.

List, C. (2018). Levels: descriptive, explanatory and ontological. *Noûs*. DOI: 10.1111/nous.12241.

List, C. & Koenig-Archibugi, M. (2010). Can there be a global demos? An agency-based approach. *Philosophy & Public Affairs*, 38(1), pp. 76–110.

List, C. & Pettit, P. (2006). Group agency and supervenience. *The Southern Journal of Philosophy*, 44, pp. 85–105.

List, C. & Pettit, P. (2011). *Group Agency: The Possibility, Design, and Status of Corporate Agents*. Oxford: Oxford University Press.

List, C. & Spiekermann, K. (2013). Methodological individualism and holism in political science: a reconciliation. *American Political Science Review*, 107(4), 629–643.

Ludwig, K. (2003). The mind-body problem: an overview. In S. P. Stich & T. A. Warfield (Eds.), *The Blackwell Guide to Philosophy of Mind* (pp. 1–46). Malden (MA): Blackwell.

Ludwig, K. (2007a). The argument from normative autonomy for collective agents. *Journal of Social Philosophy*, 38(3), pp. 410–427.

Ludwig, K. (2007b). Foundations of social reality in collective intentional behavior. In S. L. Tsohatzidis (Ed.), *Intentional Acts and Institutional Facts. Essays on John Searle's Social Ontology* (pp. 42–72). Dordrecht: Springer.

Ludwig, K. (2014). The ontology of collective action. In S. Chant, F. Hindriks & G. Preyer (Eds.), *From Individual to Collective Intentionality: New Essays* (pp. 112–133). Oxford: Oxford University Press.

Ludwig, K. (2015). Is distributed cognition group level cognition?. *Journal of Social Ontology*, 1(2), pp. 189–224.

Ludwig, K. (2016). *From Individual to Plural Agency: Collective Action I*. New York: Oxford University Press.

Ludwig, K. (2017a). *From Plural to Institutional Agency. Collective Action II*. New York: Oxford University Press.

Ludwig, K. (2017b). Methodological individualism, the we-mode, and team reasoning. In G. Preyer & G. Peter (Eds.), *Social Ontology and Collective Intentionality. Critical Essays on the Philosophy of Raimo Tuomela with His Responses* (pp. 3–18). Cham: Springer.

Lukács, G. (1984). *Prolegomena zur Ontologie des gesellschaftlichen Seins Prinzipienfragen einer heute moeglich gewordenen Ontologie*. Darmstadt u. Neuwied: Luchterhand.

Lukes, S. (1968). Methodological individualism reconsidered. *The British Journal of Sociology*, 19, 119–129.

McDowell, J. (2011). Some remarks on intention in action. *The Amherst Lecture in Philosophy*, 6, pp. 1–18.

Meijers, A. W. M. (2000). Mental causation and Searle's impossible conception of unconscious intentionality. *International Journal of Philosophical Studies*, 8(2), pp. 155–170.

Mele, A. (2003). Agents' abilities. *Nous*, 37(3), pp. 447–70.

Miller, S. (2007). Joint action: The individual strikes back. In S. L. Tsohatzidis (Ed.), *Intentional Acts and Institutional Facts. Essays on John Searle's social ontology* (pp. 73–92). Dordrecht: Springer.

Orts, E. W. & Smith, N. C. (Eds.) (2017). *The Moral Responsibility of the Firm Revisited.* Oxford: Oxford University Press.

Pacherie, E. (2002). The role of emotions in the explanation of action. *European Review of Philosophy*, 5, pp. 55–90.

Pacherie, E. (2007). Sense of control and sense of agency. Special issue on the Phenomenology of Agency, S. Siegel (Ed.), *Psyche*, 13(1), pp. 1–30.

Pacherie, E. (2014). How does it feel to act together?. *Phenomenology and the Cognitive Science*, 13(1), pp. 25–48.

Pacherie, E. (2017). Collective phenomenology. In M. Jankovic & K. Ludwig (Eds.), *The Routledge Handbook of Collective Intentionality* (pp. 162–173). New York-Abingdon: Routledge.

Pacherie, E. (2018). Motor intentionality. In A. Newen, L. de Bruin & S. Gallagher (Eds), *The Oxford Handbook of 4e Cognition* (pp. 369–388). Oxford; Oxford University Press.

Pettit, P. (1996). *The Common Mind. An Essay on Psychology, Society, and Politics.* Second edition. New York: Oxford University Press.

Pettit, P. (2003). Groups with minds of their own. In F. F. Schmitt (ed.), *Socializing Metaphysics* (pp. 167–193). Lanham: Rowman and Littlefield.

Pettit, P. (2007a). Responsibility incorporated. *Ethics*, 117, pp. 171–201.

Pettit, P. (2007b). Rationality, reasoning and group agency. *Dialectica*, 61(4), pp. 495–519.

Pettit, P. (2014). Three issues in social ontology. In J. Zahle & F. Collin (Eds.), *Rethinking the Individualism-Holism Debate. Essays in the Philosophy of Social Science* (pp.77–96). Cham: Springer.

Pettit, P. & Schweikard, D. P. (2006). Joint actions and group agents. *Philosophy of the Social Sciences*, 36, pp. 18–39.

Pinkert, F. (2014). What We Together Can (Be Required to) Do: What We Together Can (Be Required to) Do. *Midwest Studies in Philosophy*, 38(1), pp. 187–202.

Popper, K. (1944a). The poverty of historicism I. *Economica*, 11, pp. 86–103.

Popper, K. (1944b). The poverty of historicism II. *Economica*, 11, pp. 119–37.

Popper, K. (1945). The poverty of historicism III. *Economica*, 12, pp. 69–89.

Reinach, A. (1989). *Die apriorischen Grundlagen des bürgerlichen Rechtes.* In Sämtliche Werke. Textkritische Ausgabe, ed. K. Schuhmann and B. Smith, 2 vols, pp. 141–278. Munich: Philosophia Verlag. Engl. trans. by J. Crosby (2012). In *The a priori foundations of the civil law*. Along with the lecture "Concerning Phenomenology". J. Crosby (Ed.), with an introduction by A. McIntyre. Berlin: De Gruyter, (pp. 1–142).

Risjord, M. (2014). *Philosophy of social science: A contemporary introduction.* London: Routledge.

Ritchie, K. (2013). What are groups?. *Philos Stud*, 166, pp. 257–272.

Ritchie, K. (2015). The metaphysics of social groups. *Philosophy Compass*, 10(5), pp. 310–321.

Ritchie, K. (2018). Social structures and the ontology of social groups. *Philosophy and Phenomenological Research.* DOI: 10.1111/phpr.12555.

Rizzolatti G. & Sinigaglia C. (2008). *Mirrors in the Brain: How Our Minds Share Actions and Emotions.* Oxford: Oxford University Press.

Rovane, C. (1998). *The Bounds of Agency: An Essay in Revisionary Metaphysics.* Princeton: Princeton University Press.

Rovane, C. (2004). What is an agent?. *Synthese,* 140, pp. 181–198.

Rovane, C. (2014). Group agency and individualism. *Erkenntnis,* 79(9), pp. 1663–1684.

Ruben, D. H. (1985). *The Metaphysics of the Social World.* London-Boston-Melbourne- Henley: Routledge & Kegan Paul.

Rupert, R. (2005). Minding one's cognitive systems: When does a group of minds constitute a single cognitive unit?. *Episteme,* 1, pp. 177–188.

Salice, A. (2013). Social ontology as embedded in the tradition of phenomenological realism. In M. Schmitz, B. Kobow & H. B. Schmid (Eds.), *The Background of Social Reality. Selected Contributions from the Inaugural Meeting of ENSO* (pp. 217–232). Dordrecht: Springer.

Salice, A. (2015). There are no primitive we-intentions. *Review of Philosophy and Psychology,* 6, pp. 695–715.

Salice A. & Schmid H. B. (2016). Social reality—The phenomenological approach. In A. Salice & H. B. Smith (Eds.), *The Phenomenological Approach to Social Reality, Concepts, Problems* (pp. 1–14). Dordrecht: Springer.

Salmela, M. (2012). Plural emotions. *Philosophical Explorations,* 15(1), pp. 1–14.

Sawyer, R. K. (2002). Nonreductive individualism. Part I—Supervenience and wild disjunction. *Philosophy of the Social Science,* 32(4), pp. 537–559.

Sawyer, R. K. (2003). Nonreductive individualism. Part II—Social causation. *Philosophy of the Social Science,* 33(2), pp. 203–224.

Schapp, W. (1930). *Die neue Wissenschaft vom Recht. Eine phänomenologische Untersuchung.* Berlin: Rothschild.

Schapp, W. (1959). Erinnerung and Husserl. In E. Husserl, *1859-1959. Recueil commemoratif publié à l'occasion du centenaire de la naissance du philosophe.* La Haye: Martinus Nijhoff.

Scheler, M. (1954). *Der Formalismus in der Ethik und die materiale Wertethik. Neuer Versuch der Grundlegung eines ethischen Personalismus.* Translated by M. S. Frings & R. L. Funk (1973). *Formalism in the ethics and non-formal ethics of values. A new attempt toward the foundation of an ethical personalism.* Evanston: Northwestern University Press.

Schmid, H. B. (2009). *Plural action. Essays in Philosophy and Social Science.* Dordrecht: Springer.

Schmid, H. B. (2014). The feeling of being a group: Corporate emotions and collective consciousness. In C. von Scheve & M. Salmela (Eds.), *Collective Emotions* (pp. 3–16) Oxford: Oxford University Press.

Schmid, H. B. (2017a). The subject of we-intend. *Phenomenology and the Cognitive Sciences.* DOI: 10.1007/s11097-017-9501-7.

Schmid, H. B. (2017b). What kind of mode is the we-mode?. In G. Preyer & G. Peter (Eds.), *Social Ontology and Collective Intentionality. Critical Essays on the Philosophy of Raimo Tuomela with His Responses* (pp. 79–94). Cham: Springer.

Schmitz, M. (2013). Social rules and the social background. In M. Schmitz, B. Kobow & H. B. Schmid (Eds.), *The Background of Social Reality. Selected Contributions from the Inaugural Meeting of ENSO* (pp. 107–126). Dordrecht: Springer.

Schmitz, M. (2017). What is a mode account of collective intentionality?. In G. Preyer & G. Peter (Eds.), *Social Ontology and Collective Intentionality. Critical Essays on the Philosophy of Raimo Tuomela with His Responses* (pp. 37–70). Cham: Springer.

Schmitz, M. (2018). Co-subjective consciousness constitutes collectives. *Journal of Social Philosophy,* 49(1), pp. 137–160.

Schulte-Ostermann, K. (2008). Agent causation and collective agency. In H. B. Schmid, K. Schulte-Ostermann & N. Psarros (Eds.), *Concepts of Sharedness. Essays on Collective Intentionality* (pp. 191–207). Heusenstamm: Ontos Verlag.

Schweikard, D. P. (2008). Limiting reductionism in the theory of collective action. In H. B. Schmid, K. Schulte-Ostermann & N. Psarros (Eds.), *Concepts of Sharedness. Essays on Collective Intentionality* (pp. 89–118). Heusenstamm: Ontos Verlag.

Schweikard, D. P. (2017a). Cooperation and social obligation. In N. J. Enfield & P. Kockelman (Eds.), *Distributed Agency* (pp. 233–242). New York: Oxford University Press.

Schweikard, D. P. (2017b). Voluntary groups, noncompliance, and conflicts of reason: Tuomela on acting as a group-member. In G. Preyer & G. Peter (Eds.), *Social Ontology and Collective Intentionality. Critical Essays on the Philosophy of Raimo Tuomela with His Responses* (pp. 97–112). Cham: Springer.

Schweikard, D. P., Schmid, H. B. (2012). Collective intentionality. In E. N. Zalta (Ed.), *Stanford Encyclopedia of Philosophy,* https://plato.stanford.edu/archi ves/win2020/entries/collective-intentionality/. Stanford: Stanford University Press.

Searle, J. R. (1980). The intentionality of intention and action. *Cognitive Science,* 4, pp. 47–70.

Searle, J. R. (1983). *Intentionality.* Cambridge: Cambridge University Press.

Searle, J. R. (1990). Collective intentions and actions. In P. R. Cohen, J. Morgan & M. E. Pollack (Eds.), *Intentions in Communication* (pp. 401–416). Cambridge (MA): MIT Press.

Searle, J. R. (1995). *The Construction of Social Reality.* New York: The Free Press.

Searle, J. R. (1997). Responses to critics of the Construction of Social Reality. *Philosophy and Phenomenological Research,* 57(2), pp. 449–458.

Searle, J. R. (2002). Speech acts, mind, and social reality. In G. Grewendorf & G. Meggle (Eds.), *Speech Acts, Mind, and Social Reality. Discussions with John R. Searle* (pp. 3–16). Dordrecht: Springer.

Searle, J. R. (2003). Social ontology and political power. In F. F. Schmitt (Ed.), *Socializing Metaphysics. The Nature of Social Reality* (pp. 19–34). Larzham-Boulder-New York-Oxford: Rowman & Littlefield.

Searle, J. R. (2006). Social ontology: some basic principles. *Anthropological Theory*, 6, pp. 12–29.

Searle, J. R. (2007). Social ontology: the problem and steps toward a solution. In S. L. Tsohatzidis (Ed.), *Intentional Acts and Institutional Facts: Essays on John Searle's Social Ontology* (pp. 11–28). Dordrecht: Springer.

Searle, J. R. (2010). *Making the Social World. The Structure of Human Civilization.* New York: Oxford University Press.

Searle, J. R. (2014). Are there social objects?. In M. Gallotti & J. Michael (Eds.), *Perspectives on Social Ontology and Social Cognition* (pp. 17–26). Dordrecht: Springer.

Seddone, G. (2014). *Collective Intentionality, Norms and Institutions. A Philosophical Investigation about Human Cooperation.* Frankfurt am Main: Peter Lang Edition.

Small, W. (2017). Agency and practical abilities. *Royal Institute of Philosophy Supplement*, 80, pp. 235–64.

Smith, B. (2003). John Searle: from speech act to social reality. In B. Smith (Ed.), *John Searle* (pp. 1–33). Cambridge: Cambridge University Press.

Stahl, T. (2011). Institutional power, collective acceptance, and recognition. In H. Ikäheimo & A. Laitinen (Eds.), *Recognition and Social Ontology* (pp. 349–372). Leiden: Brill.

Stahl, T. (2013). Sharing the background. In M. Schmitz, B. Kobow & H. B. Schmid (Eds.), *The Background of Social Reality. Selected Contributions from the Inaugural Meeting of ENSO* (pp. 127–146). Dordrecht: Springer.

Stoutland, F. (1997). Why are philosophers of action so anti-social?. In L. Alanen, S. Heinämaa, & T. Wallgren (Eds.), *Commonality and Particularity in Ethics* (pp. 45–74). New York: St. Martin's Press.

Stoutland, F. (2002). Critical notice of faces of intention. *Philosophy and Phenomenological Research*, 65(1), pp. 238–241.

Stoutland, F. (2008). The ontology of social agency. *Analyse & Kritik*, 30, pp. 533–551.

Taylor, C. (1985). *Philosophy and the Human Sciences: Philosophical Papers 2.* Cambridge: Cambridge University Press.

Testa, I. (2011). Social space and the ontology of recognition. In H. Ikäheimo & A. Laitinen (Eds.), *Recognition and Social Ontology* (pp. 287–308). Leiden: Brill.

Testa, I. (2015). Ontology of the false state. On the relation between critical theory, social philosophy, and social ontology. *Journal of Social Ontology*, 1(2), pp. 271-300. DOI: 10.1515/jso-2014-0025.

Testa, I. (2016). La teoria critica ha bisogno di un'ontologia sociale (e viceversa)?. *Politica & Società*, 49, pp. 47–72.

Testa, I. (2017). The authority of life. The critical task of Dewey's social ontology. *Journal of Speculative Philosophy*, 31(2), pp. 231–44.

Theiner, G. (2018). Group-sized distributed cognitive systems. In M. Jankovic & K. Ludwig (Eds.). *The Routledge Handbook of Collective Intentionality*, pp. 233–248. New York-Abingdon: Routledge.

Theiner, G., Allen, C. & Goldstone, R. L. (2010). Recognizing group cognition. *Cognitive Systems Research*, 11(4), pp. 378–395.

Theiner, G., & O'Connor, T. (2010). The emergence of group cognition. In A. Corradini & T. O'Connor (Eds.), *Emergence in Science and Philosophy* (pp. 78–117). New York: Routledge.

Theiner, G. & Wilson, R. (2013). Group mind. In B. Kaldis (Ed.), *Encyclopedia of Philosophy and the Social Sciences* (pp. 401–404). Los Angeles-London-New Dehli-Singapore-Washington DC: Sage Publications.

Thomasson, A. L. (2002). Foundations for a social ontology. *Protosociology: an International Journal of Interdisciplinary Researches*, 18-19, pp. 269–290.

Thomasson, A. L. (2009). Social entities. In R. le Poidevin et al. (Eds.), *Routledge Companion to Metaphysics* (pp. 545–554). London: Routledge.

Thomasson, A. L. (2016). The ontology of social groups. *Synthese*, pp. 1–17. DOI: 10.1007/s11229-016-1185-y.

Thompson, M. (2008). *Life and Action. Elementary Structures of Practice and Practical Thought.* Cambridge (MA): Harvard University Press.

Tollefsen, D. P. (2002a). Collective intentionality and the social sciences. *Philosophy and the Social Sciences*, 32(1), pp. 25–50.

Tollefsen, D. P. (2002b). Organizations as true believers. *Journal of Social Philosophy*, 33(3), pp. 395–401.

Tollefsen, D.P. (2006). From extended mind to collective mind. *Cognitive System Research*, 7, pp. 140–150.

Tollefsen, D. P. (2015). *Groups as Agents.* Cambridge: Polity Press.

Tollefsen, D. P. (2018). Collective intentionality and methodology in the social sciences. In M. Jankovic & K. Ludwig (Eds.), *The Routledge Handbook of Collective Intentionality* (pp. 389–401). New York-Abingdon: Routledge.

Tollefsen, D. P. & Gallagher S. (2017). We-narratives and the stability and depth of shared agency. *Philosophy of the Social Sciences*, 47(2), pp. 95–110.

Tollefsen, D. P., Kreuz D. & Dale R. (2014). Flavors of "togetherness". Experimental philosophy and theories of joint action. In Knobe J., Lombrozo T. & Nichols S., *Oxford Studies in Experimental Philosophy: Volume 1* (pp. 232–252). New York: Oxford University Press.

Tuomela, R. (1984). *A Theory of Social Action.* Dordrecht: Reidel Publishing Company.

Tuomela, R. (1991). We will do it: an analysis of group-intentions. *Philosophy and Phenomenological Research*, 51(2), pp. 249–277.

Tuomela, R. (1995). *The Importance of us: A philosophical study of basic social notions.* Stanford: Stanford University Press.

Tuomela, R. (2000). *Cooperation. A Philosophical Study.* Dordrecht: Springer.

Tuomela, R. (2002). *The Philosophy of Social Practices. A Collective Acceptance View.* New York: Cambridge University Press.

Tuomela, R. (2003). The we-mode and the I-mode. In F. F. Schmitt (Ed.), *Socializing Metaphysics. The Nature of Social Reality* (pp. 65–91), Larzham-Boulder-New York-Oxford: Rowman & Littlefield.

Tuomela, R. (2005). We-intentions revisited. *Philos Stud*, 125(3), pp. 327–369. DOI: 10.1007/s11098-005-7781-1.

Tuomela, R. (2007). *The Philosophy of Sociality. The Shared Point of View.* New York: Oxford University Press.

Tuomela, R. (2008). Collective intentionality and group reasons. In H. B. Schmid, K. Schulte-Ostermann & N. Psarros (Eds.), *Concepts of Sharedness. Essays on Collective Intentionality* (pp. 3–20). Heusenstamm: Ontos Verlag.

Tuomela, R. (2011). Holistic social causation and explanation. In D. Dieks, W. Gonzalez, S. Hartmann, T. Uebel & M. Weber (Eds.), *Explanation, Prediction, and Confirmation. The Philosophy of Science in a European Perspective. Volume 2* (pp. 305–318). Dordrecht: Springer.

Tuomela, R. (2013a). *Social ontology. Collective Intentionality and Group Agents.* New York: Oxford University Press.

Tuomela, R. (2013b). Who is afraid of group agents and group minds?. In M. Schmitz, B. Kobow & H. B. Schmid (Eds.), *The Background of Social Reality. Selected Contributions from the Inaugural Meeting of ENSO* (pp. 13–36). Dordrecht: Springer.

Tuomela, R. (2017). Raimo Tuomela: Response to Bernhard Schmid. In G. Preyer & G. Peter (Eds.), *Social Ontology and Collective Intentionality. Critical Essays on the Philosophy of Raimo Tuomela with His Responses* (pp. 95–96). Cham: Springer.

Tuomela, R. (2018). Non-reductive views of shared intention. In M. Jankovic & K. Ludwig (Eds.), *The Routledge Handbook of Collective Intentionality* (pp. 25–33). New York: Routledge.

Tuomela, R. & Tuomela, M. (2003). Acting as a group member and collective commitments. *ProtoSociology*, 18, pp. 7–65.

Velleman, J. D. (1997). How to share an intention. *Philosophy and Phenomenological Research*, 57, pp. 29–50.

Vesper, C., Wel, R. P. R. D. van der, Knoblich, G. K., Sebanz, N. (2012). Are you ready to jump? Predictive mechanisms in interpersonal coordination. *Journal of Experimental Psychology: Human Perception and Performance*, 39(1), pp. 48–61.

Ware, R. (1988). Group action and social ontology. *Analyse und Kritik*, 10, pp. 48–70.

Watkins, J. W. N. (1952). Notes and comments. The principles of methodological individualism. *The British Journal for the Philosophy of Science*, III(10), pp. 186–189.

Watkins, J. W. N. (1955). Methodological individualism: a reply. *Philosophy of Science*, 22(1), pp. 58–62.

Weber, M. (1922). *Wirtschaft und Gesellschaft*. Edited and translated by G. Roth & C. Wittich, *Economy and Society: An Outline of Interpretive Sociology*. Berkeley: University of California Press (1978).

Wegner, D. M. (1986). Transactive memory: A contemporary analysis of the group mind. In B. Mullen & G. R. Goethals (Eds.), *Theories of Group Behavior* (pp. 185–208). New York: Springer Verlag.

Wegner, D. M. (1995). A computer network model of human transactive memory. *Social Cognition*, 13, pp. 319–339.

Wilby, M. (2012). Subject, mode, and content in 'We-Intention'. *Phenomenology and Mind*, 5, pp. 94–106.

Wilson, R. (2004). *Boundaries of the Mind: The Individual in the Fragile Sciences*. Cambridge: Cambridge University Press.

Wringe, B. (2019). Global obligations, collective capacities, and 'ought implies can'. *Philosophical Studies*. DOI: 10.1007/s11098-019-01272-6.

Ylikoski, P. & Mäkelä, P. (2002). We-attitudes and social institutions. In G. Meggle (Ed.), *Social Facts and Collective Intentionality* (pp. 459–474). Frankfurt: Dr. Hänsel-Hohenhausen AG.

Young, I. M. (1990). *Justice and the Politics of Difference*. Princeton: Princeton University Press.

Zahle, J. (2007). Holism and supervenience. In S. P. Turner & M. W. Risjord (Eds.), *Handbook of the Philosophy of Science* (pp. 311–341). New York: Elsevier.

Zahle, J. & Collin, F. (Eds.) (2014). *Rethinking the Individualism-Holism Debate. Essays in the Philosophy of Social Science*. Cham: Springer.

Zaibert, L. A. (2003). Collective intentions and collective intentionality. *American Journal of Economics and Sociology*, 62(1), pp. 209–232.

Zaibert, L. A. & Smith, B. (2007). Legal ontology and the problem of normativity. In S. L. Tsohatzidis (Ed.), *Intentional Acts and Institutional Facts: Essays on John Searle's Social Ontology* (pp. 157–174). Berlin: Springer.

Znamierowski, C. (1912). *Der Wahrheitsbegriff im Pragmatismus*. Warschau: Buchdruckerei von St. Niemira's Söhnen.

Index

SDC
  socially distributed cognition,
    161, 162, 163
Searle, John R., xi, xv, xvi, xvii, xviii,
    xx, xxi, xxii, xxiii, xxvi, 5, 6, 7, 16,
    21, 22, 23, 24, 25, 26, 30, 36, 38,
    42, 43, 44, 45, 46, 47, 49, 50, 51,
    58, 59, 60, 63, 68, 69, 71, 76, 89,
    90, 101, 102, 106, 108, 116, 117,
    123, 136, 137, 167, 168, 173, 189,
    192, 193, 195, 196, 199
shared action, xxvi, 5, 6, 11, 15, 32,
    37, 42, 46, 47, 50, 73, 135
shared agency, xi, xiii, xiv, xvi, xvii,
    xxi, xxii, xxiii, xxiv, xxv, xxvi,
    xxvii, 3, 4, 5, 6, 7, 9, 10, 13, 15,
    16, 19, 21, 22, 23, 24, 28, 29, 32,
    35, 37, 39, 40, 41, 42, 44, 46, 47,
    55, 56, 57, 62, 63, 65, 66, 67, 73,
    74, 75, 76, 79, 84, 87, 95, 97, 101,
    102, 103, 104, 106, 108, 111, 113,
    114, 115, 117, 119, 122, 126, 133,
    137, 138, 139, 140, 141, 142, 149,
    152, 155, 164, 167, 168, 169, 170,
    172, 179, 181, 182, 197
shared intention, 7, 10, 11, 12, 14,
    15, 16, 20, 24, 29, 30, 31, 32, 35,
    36, 38, 44, 46, 48, 50, 55, 58, 63,
    96, 97, 98, 100, 101, 102, 104,
    106, 124, 128, 139, 185, 198
singularism, 76, 82, 83, 115
social facts, xvi, xvii, xxiv, xxv, 73,
    75, 76, 77, 78, 79, 82, 86, 90, 91,
    92, 93, 94, 95, 109, 113, 116, 117,
    128, 129, 130, 131, 132, 133, 134,
    140, 144, 146, 173, 174, 175, 189,
    199
social ontology, xi, xiv, xv, xvii, xxi,
    xxiv, 3, 5, 19, 21, 22, 26, 37, 41,
    55, 59, 73, 75, 76, 77, 79, 80, 81,
    84, 90, 92, 115, 128, 130, 135,
    138, 146, 148, 151, 153, 161, 188,

190, 191, 192, 193, 194, 195, 196,
    198, 199
social reality, xv, 73, 76, 185, 189,
    191, 192, 194, 195, 196, 197, 198
social sciences, 56, 57, 74, 77, 78,
    81, 84, 93, 95, 130, 135, 148, 153,
    185, 187, 188, 197
social world, xi, xiv, xv, xvii, xviii,
    xxvi, xxvii, 21, 37, 73, 76, 78, 79,
    81, 84, 89, 90, 93, 94, 109, 113,
    117, 121, 130, 131, 133, 148, 151,
    153, 173, 177, 194, 196
speech act, xv, xviii, 44, 101, 195,
    196
status account, 66, 67, 69, 96, 115,
    143, 190
status function, xvi, 68, 69, 106,
    108
structural relation, xxi, xxii, 41, 46,
    102, 116, 118, 119, 121, 139, 140,
    169, 170
supervenience, 73, 89, 90, 91, 92,
    93, 95, 97, 98, 109, 114, 130, 131,
    132, 139, 173, 175, 176, 187, 191,
    192, 194, 199
supervenient causation, 108, 130,
    133

T

TMS
  transactive memory system, 162
Tuomela, Raimo, xi, xiii, xvii, xxi,
    xxvi, 5, 6, 16, 20, 21, 26, 27, 28,
    29, 30, 36, 37, 38, 39, 45, 46, 47,
    49, 50, 56, 58, 59, 60, 62, 63, 69,
    70, 71, 73, 74, 75, 76, 80, 90, 97,
    99, 101, 103, 104, 105, 106, 107,
    108, 109, 115, 116, 117, 118, 122,
    123, 124, 125, 126, 128, 130, 136,
    137, 138, 139, 140, 147, 172, 173,

174, 176, 189, 190, 191, 192, 195, 197, 198

W

we intention, xvi, 5, 23, 26, 28, 29, 37, 38, 39, 55, 58, 59, 60, 62, 99, 103, 136, 137, 167, 169, 194

we intentionality, 6, 10, 39, 49, 59, 96, 99, 137, 167

we mode, 16, 20, 21, 22, 26, 27, 28, 29, 37, 40, 46, 49, 50, 58, 59, 65, 90, 96, 98, 99, 103, 104, 105, 107, 119, 123, 124, 125, 139, 163, 171, 185, 191, 192, 194, 197

Weber, Maximilian, 77, 78, 79, 198

www.ingramcontent.com/pod-product-compliance
Lightning Source LLC
Chambersburg PA
CBHW072119020426
42334CB00018B/1649